Resolving Racial Conflict

Resolving Racial Conflict

The Community Relations Service and Civil Rights, 1964–1989

Bertram Levine

University of Missouri Press   Columbia and London

Library of Congress Cataloging-in-Publication Data

Levine, Bertram J.
    Resolving racial conflict : the Community Relations Service and civil
rights, 1964–1989 / Bertram Levine.
        p.   cm.
    Includes bibliographical references and index.
    ISBN 0-8262-1558-0 (alk. paper)
    1. United States. Community Relations Service—History.
2. United States—Race relations.   3. United States—Ethnic relations.
4. African Americans—Civil rights—History—20th century.   5. Race
discrimination—United States—History—20th century.   6. United States.
Civil Rights Act of 1964.   7. Civil rights—United States—History—20th
century.   8. Discrimination—United States—20th century.   I. Title.
    E184.A1L468   2005
    323.1196'073'009045—dc22   2004022372

Designer: Jennifer Cropp
Typesetter: Phoenix Type, Inc.
Printer and binder: The Maple-Vail Book Manufacturing Group
Typeface: Basilia

For permissions, see p. 261.

To Muriel

who decorated my life

Contents

Preface ix

Acknowledgments xv

Introduction 1

One.   Lyndon Johnson Sets the Stage 3

Two.   Learning Intervention:
          Intuition, Courage, and Goodwill 21

Three.   Selma Blow by Blow:
          A Dissection of the Community Crisis
          That Turned the Tide for Voting Rights 45

Four.   Equality of Results:
          The Revised Civil Rights Agenda 74

Five.   When Cities Erupt 101

Six.   Police-Minority Relations:
          A Lightning Rod for Racial Conflagration 125

Seven.   Education amid Turmoil 155

Eight.   Mediation:
          The Road Less Traveled 181

Nine.   Not All Black and White:
          Varieties of Civil Rights Conflict 193

Ten.   Minorities and the Media:
          The Conversion of the Image Builders 218

Eleven.   The Quest for Value 226

Selected Bibliography 247

Index 251

Preface

Two lines of American graffiti explain the impulse that generated this book. *"Pasado por aqui—*I passed by here" is how the awestruck conquistadores recorded on canyon walls their wonderment at being the first Europeans to behold the magnificence of the American Southwest. "Kilroy was here" is how the American GI chose to attest his presence as a participating witness to the cataclysmic events of World War II.

From 1964 to 1989, I was a participating witness to a different kind of American adventure—not comparable in scale, but certainly worthy of a footnote in history, which it did not seem likely to get. This book was written to provide that footnote—and because I wanted to record that I was there.

Sometime in 1988, about a year before my retirement from the Community Relations Service (CRS) of the Justice Department, Calvin Kytle called to ask if I had ever considered writing a book about CRS. Kytle was then a book publisher. We had first met when I joined CRS, a pinpoint of a federal agency, during the year of its birth, when he was the deputy director. That call fertilized the seed of an idea that had just begun to tease me.

The Community Relations Service of the Justice Department had provided the nation with a unique and important service during a critical—and dangerous—period of history, and virtually nobody knew anything about it. Here was a book that cried out to be written.

The brainchild of President Lyndon Johnson, CRS was created to work behind the scenes to reduce racial violence and to speed peaceful acceptance of the changes that the new civil rights laws demanded. The strictures of the law that created CRS, and the modus operandi of the agency, which included respect for confidentiality and the avoidance of unnecessary publicity, fostered a self-effacing style of operation. As a result, CRS became one of Washington's best-kept secrets.

My original idea was to tell the story of a small band of men and women—black, white, Hispanic, Asian, and Native American—whose duty every day was to rush to the heart of racial controversy to lessen the violence and move the scene of action from the streets to the conference table. These were the conciliators and mediators through whose efforts CRS addressed more than a thousand hostile encounters a year in hundreds of cities and towns in every state of the union. But it soon became apparent that the story was larger than the sum of individual achievements and adventures.

During its first twenty-five years the agency had done more than calm troubled waters in individual locales. The weight of so many healings in so many places for so many years clearly affected many behavioral patterns as well as the quality of intergroup relationships nationwide. In the process, the agency itself had developed a unique ethos and persona that had to be depicted, and a record that needed to be brought to light.

From the outset I wanted to avoid making this a personal memoir. I had not been hired to be one of the peacemakers. My job was to aid and abet. The "I" began to crawl into the narrative only when my own infrequent ventures into "the field" provided me with the best available data about a particular circumstance. My use of the first person also crops up when my duties as a "chairborne commando" made me central to certain operations essential to the story.

My relative anonymity, however, left a gap in the book that was pointed out by Robert Dentler, one of the outside scholars called upon by the publisher for an evaluation of the manuscript. Dentler, whose long involvement in civil rights matters had made him familiar with the Community Relations Service, suggested that "Levine describe his own role in the CRS, his relation to the actors in his book, and above all his methods in preparing this history." I took his point to mean that the reader deserved to be informed just how the author derived the authority to write what he wrote. Hence this preface of how I became qualified to relate the life and times of the CRS.

That requires a trip behind the scenes.

I joined the Community Relations Service early in 1965 when a still-skeletal staff of conciliators was rocketing from crisis to crisis, mostly in the rural South. My job was to provide liaison with the private sector. That meant to cultivate a symbiotic relationship with national membership organizations whom we might be able to help and who might be able to help us. Religious social action agencies and civil rights organizations needed to let their local constituents know that federal troubleshooters were available, and we needed to have access to their local leaders. Organizations like the U.S. Chamber of Commerce could put us in touch with influential local business leaders who knew that racial controversy was bad for business. This linkage with national organizations, so important when the infant CRS needed to develop resources, was always a useful tool. The American Jewish Committee, the National Urban League, the International Association of Chiefs of Police, the AFL-CIO, the National Council of Churches, and the National Education Association were typical of groups that partnered with CRS on various projects to reduce racial bias and support compliance with civil rights laws.

Within months, I was part of a CRS team that became the spearhead of a special multiagency federal effort, headed by Vice President Hubert Humphrey, to help the most troubled cities get through the summer of 1965 without the civil disorder that had flared up the previous summer.

In less than a year my boss, Roger Wilkins, was appointed by President Johnson to be the director of CRS. Roger picked me to fill his old position as assistant director in charge of the Office of Community Action. "Community Action" was a euphemism for "doing whatever it takes to speed compliance with civil rights law beyond what the conciliation staff did in local communities." Mostly we worked to find, motivate, assist, and help target the resources of potent allies. We enlisted other federal agencies in the fight and helped local governments to create and improve human relations commissions. We joined with private sector organizations in national programs to support human rights objectives.

I continued to work for CRS for the next twenty-three years, mostly as assistant director or associate director. While titles and portfolios changed, at one time or another I directed almost every area of activity that supported the conflict resolution program, except for the conciliation staff itself. The following description of three of these management systems may illustrate the extent and variety of my exposure to racial conflict in America and how CRS addressed it.

(1) Information flow. In a typical year CRS might be alerted to about two thousand racial confrontations in four to five hundred communities. After an initial assessment of causes and possible consequences, we tried to resolve about half of them, recording the effort in carefully structured case reports. All of these data were accumulated in the Management Information System, where it was studied to monitor case process and staff performance and analyzed for insight into what was happening in America. The

data were also mined for information that enabled CRS to use its experience to develop training activities that continually upgraded our conflict resolution abilities.

(2) Program development. Since the demand for CRS's services always exceeded its capacity to perform, limited resources had to be focused in areas and on problems where they would do the most good. Annual work plans for each region, and nationally, identified needs, set priorities, and made choices as to program emphasis: a short-range focus to quell violent symptoms or a long-range focus to address causes of conflict; working for a quick settlement and then moving on or striving for a problem-solving process that would build relationships and enable antagonists to work out future problems on their own; responding to a freedom-of-residence conflict in one town or to a Ku Klux Klan demonstration in another. For many years the information and program development activities were supplemented by the Annual Assessment of Racial Tension. When the nation was concerned with the high incidence of urban civil disorder, CRS eschewed the popular guessing game of riot prediction. Nevertheless, for our own planning purpose, veteran conciliators, in and out of troubled areas all year long, were called upon to hone their intuitive judgments with supporting data, to help identify places of concern. In the eighties this process evolved into a fairly accurate system of identifying cities of greatest risk. It required that every field representative study a specially constructed battery of quantifiable social indicators that, in their aggregate, CRS had found to be significant in distinguishing risk levels. These data were used by regional offices in preventive planning for work in critical cities. The findings were always treated with great secrecy to avoid self-fulfilling prophecy or political exploitation.

(3) Accountability. The CRS field representative has been likened to the Lone Ranger, the stranger, armed with nothing but his own resources, who comes to help a beleaguered community. An apocryphal story from CRS's early years has a neophyte conciliator calling on the titan of American police chiefs, William H. Parker of Los Angeles—ace crime fighter, dominating administrator, national political mogul. The conciliator said, "Chief, I'm here to help with your police-community relations. Tell me your problems, and then give me a list of your worst troublemakers so that I can get their side of the story." Parker immediately phoned the attorney general and said, "General, this is a courtesy call to thank you for the man from CRS—whom I'm about to throw out of my office."

Literally, there are just three degrees of separation between a CRS field representative and the attorney general. The relationship is symbolized by a black leatherette ID folder with gold lettering: "Department of Justice." While it rarely needs to be shown, this badge of office conveys great authority. It is a license to intervene, on the agency's own motion, in the affairs of a community and to act as a catalyst that may alter the community chemistry. This short chain of command (attorney general—CRS director—regional director—field representative) imposes a heavy responsibility on the CRS actors to be worthy of the trust. Systems were emplaced to guide the exercise of discretion and assure accountability. An Operational Planning System clarified the rules of engagement, determining criteria for opening and closing cases and specifying how progress would be reported and monitored. Various quality-assurance programs were employed to make sure that fieldwork accorded to the highest standards of case practice. Peer review panels were used to backtrack a sampling of cases, reviewing paperwork and interviewing antagonists and observers in the field, so that when the director reported to the attorney general or to Congress he knew he could rely on the quality of the casework and the accuracy of its reporting.

This rendering of account by the director was an institutionalized ritual that CRS always approached as though its life depended upon it—as it sometimes did. As a tiny agency, working outside the limelight, with no significant constituency or political sponsor, it often had to struggle for political and budgetary support. With every new administration, with the accession of every new attorney general, with every annual budgetary submission, there came an opportunity and a requirement for the director of CRS to analyze the state of race relations in America, to recount CRS's record in ameliorating racial violence and resolving conflict, and to define the continuing need for its services. For many years coordination of the task of making the case for the director's presentation fell within my portfolio.

With this background as my base, writing the book should have been easy. From the outset I knew the themes I wanted to touch on and was informed about many of the cases that could illustrate them. I knew the personalities of most of the CRS actors and had worked side by side with many of them. I understood the community dynamics that impacted on the CRS mission and that, in turn, were impacted by CRS.

In one way, I felt hampered by information overload. Selection of material was painful, involving the reduction of an original outline of eighteen chapters to a book with eleven. Another hazard was the need to distinguish between memory and lingering impression. The burden of my research, therefore, was to confirm or correct what I thought I knew, to find enriching detail, and to better inform my understanding of the social climate in which events took place.

My principal resources for CRS activities were of three types. One was the interviews I conducted, specifically for this purpose, with many of my CRS colleagues. For further understanding of the skills and techniques employed by CRS mediators, I reviewed the online collection of interviews of CRS former mediators that compose the Oral History Project conducted by Richard Salem and Heidi and Guy Burgess.[1] I also interviewed a number of government officials and civil rights leaders to develop my account of the conception and creation of CRS. My second resource was my collection of materials pack-ratted for more than a quarter of a century, including a variety of internal memorandums, informal CRS communications, operations manuals, staff training material, and case evaluation reports, as well as a sampling of CRS publications and relevant publications of other government agencies and national organizations. Third was my collection of CRS Annual Reports, each of which recounts the agency's major concerns and summarizes a good variety of each year's cases. For details of date, local color, and chronology, I most frequently went to the files of the *New York Times* and the *Washington Post*.

That's how I learned about what CRS did and how it did it. I also had the benefit of twenty-four years of professional and personal interaction with my CRS colleagues.

While I share with the reader the obvious question as to whether familiarity may have clouded the author's objectivity, I trust that my many years of studying CRS's performance for shortfalls as well as achievements has resulted in a reasonably balanced report.

1. Http://www.colorado.edu/conflict/civil_rights/interviews.

Acknowledgments

Many people who worked for the Community Relations Service between 1964 and 1989 consented to be interviewed by me, and I am grateful for their help and encouragement. While the contributions of only some are identified by name in the text, the work of all is meant to be represented. The picking and choosing was not value-based but opportunistic—a function of what fit with memory and with other sources of information and of a practical need to boil eighteen chapters of original intent down to a doable eleven.

I also enjoyed reading, and benefited from, the interviews of former CRS mediators that appear online as the Civil Rights Mediation Oral History Project.

I am indebted to all I interviewed, as well as to the many other CRS staff members whose experiences and insights during a quarter century enriched my understanding of the matters I have chosen to write about.

The CRS staff members I interviewed include: Gonzalo Cano, Leo Cardenas, Jonathan Chace, LeRoy Collins, James Draper, Nancy Ferrell, Harold Fleming, Robert Greenwald, John Griffin, Silke Hansen, Ben Holman, Robert Hughes, Jay Janis, Julian Klugman, Calvin Kytle, Robert Lamb Jr., James Laue, Ephrain Martinez, Art Montoya, John Perez, John Perry, Wilbur Reed, Dennis Renault, Victor Risso, Richard Salem, Manuel Salinas, Seymour Samet, A. M. Secrest, Ozell Sutton, Jesse Taylor, Abraham Venable, Martin Walsh, Wallace Warfield, Roger Wilkins.

The story of CRS's creation and first years was greatly illuminated for me as a result of interviews with several participants in, or close observers of, that process. These include: Arnold Aronson, Hyman Bookbinder, John Doar, David Filvaroff, Nicholas Katzenbach, Burke Marshall,

Harry McPherson, Joseph Rauh, Gerald Siegel, John Siegenthaler, Theodore Sorensen, John Stewart, Lee White.

James Laue enriched his interviews with the gift of relevant CRS papers from his personal collection. His widow, Mariann, later gave me the bulk of his CRS files. Harold Fleming augmented his interviews by later sending me a copy of the CRS chapter of his then work in progress, *The Potomac Chronicle,* which was ultimately completed by his widow, Virginia, and published by the University of Georgia Press.

The program, performance, and ethos of the Community Relations Service described in this book were shaped and influenced by many members of its staff. None had a more significant impact on it than the founding director, LeRoy Collins, who invested it with his reputation for rectitude, fairness, and goodwill; Roger Wilkins, who imbued it with the sense of mission that continued to energize the organization for many years after his incumbency as director; and Gilbert Pompa, whose earlier experience as a CRS conciliator gave a sense of reality to his drive as director to continually elevate the standards of professional performance. Although this narrative focuses on the work of CRS field representatives, the character and quality of that work were enhanced by a leadership cadre that helped to provide guidance and essential "body English." Among those who provided this distinguished service over the years are Jonathan Chace, George Culberson, Harry Martin, Roscoe Nix, Gail Padgett, and Wallace Warfield. Perhaps the most underappreciated heroes of the service were its regional directors, who, because of the small size of the agency, contributed significantly to the formulation of national programs, while they bore responsibility for all conflict resolution in their multistate regions and personally mediated some of the most critical cases. Representative of this group are: Leo Cardenas, Julian Klugman, Robert Lamb Jr., John Perez, Richard Salem, Ozell Sutton, Jesse Taylor, and Martin Walsh. Senior mediators Edward Howden and Lawrence Turner were master trainers who could be counted on for exemplary work in the most demanding of special assignments.

My writing efforts were vastly improved thanks to the critical analyses of Caroline Eisenberg, Daniel Fischell, Gerson Goodman, and Rebecca Salokar. l am indebted to the companionate professional interests of my sons, David and Neil, who provided ever available sounding boards during the full length of an overlong writing journey. The continuing faith of my daughter, Susan Rae, and the encouragement of friends Sandra and Andrew Boots, Marjorie Eiseman, and Maxine Fischell always provided a boost. Elizabeth Lewis was a pillar of support when the going was tough.

Resolving Racial Conflict

Introduction

This book is about twenty-five years of racial conflict in America (1964–1989), and what was done by federal conciliators to help resolve it. It recounts America's civil rights struggle as seen through the eyes of the federal agency whose observers were almost always at ground zero working with antagonists to find solutions and to avoid or lessen violence.

The book looks at the celebrated breakthroughs that made change possible and the countless follow-throughs that converted possibility to reality. It tells of what happened when "the movement" played out—after bitter and triumphant demonstrations, after great court decisions and the passage of new laws, but somehow things didn't seem to get much better. Through the lens of conflict analysis it looks at the hedgerow warfare that followed the movement's victories—where every change toward a fairer balance of equity had to be defined, demanded, and fought for—issue by issue, institution by institution, city by city. It is about the struggles to consolidate the victories.

The data are drawn largely from the eyewitness experience of the handful of men and women whose job was to be there, at the center of the storm, to help forestall or resolve racial and ethnic disputes. Based in the Community Relations Service (CRS) of the Department of Justice, this multiracial cadre of conciliation and mediation specialists worked behind the scenes in more than twenty thousand confrontations involving racial and ethnic minorities. These have ranged from the disputes that attracted worldwide attention to the everyday affronts, assaults, and upheavals that marked the nation's adjustment to wider power sharing within an increasingly diverse population.

Created by Congress in the Civil Rights Act of 1964 to deal with civil rights disputes, the Community Relations Service dispatched its trouble-shooters to help at the march from Selma to Montgomery; at the urban riots of the sixties, seventies, and eighties; at the siege of Wounded Knee; at the school desegregation battles in the North and the South; and at the Gulf Coast fishing wars between Southeast Asians and Anglos. It helped to lessen the atmosphere of racial violence in every major American city and in many thousands of smaller communities.

CRS was not quite a year old on the night of June 4, 1965, when President Johnson spoke to the nation by radio from Howard University. He concluded by pronouncing a new civil rights goal.

> But freedom is not enough. You do not wipe away the scars of centuries by saying: now you are free to go where you want, do as you desire, and choose the leaders you please . . . it is not enough just to open the gates of opportunity. All our citizens must have the ability to walk through those gates. . . . This is the next and more profound stage of the battle for civil rights. We seek not just freedom but opportunity—not just legal equity but human ability—not just equality as a right and a theory, but equality as a fact and as a result.

The definition of the American condition as set forth by the president that night, and the new civil rights goal he specified, was to forecast the role of the Community Relations Service for the next quarter of a century and more. The battle for equality as a right and a theory had largely been won. The battle for equality as a fact and as a result lay ahead. It would have to be fought in all walks of life, especially on the local scene—in cities, counties, neighborhoods, and individual institutions. CRS would be there to witness the conflict and to help ease its pains.

One

Lyndon Johnson Sets the Stage

It was July 2, 1964. After a decade of racial turmoil, after a year of anguished debate, including a record eighty-three-day filibuster in the Senate, Congress—in the face of still solid southern resistance—had passed the most sweeping civil rights legislation since the post–Civil War period. President Lyndon Johnson was about to sign it, and the White House spared no effort to dramatize the moment.

The Civil Rights Act was rushed to the president within hours of final congressional approval. In the East Room the stage had been set for a full-production signing ceremony at which the president's message would be loud and clear. The media had been alerted so that the word would go forth during prime time. All the leaders of the civil rights movement, the most powerful members of Congress, and the key figures of the Justice Department had been invited to share the moment that would crown their labors and establish the law.

The citizens of a concerned nation were looking on, many with grave doubts and questions. For minorities—particularly blacks—the question was: would the federal government make sure that the law was obeyed? For southerners, it was: would federal enforcement bring the "police state" that some of their spokesmen had decried? For conservatives, it was: how much federal intrusion would there be in local affairs? For most Americans—and for the president himself—there was one overarching question: would this end the violence, or would defiance of the new law require harsh federal enforcement that would add fuel to the already inflamed passions that had been tearing the country apart?

To Help the Medicine Go Down

The Civil Rights Act of 1964 was strong medicine. It reached into the fiber and tissue of American society, creating new channels for redress of racial discrimination. It declared job discrimination unlawful and created the Equal Employment Opportunities Commission. It outlawed segregation in all publicly supported facilities and certain establishments serving the general public. It strengthened protections of equality in voting and in education. It required policies of racial equity in every institution that accepted a dollar of federal assistance.

The president's remarks were a plea for reconciliation. He sounded a call for voluntary compliance. He made little reference to the substance of the new law; he spoke, instead, of how he was going to help the medicine go down. He discussed none of the details of what the legislation contained save for one of its lesser—and little-debated—provisions. This was the establishment in the Department of Commerce of a federal mechanism for the conciliation of racial conflict. The Community Relations Service had been created to help communities voluntarily reduce racial violence and comply with civil rights laws.

The reason for his special emphasis was rooted in his understanding of the times. It also reflected the impact of the previous ten years on Lyndon Johnson the man and Lyndon Johnson the politician.

Racial conflict born of resistance to the Negro thrust for social and economic equity had been searing the American consciousness for a full ten years. It started with the Supreme Court's landmark school desegregation decision in May 1954, which was followed two months later by the formation in Mississippi of the first fortress of opposition, the White Citizens Council. Similar organizations then mushroomed throughout the South. Massive resistance to school desegregation followed. This was marked by violence, intimidation, school closings, and confrontations between blacks and whites, between federal law enforcement agents and local communities.

The killing of fourteen-year-old Emmett Till in 1955 had been headlined around the world as symbolic of brutally enforced repression of blacks in America. Ensuing years were marked by a string of dramatic events. There was the Montgomery bus boycott and the consequent birth of the Southern Christian Leadership Conference (SCLC). There were the sit-ins and freedom rides and the birth of the Student Nonviolent Coordinating Committee (SNCC). There were the torchings and bombings of black churches and the homes of civil rights leaders. There were the murders of civil rights activists. There was the application of federal force: to enforce school desegregation in Little Rock; to face down Governor George Wallace's effort to bar the entry of a black student at the University of Alabama; to assure safe entry of blacks at the University of Georgia and the University of Mississippi. There were the assaults by law enforcement agencies on peaceful protesters in Birmingham. And there was the 1963 March on Washington by a quarter-million advocates of civil rights legislation.

In June 1964, at the very time that Congress was bringing the Civil Rights Act to its culminating votes, the nation's headlines reflected a fever of racial violence. Eight hundred whites assaulted a civil rights demonstration in St. Augustine, Florida, hospitalizing nineteen Negroes. The disappearance (and suspected murder) of three civil rights workers in Mississippi alarmed the nation, causing the president to send hundreds of military personnel to help search for the bodies. Thousands of northern college students were recruited and trained for civil rights work in the South that summer. The Justice Department warned that the federal government lacked the jurisdiction and resources to guarantee their safety.[1]

The disproportionate attention given by Johnson at the signing ceremony to the Community Relations Service and to voluntary compliance reflected his reading of the temper of the times. Millions of whites bitterly resented, and many feared, the imposition of federal law that would wipe away a cherished way of life. Millions of blacks—and whites as well—were determined that the new law, won after ten years of protest in the face of violent resistance, must be obeyed. Many Americans saw the potential for new violence. As a pragmatist, Johnson believed in the value of persuasion and negotiation. As a politician facing nomination and election challenges later in the year, he knew he had to stand four-square behind the nation's now highly popular civil rights goals. At the same time, he must, at all cost, avoid circumstances that might require him to order U.S. troops to take action—at gunpoint if necessary—against a resistant South.

Legislative History

Johnson's advocacy of a federal conflict resolution capability contrasted sharply with the less-than-major priority assigned to that provision by the civil rights bill's staunchest advocates. Most of them looked upon it

---

1. Remarks of John Doar, assistant attorney general for civil rights, at a training session in Oxford, Ohio, to prepare two hundred college students for the 1964 summer project.

as a useful adornment but not critical. LBJ, on the other hand, was personally committed to nurturing it and assuring achievement of its full potential. For the next two years he gave it closer personal attention than he did any other federal agency of such relatively microscopic proportions. He gave it higher priority than did any president who followed him.

Johnson had first envisioned a federal agency to mediate racial conflict seven years earlier, during Senate consideration of the Civil Rights Act of 1957. It reflected his conviction that most conflict could be negotiated. "Let us reason together" was a well-worn phrase in his Senate—and later in his White House—vocabulary. Why not create a racial conflict resolution service similar to the Federal Mediation and Conciliation Service, which mediated labor disputes? He took his idea to Arthur Goldberg, a distinguished labor relations lawyer (later to serve as a Supreme Court justice and as U.S. ambassador to the United Nations). At Johnson's request Goldberg and Gerald Siegel, counsel to the Senate Policy Committee (which Johnson chaired as majority leader), worked up proposed legislation. But Johnson did not introduce it. Rowland Evans and Robert Novak reported: "Ben Cohen had told Johnson repeatedly that it would never satisfy the liberals. The proposal never left Johnson's pocket."[2] The civil rights bill that was enacted in 1957 authorized the creation of two other agencies—the independent Civil Rights Commission and the Civil Rights Division of the Department of Justice.

Johnson waited until the next session of Congress to introduce a bill calling for creation of a Community Relations Service. It envisioned a race relations agency with a staff of one hundred working out of regional offices to help local communities when disagreement threatened to disrupt peaceful relations among citizens.

Johnson's speech introducing that bill—considered by the Senate Judiciary Committee, but never acted upon—reflected an acute understanding of the dynamics of community conflict and a vision of the inevitability of civil rights changes. It was years ahead of what the public would hear from any other high-ranking official.

The idea of a federal conciliation effort in the civil rights field caught on in other quarters. The Civil Rights Commission proposed that a conciliation function, to be focused on school desegregation, be added to the commission's own responsibilities. Harris Wofford, counsel of the commission, (later to be the civil rights flag bearer of the Kennedy White House and still later a U.S. senator from Pennsylvania), reported in his book *Of Kennedys and Kings:*

2. Evans and Novak, *Lyndon B. Johnson: The Exercise of Power,* 126.

The Commission also recommended that it be authorized "to establish an advisory and conciliation service to assist local school officials in developing plans designed to meet constitutional requirements and local conditions and to mediate and conciliate, upon request, disputes as to proposed plans and their implementation." This was an idea that Lyndon Johnson had been advancing for several years. Civil rights leaders tended to look askance at any such approach that implied mediation instead of enforcement, but the Northern Commissioners joined their Southern colleagues in thinking such a service could be constructive.[3]

In the Eighty-seventh Congress (1961–1962), bills calling for a Community Relations Service were submitted by various liberal representatives and senators. None were reported out of committee.

The comprehensive civil rights bill that the Kennedy administration submitted to the Eighty-eighth Congress on June 19, 1963, did provide, in its original Title IV, for the establishment of a Community Relations Service. It was consistent in form and function with the original Johnson proposal of 1959. It had not been included in the White House staff's original conception of the bill but had been added as an afterthought.

Even though Vice President Johnson was chairman of the President's Committee on Equal Employment Opportunity, White House staff had failed to include him in the earliest discussions of the proposed civil rights legislation. Lee White, who served as presidential counsel and civil rights point man under both Kennedy and Johnson, recalls that Johnson brooded about this. "He was a proud and in some ways a sensitive guy. He did not want to insinuate himself. But if President Kennedy asked him to do something, he was delighted."[4] Finally, in the last days before the bill was sent to Congress, President Kennedy directed that LBJ be drawn into the circle, and for the duration of the Kennedy administration he energetically served as a major civil rights strategist.

Theodore C. Sorensen, one of President Kennedy's closest advisers, recalls Johnson proposing the creation of the Community Relations Service in the course of a long telephone conversation between Sorensen and LBJ on June 3, 1963. Sorensen had called to get the vice president's input for the civil rights bill then reaching its final stages of refinement. In his book *Kennedy,* Sorensen notes that the bill, as finally submitted, "was different in several respects from the bill we had first discussed with Justice the previous month. . . . With the backing of the Vice President, a Community Relations Service had been added to work quietly with local communities in search of progress. (Negro congressmen had urged that the words

3. Wofford, *Of Kennedys and Kings: Making Sense of the Sixties.*
4. White, interview with the author.

'mediation' and 'conciliation' had an 'Uncle Tom' air about them and should be stricken from the title.)"[5]

Burke Marshall, who was Robert Kennedy's assistant attorney general for civil rights, headed the Justice Department's effort to draft a bill that would be both effective and passable. He, too, credits Johnson with primary influence in putting the CRS provision into the legislation.[6]

Johnson's 1958 advocacy of a Community Relations Service is one of the early bits of data that must be considered in the long-running debate of whether LBJ came to be a civil rights partisan as a result of nurture or nature—of politics or commitment. In the late fifties, Johnson was regarded by the civil rights community as "the enemy." Starting as a Texas congressman in 1939, and then as senator, he had voted against every civil rights measure that had been proposed. As majority leader of the Senate, he had orchestrated the fight against all efforts to weaken the filibuster—the parliamentary device by which the southern minority had been able to resist all civil rights proposals.

Then Johnson made a 180-degree turn on civil rights, according to his most bitter foes. Arnold Aronson, who for almost three decades had been the executive secretary of the Leadership Conference on Civil Rights, said:

> Lyndon Johnson was the one who beat us all the time. So from that point of view we regarded him as the enemy. And in '57 it was Lyndon Johnson who engineered the act's passage by removing what we regarded as the most important part, which was Title III, which was injunctive power. So Johnson was the enemy. My own feeling, based on what happened later, was that we were wrong. Lyndon Johnson in the early years really identified primarily with his experience with Hispanics more than with blacks. And you find in the early period, long before he became prominent, that there were evidences that he really felt something which as a southern politico he couldn't show. Remember, there were only three southern members of the Senate who didn't sign the Southern Manifesto.[7] One of them was Lyndon Johnson. My feeling is that he did what he could. And as soon as he had the clout of the presidency, he went all the way. I think it was genuine. There's no question he was the greatest president so far as civil rights is concerned. Whether we could have gotten this bill through in the shape that it is with Kennedy, I doubt very much. Johnson addressed the joint session five days after the assassination. He said, "This is the Kennedy legacy and we are going to pass it." It was the first priority that he took on. We didn't have to pressure the White House the way we normally did. He was after us. He'd be calling all the time. Have you done this, have you

5. Sorensen, telephone interview with the author; Sorensen, *Kennedy,* 496.
6. Marshall, telephone interview with the author.
7. On March 12, 1956, one hundred southern senators and congressmen issued the Southern Manifesto, opposing the Supreme Court's 1954 decision on school desegregation.

been in touch with X, have you thought about Y. He used all of his political pressures and leverage and know-how.[8]

Joseph Rauh, as counsel for the Leadership Conference on Civil Rights, had been at the forefront of those lobbying for congressional action. He saw Johnson as struggling between his dues-paying obligation to his southern constituency and the requirement of his political ambition to win acceptance within the broadest spectrum of both the party and the electorate. To find and focus on "safe" civil rights issues appealed to him as an acceptable risk. One such safe issue was the Civil Rights Commission, whose creation he had supported in the Civil Rights Act of 1957. A second was the Community Relations Service. Both might be defined as procedural rather than substantive. They did not, by their creation, change anything. As Rauh put it:

> In '56, or '57, a House bill came over that was very strong on civil rights, and Johnson flattened it. He wanted a bill that could be called a civil rights bill that wouldn't get him in dutch with Texas. So what he did was to say to guys like us—Clarence Mitchell and me, primarily—who were the chief lobbyists for the Leadership Conference, "I'm giving you these things."
>
> What he "gave" us were largely things for which people couldn't hit him too hard: a Civil Rights Commission and an assistant attorney general for civil rights. (Which also meant a Civil Rights Division.) He had to fight us on the important things like school desegregation.
>
> In '59, when he proposed the Community Relations Service—that, too, was of a character that doesn't get Texas anti–civil rights people up in arms. You've got to have people who try to keep the peace. It was the perfect Johnsonian thing. He needed things to help his national ambition to be president, but as a Texas senator he also needed to make sure the right wing down there wouldn't beat him up politically.

Johnson's role as an advocate of the 1964 legislation first became apparent to the civil rights leaders when a group of them were invited to meet with President Kennedy and his staff for a briefing on the new bill. Rauh remembered:

> On the twenty-first of June 1963, President Kennedy called the leaders of the civil rights groups to the White House. He left that meeting after about an hour, and Johnson, the vice president, and Robert Kennedy, the attorney general, remained. I didn't know who was in charge. They hated each other's guts. I knew Bobby Kennedy was not sympathetic to strengthening the bill. I didn't know anything about Johnson. Each of us got a chance to say something. I said, "Mr. Vice-President, will we be able to work together, with us seeking strengthening amendments which you have not put in the

8. Aronson, interview with the author.

bill, the most important of which, of course, would be the Equal Employment Opportunity Commission?"

I held my breath. And Johnson said, "I don't see why that's inconsistent at all. It never hurts for us to have pressure from the left." He gave my dream answer. He was free of all the constraints of Texas politics. He now was going to go to the left of the administration and say that we could work for those additions. And of course we did get them.[9]

Johnson's advocacy was only one of several factors arguing for inclusion of a conflict resolution capability in the Civil Rights Act. There were two others. The first was the example of effective third-party mediation in the recent settlement of conflict in Birmingham. The second was widespread concern that there would be massive resistance to the desegregation of public accommodations, and conciliation teams would be needed in countless communities to limit controversy and reduce violence.

The logic of using federal mediation to resolve community conflict had been demonstrated a number of times in the early sixties, but nowhere more dramatically than in Birmingham, where the Justice Department, at the bidding of the president, went outside its normal responsibilities of law enforcement and prosecution and sought to bring antagonists together to negotiate a settlement.

Birmingham had represented the high-water mark in protest, in anti-Negro violence by law enforcement officers as well as by lawless whites, and in worldwide notoriety. Martin Luther King Jr. and six thousand others had been jailed. Public Safety Commissioner Bull Connor had become a world-class bully overnight by unleashing dogs and fire hoses on protesters in the view of television cameras.

At the same time that the protest and violence in Birmingham were reaching a crescendo, Burke Marshall had painstakingly sought to develop a negotiating dialogue. Amid a setting in which passion and posture made true communication between antagonists impossible, he discreetly worked behind the scenes to engineer confidential negotiations between a few of the more conservative Negro leaders and influential pillars of the white business community. The resulting peace formula became the basis for the ultimate agreement. Recalling that venture in 1989, Marshall said:

We had just gone through a period of demonstrations in Birmingham, which showed one thing: that is there was no way legally for the federal government to get at that problem. The demonstrations had to do with employment problems, lunch-counter problems, street problems, a whole array of disparate problems that weren't covered by the existing statutes. I spent a lot of time myself, in Birmingham, doing something that had nothing to do

9. Rauh, interview with the author.

with my job—just to try to bring some kind of racial understanding. So there was a common understanding within the administration that that kind of work needed to be done. The only question was whether it should be institutionalized. I was in favor of institutionalizing it because it was a burden on my own time in addition to all the litigation work.[10]

In his message transmitting the civil rights bill to Congress, President Kennedy specifically cited the effective conciliation work of the Department of Justice in Birmingham. He went on to say that "dialogue and discussion are always better than violence—and this agency (the Community Relations Service), by enabling all concerned to sit down and reason together, can play a major role in achieving peaceful progress in civil rights." He wanted the new agency to "work quietly to improve relations in any community threatened or torn with strife."

In Kennedy's mind and in the minds of congressional leaders, the fear that communities might be "threatened or torn with strife" was rooted primarily in concern that throughout the South there would be widespread resistance to the provision of the new law that barred discrimination in places of public accommodation. These facilities—hotels, restaurants, gas stations, theaters, retail stores—were precisely the ones where denial of racial equality had triggered bitter protest and violent resistance in the past decade.

A confidential survey of opinions in almost six hundred southern communities indicated that while there had been some desegregation of public facilities, one-third of these towns were "dead set against all form of desegregation."[11]

It was certain that access to segregated premises would be tested by America's Negro population just as soon as the law was enacted. If there was no compliance, not only would protests be resumed, but it would be incumbent on the federal government to enforce the law.

Burke Marshall could visualize a litigative nightmare. He recalled: "I was very concerned, fortunately without reason, that the bill would be signed and we would have racial discrimination in public places throughout the South made illegal overnight, and that nobody would comply with it. It would be like schools. We would have to bring a hundred thousand lawsuits. I could foresee an enormous law enforcement problem. I wanted to push every button I could find to lead people toward voluntary compliance with Title II."[12]

10. Marshall interview.
11. Reported by Evans and Novak in the *Washington Post,* May 27, 1964.
12. Marshall interview.

Negotiation and persuasion seemed to be a far better course for the federal government than legal action. The latter option would require the employment of hundreds of additional Department of Justice personnel: FBI agents to investigate charges, prosecutors to prepare the cases, marshals to enforce court orders, to say nothing of the hundreds of courtroom years.

To political leaders North and South the prospect of federal law enforcement pitted against many southern institutions for many years was one to be avoided at all cost. Also, the idea of first trying to settle conflict by negotiation was seen by many as a spoonful of sugar that might help the bitter medicine of the civil rights law go down a bit more smoothly.

To some political analysts the spoonful of sugar theory was applied even further. Cabell Phillips, writing in the *New York Times* on July 3, 1964, the day after President Johnson signed the bill into law, said:

> The Community Relations Service called for in the bill is intended primarily as a mediator that will compose the intense local feelings certain to arise under application of the public accommodations and fair employment sections of the bill. The new agency is not only to be headed by a Southerner, Governor Collins, but it is to be set up administratively in the Department of Commerce where another Southerner presides, former Governor Luther Hodges of North Carolina. Thus a conspicuous effort has been made at the *outset* to make the mediation agency acceptable to Southern leaders in whose communities its greatest effort will be concentrated.

The Winning of the Civil Rights Act

The Civil Rights Act of 1964 emerged from Congress with wide bipartisan support, but only after a year of debate marked by bitter conflict, heartening cross-party cooperation, and skillful dealing and manipulation within the legislative process. The proposal for a Community Relations Service, originally known as Title IV of the administration's bill, encountered little serious opposition. Neither friends nor foes of civil rights saw it as a major new protection for minorities. It was regarded merely as a possible cure for the side effects of conflict that the new law might engender. Nevertheless, the proposal almost died before birth—a victim more of neglect than of opposition.

Because of the importance attached to it, the civil rights bill was introduced jointly in Congress by Emanuel Celler, Democrat of Brooklyn, New York, and chairman of the House Judiciary Committee, and William McCulloch, Republican of Ohio and ranking minority member of the committee. Speaker John McCormick assigned it to the Judiciary Committee, where Chairman Celler assigned it to Subcommittee 5, which he himself chaired. The subcommittee consisted of seven Democrats and four Republicans. Liberals of both parties were clearly in the majority. The overall result of the subcommittee's work was a stronger bill than the administration had proposed.[13] It was so strong that the attorney general requested a hearing before the full committee to ask that it be watered down. The administration feared that too strong a bill might impede its chances of approval by the full House and Senate. In the subcommittee hearings the CRS proposal enjoyed a modest show of support. The only specific opposition came from Representative Armistead I. Selden, an Alabama Democrat. He stated that it was not appropriate for the federal government to be involved in community relations.

The highly organized and effective civil rights lobby had been primarily concerned with preserving and strengthening the more substantive provisions of the bill. The focus of its members was on the achievement of major breakthroughs in voting rights and public accommodations. They wanted to empower the attorney general to bring suit against segregated schools and public facilities. They sought an end to discrimination in all federally assisted programs. Community relations was a far lower priority.

Arnold Aronson recalled: "[W]e were concerned primarily with prohibiting discrimination—whether it was in public accommodations, whether it was in employment, or housing. Our interest was in establishing a body of law—and in overturning existing law—which was segregation. That was tough enough, so that we didn't give CRS any priority."[14]

Thus propelled by no more than mild favor and slight criticism, the provision for a Community Relations Service apparently became lost in the shuffle of highly charged debate. It was not part of the bill that the committee reported to the full House of Representatives. It was restored in a last-minute maneuver that has never been fully explained.

At 6:00 p.m. on February 10, 1964, after nine full days of House debate, and only two hours before the final enactment would occur, Representative Robert T. Ashmore, Democrat of South Carolina, introduced an amendment providing for a Community Relations Service.

Apparently by prearrangement, and to expedite final passage of the bill that night, Cellar and McCulloch both declared the measure to be merely technical, and acceptable to them. It was promptly adopted. According to Charles and Barbara Whalen, "This ready concurrence was a deliberate

13. Charles Whalen and Barbara Whalen, *The Longest Debate: A Legislative History of the 1964 Civil Rights Act.*
14. Aronson interview.

move by the two leaders to appease conservative house members by incorporating into the law a mechanism which, if effective, would greatly reduce federal involvement in local civil rights disputes. The new title [Title X] was quickly adopted by voice vote."[15]

The big fight over the Civil Rights Act took place in the Senate, where an eighty-three-day filibuster, the longest on record, was broken by the required two-thirds vote. To weaken the traditional anti–civil rights alliance between southern Democrats and conservative Republicans, careful and convoluted political manipulation was needed. A primary focus of strategy was on winning over the minority leader of the Senate, William McKinley Dirksen. He was subjected to the massed persuasive power of Lyndon Johnson, Senate Majority Leader Mike Mansfield, and Senator Hubert Humphrey, the floor manager of the bill. The vehicle for victory was a Mansfield-Dirksen substitute for the House bill. The substitute did little damage to the measure passed by the lower chamber.

The CRS provision was strengthened in the Mansfield-Dirksen substitute. It differed from the House measure in four respects: It eliminated a ceiling of six on the number of regular employees. It specifically added voluntary associations to the state and local public agencies with which CRS was encouraged to cooperate. It imposed penalties of up to a year in prison and a $1,000 fine on employees who failed to hold confidential all information so imparted to them in the course of conciliation. The substitute bill also gave the Community Relations Service an additional role by writing it into Title II, which provided for injunctive relief against discrimination in places of public accommodation. The federal courts were authorized (but not required) to refer such cases to CRS for a period of up to 120 days, for purposes of working out voluntary compliance. The CRS provision received little attention in the ensuing Senate discussion. Initiating formal debate on the House bill on March 30, Senator Humphrey commented on each title. All he had to say about the CRS proposal was: "In many cases mediation and litigation work together effectively. Individual restaurant or hotel owners may be reluctant to admit Negroes unless assured that their competitors will do likewise. Through the good offices of the Community Relations Service, or of comparable state or local organizations, it may be possible to achieve agreement among all or substantially all of the owners."

During the debate, five amendments pertaining to CRS were defeated by large majorities. Senator Sam Irvin of North Carolina proposed elimi-

15. Whalen and Whalen, *Longest Debate,* 120.

nation of the Community Relations Service because it would be redundant to the Civil Rights Commission and the Civil Rights Division of the Department of Justice. Senator Strom Thurmond of South Carolina offered four CRS amendments. One would have permitted breaches of confidentiality in providing information to Congress. The second would have limited the number of employees to ten. The third would have limited CRS's jurisdiction to cases affecting interstate commerce, rather than to those that *might* affect interstate commerce. The fourth would have barred CRS from entering a case except on invitation of the community.

The CRS amendments offered by Senator Thurmond were among a hundred or so he proposed covering every feature of the act. To his colleagues he was "just going through the motions," since the South had lost its case when cloture had been voted. John Stewart, legislative aide to Hubert Humphrey during both his senatorial and vice presidential years, recalls sitting next to Humphrey and Senator Richard Russell, leader of the southern wing of the Senate, during the consideration of the Thurmond amendments. Russell leaned across to Humphrey and said: "Can't we shut him up somehow?"

Efforts to Soften Southern Resistance

Even before the congressional battle over the civil rights bill was won, the bill's backers saw the need to build massive public support. This support would be necessary not only to win passage of the law but also to win voluntary compliance with it after it was passed. Strategists in the Justice Department, the White House, and the civil rights community believed that the massive resistance that had followed the Supreme Court's school desegregation decision in 1954 had resulted in part from the silence of the more responsible political and business leaders of southern communities. The false dream that somehow delay and obstruction would prevent the inevitable change had been allowed to blossom so that the leaders themselves became prisoners of the call for resistance. To avoid that scenario when the Civil Rights Act was passed, southern community leaders—and responsible leaders throughout the country—would have to be prepared in advance.

The first step in this strategy had been initiated by the Kennedy White House in the summer of 1963. President Johnson continued and embellished it. It had started with a series of gatherings at the White House at which the president met with the foremost leaders of public opinion in various walks of life. Separate sessions were held with the nation's most prominent lawyers, business leaders, prelates of the religious communities, and educators, as well as with civil rights and civic organization heads. In these meetings the president shared his knowledge and fears as to the potential for violent resistance and sought to persuade his listeners to use their influence to make the inevitable civil rights changes work. A total of eleven White House meetings, with sixteen hundred of America's most influential citizens, were held by both Kennedy and Johnson.

Early in 1964 the administration launched another behind-the-scenes unofficial endeavor. Called Project Compliance, it was designed to persuade government and business leaders throughout the South to use their influence to encourage voluntary compliance with the impending legislation. An informal network of civil rights advocates in the federal government and in the private sector had been consulting together regularly on civil rights strategies. Within that framework Burke Marshall had proposed the idea of Project Compliance to Harold Fleming of the Potomac Institute. The institute thereafter served as the secretariat of the program.

The effort was headed jointly by Fleming and Louis Oberdorfer, then an assistant attorney general and later a federal judge. The project enlisted teams of important businessmen and government leaders and assigned them to visit with their counterparts in selected southern cities. They presented the president's appeal that, as a patriotic duty, they use their influence to prepare their communities for peaceful compliance with the new law.

Special emphasis was placed on appeals to the business community. Discussions with chambers of commerce emphasized two points: first, that the law would be enforced; second, that resistance, with its potential for confrontation and violence, would be bad for business. The community leaders were asked to use their influence with the political leadership to establish a community ethos of peaceful compliance. According to Fleming:

> When the Civil Rights Act was pending, the anticipation was that the biggest danger would be massive resistance to Title II—public accommodations. So the thought about controlling the degree of resistance started months before the Act actually passed. We built profiles of many of the southern communities—what the climate of opinion was, the public facilities under siege, what the political leadership and newspapers were like. We had files on possibly one hundred places in the South. An informal steering committee made the decisions as to which places seemed to warrant high priority and who among the business types could wield the most effective personal influence upon the business and official leadership of the targeted city.[16]

16. Fleming, interview with the author.

Some thought the southern business community did not need a lot of convincing. Lee White recalled that chambers of commerce were already reporting drops in convention business resulting from the civil rights turmoil.

It was apparent that Johnson saw the Community Relations Service as the final link in this strategy for winning voluntary compliance with the law. But before he would let it undertake its duties, he felt it necessary to give his personal direction and support to two additional efforts. The first was to win the cooperation of the southern state governments.

Focus on the Southern Moderate

When he signed the act on July 2, President Johnson announced his intention to appoint LeRoy Collins, a former governor of Florida, as the director of the Community Relations Service. At the same time, he gave Collins his first assignment. He was to form a team with two other former southern governors as the president's personal emissaries to each of the governors of the southern states. Their mission was to enlist their maximum efforts and influence to assure peaceful compliance with the new law. Serving with Collins were Buford Ellington of Tennessee and Luther Hodges of North Carolina. The three were chosen not only because of their records as racial moderates but also because of their personal influence with the state chief executives. Each was a former chairman of the Southern Governors Association.

President Johnson's second effort to win voluntary compliance was to mobilize America's most prominent citizens to be active supporters. To generate peer influence at the highest levels, he created the National Citizens Committee for Community Relations (NCC) as an adjunct of CRS. For this, he and his aides picked 450 leaders from all walks of life. Some, like Roger Blough, chairman of the U.S. Steel Corporation, and Charles Keller, president of the National Association of General Contractors, were included to note the stamp of approval of American industry. Others, such as Morris B. Abram, president of the American Jewish Committee, and George Meany, president of the AFL-CIO, were included as a link to the committed energies of the liberal community. Also included were the executive officers of Protestant, Catholic, and Jewish religious institutions, in order to harness the nation's moral commitment. Civil rights leaders and other prominent black and Hispanic individuals were part of the group. The presence of Conrad Hilton of Hilton Hotels, Kemmons Wilson of Holiday

Inns, and Julius Manger of Manger Hotels acknowledged the administration's special concern about discrimination in public accommodations.

For chairman of the NCC, Johnson chose a man of towering personal influence in America's corridors of power. He was Arthur Dean, senior partner in the Wall Street law firm of Sullivan and Cromwell. His reputation as a negotiator had long since been acknowledged by his selection in 1952 by President Eisenhower to head America's delegation to the truce negotiations ending the Korean War. The executive vice chairmen was Julius Manger. Vice chairman was John Wheeler, one of America's foremost black bankers.

On August 18, barely seven weeks after signing the civil rights act, Johnson met in the Rose Garden with the four hundred and fifty members of the NCC. They had assembled at short notice in response to telegrams of invitation from the president. Johnson appealed for their participation in a service of historic significance. He said, "We all know that the Emancipation Proclamation was signed 100 years ago, but emancipation was a proclamation, it was not a fact. So, upon you in your own communities falls the great task of these times, the task of fostering understanding, the task of securing observation and compliance, the task of assuring justice for all Americans."

On this hortatory plea—to achieve fulfillment of the Emancipation Proclamation—the members of the NCC departed the Rose Garden. Exactly how this endeavor was to be pursued was not made clear. Ultimately, as we shall see in the next chapter, members of the NCC were to exercise their influence and "clout" to further a number of activities aimed at advancing racial justice.

As these matters were proceeding, LeRoy Collins was enduring a minor but unanticipated harassment in winning confirmation in the Senate. Johnson had picked Collins, widely respected as a "moderate" southern leader, as the ideal symbol of reconciliation. As governor of Florida from 1954 to 1960, he had been able to make clear his respect for the rights of minorities and their claim for greater equity without losing the support of his white constituency. In 1960, when Tallahassee was threatened with racial violence, he calmed the storm by going on television to state that the issues would not be resolved by mobs, whether they were black or white. He acknowledged that while store owners might legally refuse service to Negroes if they chose, it was "unfair and morally wrong" to deny service at lunch counters to those whose trade they were willing to accept.

Collins had also shown himself willing to take political risks in the civil rights arena. Thurgood Marshall and Jack Greenberg of the National Association for the Advancement of Colored People (NAACP) had in 1952 unsuccessfully defended a black man accused of murder before an all-white jury in Orlando. In a community atmosphere of screaming racial invective, the jury, without supporting evidence, had handed down a verdict of death. The Supreme Court twice declined to hear the NAACP's appeal. Finally Collins, as governor, commuted the death sentence.

His influence beyond the borders of Florida had been demonstrated by his election as chairman of the Southern Governors Association. During the same time he also served as chairman of the National Governors Association. He was known to Americans across the nation who had watched on television his skillful and urbane performance as permanent chairman of the 1960 Democratic National Convention, which had nominated Jack Kennedy. Collins was credited with helping to bridge the factional differences between northern and southern delegates.

At his confirmation hearing on July 7 before the Senate Commerce Committee, Collins's nomination was opposed only by Strom Thurmond. In a two-hour interrogation, Thurmond accused Collins of turning his back on the South and also of changing his stand on issues after achieving national prominence. Collins defended his love for the South but conceded some changes in viewpoint. "We all grow and change," he said, "and have to meet new responsibilities. And I will not contend that I have not changed some of my positions as a result of better understanding."[17]

Collins and Thurmond were no strangers to each other. They represented the opposite poles of social viewpoint among southern politicians. The two had faced each other seven months earlier when Thurmond had been in the audience as Collins, then president of the National Association of Broadcasters, addressed the Greater Columbia (South Carolina) Chamber of Commerce. The date was December 3, less than two weeks after President Kennedy's assassination. Collins discussed problems of the South in the context of the violence and extremism abroad in the nation. His speech was studded with phrases that awakened controversy throughout the South:

> We have allowed extremists to speak for the South. . . . too many of the rest of us have remained cravenly silent or lamely defensive while Dixie battle cries have been employed to incite sick souls to violence. . . . How many Sunday school children have to be dynamited to death? How many Negro leaders have to be shot in the back? How many governors have to be shot in the chest? How many presidents have to be assassinated? . . . Any rational man who looks out at the horizon and sees the South of the future segregated is simply seeing a mirage.

17. *New York Times,* July 8, 1964.

At the first day of a favorable confirmation hearing, the subcommittee's endorsement of Collins was prevented only by Thurmond's calling attention to the absence of a quorum. At the next day's meeting, Thurmond lingered outside the door rather than entering and thus making the nine-member quorum. Senator Ralph Yarborough, of Texas, took him by the arm and urged him to come in. Thurmond then tried to keep Yarborough out. Thurmond twice threw Yarborough to the floor. With his shoulders pinned, Yarborough refused Thurmond's demand that he ask for release. Only when the chairman, Senator Warren Magnuson, rushed from the committee room and demanded that the two sixty-one-year-old senators break it up, did they rise, clap each other on the back, and enter the meeting room. Collins, on learning of the incident, said, "I've been hoping for support from the Senate floor but I was not expecting that kind of support from that kind of floor."[18]

The committee thereafter voted 16–1 to recommend Collins's confirmation. The full Senate followed suit with a 53–8 vote.

As further evidence of his concern with the role of the newborn agency, President Johnson personally handpicked Collins's deputy director, Harold Fleming. Fleming was president of the Potomac Institute in Washington, D.C., which had been established in 1961 to provide liaison and access between the civil rights community and federal agencies that were beginning to take on civil rights responsibilities but knew little about the problems, program needs, or players on the civil rights stage. A founder and past president of the National Association of Intergroup Relations Officials (NAIRO), Fleming had been executive director of the Southern Regional Council, an agency respected throughout the South for its research and education about social and economic problems impacting on blacks and on interracial problems in the region. The administration had previously called on him to serve as coleader of Project Compliance. Fleming was loaned to the Community Relations Service for a six-month period.

Thus launched by a powerful presidential shove, the good ship CRS sailed off on its mission. It had a captain and a first mate. No one knew better than they that despite the ceremonial launching and high expectations, there were no charts in the chart room and no clear star by which to steer.

18. *New York Times,* July 10, 1964.

Two

Learning Intervention

Intuition, Courage, and Goodwill

With racial controversy crackling throughout the South, the new conciliation agency found itself with a waiting list of calls for help from the moment of its creation in July 1964. The early conciliators plunged into the
peacemaker role armed with little more than goodwill, courage, intuition,
and faith in the power of persuasion. Despite a large measure of improvi-
sation, their efforts were, by and large, successful in helping to lessen conflict and violence. But it would take more than a year of learning and testing before the collective experience could be drawn together and take form
as a body of professional case practice.

By the end of 1965 assistance had been given to almost two hundred
communities. Seventy-eight percent were in fifteen southern and border
states. Most of them had populations of less than twenty-five thousand.
During that first year and a half, CRS acquired form and function while it
intervened in and witnessed events that marked historic social change. The
neophyte troubleshooters began to develop a methodology and to hone
their skills. While some also began to wonder about how much the role
of peacemaker could or should involve the role of change agent, national
events would be redefining their priorities and objectives.

Public Accommodations—A Better Outcome Than Expected

Minority access to public accommodations—the part of the Civil Rights
Act that its authors had feared would generate the most violent resistance—took center stage as soon as the law was signed.

The law and its enforcement were quickly challenged. In Atlanta, the Heart of Atlanta Motel sued to have the public accommodations provision declared unconstitutional. In Birmingham, the Justice Department, eager to establish the law's validity before the highest court, sued Ollie's Barbecue for violating the public accommodations clause. The issues in the two cases were slightly different and resulted in opposing decisions as to constitutionality from two different U.S. District Courts. The Heart of Atlanta Motel lost its fight, but Ollie's Barbecue prevailed. Both suits were appealed. They were argued together before the U.S. Supreme Court, which, on December 14, 1964, by unanimous decision, upheld the constitutionality of the law.[1]

At the same time that opponents were trying to get the law overturned, civil rights groups were testing to make sure it would be obeyed and enforced. The Congress of Racial Equality (CORE), long a major generator of social action in behalf of civil rights, was holding its national convention in Kansas City, Missouri, on July 2. One minute after President Johnson signed the act, a teenage delegate from Jackson, Mississippi, asked for a haircut in the Muehlebach Hotel barbershop. When he was refused, CORE members conducted a protest demonstration on the spot. The next morning, following brief negotiations between CORE and the hotel management, the young man returned to the barbershop and was served. Heartened by its success, CORE immediately sent testing instructions to its 114 affiliates around the country.

Within a week of the act's passage, the *New York Times* reported successful testing of public accommodations by black activists in cities and facilities across the South where there had formerly been unsuccessful protests of segregation. The major hotel chains set the pace for desegregation in city after city. All their chief executives had been taken into the administration's civil rights camp starting with the White House meetings in 1963–1964. Local managers had been softened up by the Project Compliance teams. They were particularly sensitive to the suggestion that conflict in the community was bad for business. As former Attorney General Nicholas D. Katzenbach reflected twenty-five years later: "The hotel people said they were all behind it [passage of the Civil Rights Act]. . . . They

1. Eighty-one years earlier, in 1883, the Supreme Court had ruled against Congress's authority to enact a public accommodations law, which had been defended then on the basis of the Fourteenth Amendment. In 1964 the Justice Department based its defense on the constitutional right of Congress to regulate interstate commerce. This the court found acceptable.

couldn't get a convention down there. . . . They weren't willing to do much in Congress, but they were willing to guarantee that when the law was passed they would comply from the first day."[2]

In August 1964, CRS surveyed fifty-three southern cities. Most of them reported compliance by about two-thirds of the affected establishments. By January 1965, other surveys showed continuing progress, albeit short of full compliance.[3] Thus, within six months of passage of the law desegregating public accommodations, it was apparent that voluntary compliance would prevail and that the tens of thousands of court cases that Burke Marshall had feared would not eventuate. It also became clear that public accommodations cases would not provide the overwhelming number of the confrontations that federal conciliators would have to defuse.

Despite the failure of public accommodations cases to hit the levels expected, persistent hard-core resistance to the law still overtaxed the government's ability to deal with it. The Justice Department's Civil Rights Division received six hundred complaints in six months. Hundreds of other conflicts that didn't lend themselves to resolution through the courts were also flaring.

The Growth of the Program and Its Methodology

Requests for federal conciliation assistance had begun to roll into the Commerce Department from communities torn by racial confrontation even before the new civil rights law had been signed. Anticipating that the Community Relations Service would be expected to perform from day one, the Commerce Department pulled together an informal task force ready to go into action the moment the ink on the president's signature was dry. Within forty-eight hours—on July 4, 1964—a special command post had been set up to monitor any violent protests that die-hard opponents of the law might generate on Independence Day. Hotlines were set up with the White House, the Justice Department, and other agencies so that all reports of trouble would be routed to one place and response could be coordinated. Jay Janis and Jerry Heilbron staffed the command post. Janis was later to recall: "We arrived at 7:00 a.m. ready for a hectic day but not knowing what to do. Especially me. At least Heilbron had worked for the Justice Department. We waited all day. Finally, about four in the

2. Katzenbach, telephone interview with the author.
3. As reported in the *New York Times* and *Wall Street Journal*.

afternoon, one call came in from a lady in the South wanting information about the Civil Rights Act. There were no disruptions, no protests."[4]

This experience was the first of scores that taught CRS two lessons. One was that when it came to forecasting how racial tensions would be acted out, there were no experts. The second was an obvious truth that was to become an article of faith: in the absence of predictability, contingency planning is a must.

Collins and Fleming rushed to recruit and deploy conflict conciliators even before a budget or position descriptions were developed and approved. As a brand-new federal organism, and one known to have the personal blessings of the president, CRS had access to all the strategies and resources that enable the federal government to achieve bureaucratic wonders overnight. The Commerce Department made operational funds immediately available from its own resources until a formal appropriation would be forthcoming. John Macy, chairman of the Civil Service Commission, personally visited with Collins to help plan the staffing and to grease the skids for a quick start. He convinced the new director that his initial personnel request was too modest, as was his request for hard-to-get supergrade positions. He then helped work out special hiring authority to speed recruitment.

While the early cadre was drawn from a variety of vocational backgrounds—law, education, journalism, religion, social service—it was by and large a homogeneous group. This was a consequence of the vision of CRS's role shared by the early managers and the usefulness of personal contacts when time is of the essence in recruiting a team that has to hit the ground running. For the most part, as the following portraits of a few of them show, the first employees were white males, sympathetic to civil rights goals, familiar with community dynamics in the South, and comfortable in dealing with the power structure elite.

Andrew MacDowd (Mac) Secrest, who published a South Carolina county newspaper, had been a Nieman Fellow at Harvard. He was frustrated by the racial inequities about him and believed that his knowledge of the rural South might be useful to the racial conciliation group about to be formed. He wrote to his cousin, Luther Hodges, the secretary of commerce, and asked if he could help. He was the first person named to the CRS task force.

Jay Janis, a Miami builder, was a volunteer civil rights activist for the American Jewish Committee in Miami. Exploring for public service oppor-

---

4. Janis, telephone interview with the author.

tunities in Washington brought him to the Commerce Department just as the task force was being formed. He signed on.

Seymour Samet was recruited by Janis. Samet was regional director of the American Jewish Committee in Florida and the first executive director of the Dade County Board of Human Relations. He was the only early worker with professional experience in community conflict resolution.

Jerome Heilbron, an Arkansas attorney, transferred from the Civil Rights Division of the Justice Department, where he had been seen as the leading advocate of negotiation—as opposed to litigation—for winning more rapid compliance with civil rights laws.

John Griffin, who arrived in September, was picked by Collins to be the first director of the conciliation field staff. Griffin, who had experience in labor arbitration, had been vice president of Florida State University at Tallahassee, where he had dealt with civil rights matters.

Abraham Venable, an MBA graduate of Howard University, was working with Undersecretary of Commerce Franklin D. Roosevelt Jr. on a program to enhance business opportunities for blacks. He was the first, and one of only a few, Negro conciliators taken on in the first year and a half.

Their initial approaches were as diverse as the personalities and experiences of each individual. The early cases provided a trial-and-error cram course in the processes and pitfalls of community dispute resolution. Gradually, as seat-of-the-pants intervention became validated by experience, a number of approaches were drawn into frequent use. Among them were establishing a "federal presence"; employing fact-finding and assessment; evoking peer pressure; activating higher authority; energizing civic responsibility; and motivating the power elite.

Immediately, the conciliators learned that outside intervention in a dispute, by its mere appearance, can sometimes alter the relationship and behavior of the antagonists. This was especially true when the intervener was a representative of the federal government. It was that principle that enabled the first conciliators to be at least minimally effective in winning compliance with the law and in lessening conflict. As one of them said, "In the rural south, the minute I step out of the rent-a-car, the scenario changes." It was important to learn where and when to use the federal presence. Local authorities were sometimes antagonized; minorities were sometimes mistrustful.

Even a simple phone call from a federal official signaled to the participants that someone was watching. It sometimes could encourage parties to make sure that their adherents were on good behavior. It often provided an opportunity for improved communication, fresh thinking, or modification of hardened positions. This kind of brief intervention was often necessary when scant resources had to be spread very thin.

A typical example involved a Negro family in a rural southern community that was being subjected to abuse and vandalism after moving into a white neighborhood. A CRS phone call to the sheriff inquiring about allegations that he had failed to provide protection resulted in periodic squad car patrols that discouraged the harassment.

A second approach was to trigger the involvement of higher authority. Sometimes an inquiry through the governor's office might result in a more diligent response from the sheriff.

"On-site assistance" was the buzz phrase denoting the preferred form of intervention, and "improved communication" was an invariable objective. Communication assistance took many forms, as needed. These included: identifying the parties who needed to communicate, carrying messages, clarifying issues, teaching both sides to listen, providing a reality check for participants, moving confrontation from the streets to the conference table, and transforming posturing to good-faith negotiating.

Seymour Samet, who had reservations about overreliance on federal presence, whether provided by telephone or by on-site service, would cite a favorite case to illustrate that more was often required. In late August 1964, CRS was asked to deal with the case of a drive-in movie theater in Fort Lauderdale. The theater segregated the audience by means of separate entrances for blacks and whites and a fence dividing the viewing area and refreshment stand. CORE had declared its intention to demonstrate in order to desegregate the facility. Samet phoned the owner and advised him of the requirements of the law.[5]

The proprietor remained adamant, so Mac Secrest was assigned to go on-site for face-to-face negotiation. He arrived at the Miami Airport just as Hurricane Cleo was approaching. He met with the protest group that night but could not get to see the theater operator. When he arrived at the drive-in the next morning, he found the owner ruefully surveying the storm damage, including a shattered fence. "I didn't know you fellows had the almighty on your side," he told Secrest. "The fence stays down. The place is integrated."[6]

Use of influential allies was another productive approach, including a number of the "movers and shakers" whom the president had enlisted in the National Citizens Committee for Community Relations. Julius Manger, for one, could always be counted on. On more than one occasion a per-

5. Samet, interview with the author.
6. Secrest, interview with the author.

sonal phone call to one of his hotels prompted the manager to take the lead in getting the local chamber of commerce to lean on city hall. A fuller appreciation of how demonstrations were bad for business often contributed to a local government's readiness to negotiate. Similarly, when Dick Gregory was turned away from the Holiday Inn in Selma, where he had gone to encourage the demonstrators, conciliator Mac Secrest called NCC member Kemmons Wilson, the Holiday Inn board chairman. The Selma Holiday Inn's discrimination policy was reversed in minutes.

Assessment—learning the facts and figuring out what they meant—was an obvious first step in conciliation.[7] It was more than just an information-gathering prelude. It had its own impact on the conflict resolution process.

From the outset, conciliators learned that perceptions were often as important as facts. In conflict situations it was how the facts were perceived that moved the parties to action. The search for facts and perceptions forced CRS to cast a wide net in seeking information. The immediate antagonists, generally white authorities and black complainants, saw the issues from their own highly focused—and sometimes very limited—points of view. Consequently, other factions and observers in both communities also had to be contacted. In the minority community, conciliators reached out beyond the recognized leaders and civil rights activists. They also consulted with informal spokespersons for the disenfranchised as well as with rank-and-file members of the victimized group.

This assessment process often irritated local authorities. They were not accustomed to having their word questioned and were discomfited by having to address long-ignored realities. They resented federal officials dignifying the "disreputable" by seeking their information and treating it with equal respect. But only in this way could the conciliator get a feeling for the phenomenon of multiple truths.

Another early approach was to energize civic responsibility. Members of the business and civic community—church federations, women's groups, chambers of commerce, and the like—were skilled in advocating their own social agendas. Frequently, however, they remained on the sidelines of racial controversy. Discussion with a federal conciliator often helped them to clarify their views and to be more comfortable in playing an active role in resolving the difficulty. Sometimes it worked the other way around; local business interests, valuing a stable community, would call on CRS for assistance.

7. Years later, assessment was to become a formal pillar of CRS's casework, including a written statement of the conciliator's objectives and his plan for achieving them.

Such a call came from Hilton Head, South Carolina, which was experiencing racial violence early in 1965 over issues of segregated schools. CRS was asked to intervene by Charles Frazier, a developer who planned to create a major resort community on the island. He saw his investment endangered if the island became the scene of racial violence. Jay Janis, who worked the case, recalled Frazier telling Collins: "It's bad for business. Besides, I don't want to see the Negroes get beat up."[8]

Janis was teamed up with John Wheeler, the black vice chairman of the National Citizens Committee. President of the Farmers and Mechanics Bank of Durham, North Carolina, Wheeler agreed to work as a volunteer conciliator as part of his commitment to the NCC. The combination of Wheeler and Janis—a Carolina-raised black banker and a white builder—struck Collins as a well-balanced team for the case. Janis recalls his first venture into the trenches for CRS as a learning experience:

> After a discussion with Frazier we set out to meet with the Negro community. It was eight or nine at night—in a real rural part of Hilton Head. In an old barn. Only one white face in the crowd—me. I was absolutely certain that the Ku Klux Klan was waiting outside to burn the place down. I had done a lot of civil rights work, but I had never been in quite that position before, in the rural South. Then we met with the white group, which was the school board. John's was the only black face in the room. I guess that John had felt there, and all of his life, like I had felt out there in the barn with the blacks. It was a great lesson to me how somebody like John had to feel. . . . As to what we accomplished—we got some conversation going between the blacks and whites. We followed up by telephone. Later, other conciliators went in. The situation was ultimately resolved.[9]

It was not long before the CRS troubleshooters came up against a dilemma the agency was never fully to resolve: what role does the conciliator play when conflict resolution and civil rights progress may be at cross purposes? Jim Draper first faced the problem in Jonesboro, Louisiana, a racial tinderbox at that time. Thirty years of experience as a reporter, advertising executive, and publisher had equipped Draper with hundreds of business and political contacts throughout Mississippi. As the onetime publisher of *Livestock Weekly,* he had personal credibility in rural areas among both blacks and whites. His strong views in favor of civil rights prompted him to enlist in CRS. Working out of Memphis, he was often the sole federal peacemaker in the back woods of Mississippi and Louisiana. As he remembered Jonesboro a quarter of a century later:

8. Janis interview.
9. Ibid.

The situation was explosive. There was a railroad that ran diagonally through the town. Whites lived on one side and blacks on the other. The Negro grievances were—everything: no mail delivery, garbage pickup, sewers, or street paving. The black schools were a travesty. In 1965 there was quite an organization going among the black people—started by CORE—two or three young people from Grambling. They had a little freedom house.[10] They decided they were going to march from the high school in the black part of town up over the railroad and meet at the courthouse, where demonstrations were off-limits. The Sheriff of Jackson Parish had a mounted posse of about fifty. I learned from a confidential source that they knew about the proposed march and intended to ambush the marchers just as they came over the railroad track. That could have been pretty bloody. I went back to Freedom House and, without telling them what I had learned, I persuaded them to change their route of march to the courthouse.[11]

Later somebody working with CORE berated Draper: "Nothing worthwhile ever happened in Jonesboro after that. Nobody was killed, shot, or put in jail that day. It stopped the movement." Years later, Draper wondered whether intervention that forestalled violence may have made CRS a role player rather than just a dispute resolver. He asked, "Did we slow down the pace of change by not letting events flow as they might have flowed?"[12]

Dealing with Political Influence

The need for federal conciliators to be insulated from political influence was learned early in the program. The desegregation of the schools in St. Helena Parish, Louisiana, provides an example. During one of Collins's out-of-town trips, Fleming fielded an urgent call from the White House. He was told that the St. Helena Parish school board had been required by the U.S. Court of Appeals to end its ten years of resistance and integrate

10. A variety of "freedom houses" were set up in the rural South as needed, to serve as headquarters and/or lodgings for civil rights workers and activities.

11. Draper, telephone interview with the author. The safeguarding of information given in confidence is an inviolable obligation of the intervener. Any conciliator would be limited in resolving conflicts without the full trust of the contesting parties. For the federal government's racial peacemakers, the obligation was reinforced by law. A year in jail and a $1,000 fine faced the CRS conciliator who revealed information gained in confidence. Congress put the provision into the Civil Rights Act to protect blacks from intimidation and reprisal as a result of talking to CRS representatives. But the sword cut both ways. To be an effective intermediary, CRS, as an agency, had to maintain a reputation of trustworthiness not only with the minority groups but with their antagonists as well.

12. Ibid.

its school system in September 1964. Violent opposition was certain. Fleming was advised to have CRS discuss the matter with the congressman from that district, Hale Boggs. The White House interest was clear. Boggs, as the majority whip, was a key player in pressing the president's program in Congress. He was currently struggling to maintain his seat in a close race against a white supremacist opponent. In recording his meeting with Boggs many years later, Fleming wrote:

> He made no bones about his political stake in the situation. Yet he wanted Governor Collins to understand that he was concerned about more than his own political fortunes. His position in the House could be vital to the success or failure of the Administration's legislative program. This included the social agenda, which was of even greater significance to blacks than to whites. He wanted the law of the land to prevail, but not at the needless price of his defeat and all that would entail. Besides, he concluded, it was a fact that St. Helena Parish was woefully unprepared for a sudden dismantling of its dual school system. The safety and well being of the black children, as well as the general community, would be served by delaying the effect of the ruling for at least a semester, thus allowing time to prepare the ground for a peaceful transition. . . . Boggs' argument struck me as an eloquent variation on the familiar refrain "the time isn't ripe." Still, I was impressed by the evident sincerity and effectiveness with which he made his case. I responded mildly that blacks might find it difficult to believe that the parish, after all those years of delay and inaction, would put more time to constructive use.[13]

Boggs asked Fleming to convey the situation to Collins and ask him whether CRS would consider appealing to the judge to delay implementation of the integration order for six months in order to reduce the likelihood of violence. He wanted Collins to know he would accept his decision. "You people have your job to do," he said.

Before making a judgment, Collins wanted CRS to conduct its own on-site assessment. In the absence of available staff, a distinguished educational consultant was engaged for the task. His report was grim. Segregationist passions were indeed inflamed. Desegregation in September would likely lead to violence. Black children would certainly be at risk. He recommended that desegregation be delayed and proposed a program for preparing the community for change in the interim.

Collins recognized the high stakes of this judgment call. For CRS to take a "go-slow" posture in its first major case might undercut the credibility of the agency in the civil rights community. On the other hand, consider-

13. Harold C. Fleming with Virginia Fleming, *The Potomac Chronicle: Public Policy and Civil Rights from Kennedy to Reagan*, 109.

ation had to be given to preventing the violence and psychological trauma that the black children would face.

In any event, the decision did not rest with CRS. If the federal government was to intervene with the court, it would have to be through the Department of Justice. Fleming was instructed to present Collins's viewpoint to Attorney General Robert Kennedy. Kennedy's conclusion was recounted by Fleming: "He explained that he had learned from hard experience that blacks were determined to decide for themselves what risks they should take in asserting their rights. This was as it should be. They would deeply resent it, he said, if the government, however well intentioned, should step in at this point and try to undo what they had fought so hard to achieve. All the Justice Department could do, he concluded, was to make every effort to prevent violence and intimidation." Fleming had no problem with that decision. He thought that Kennedy "now seemed a far cry from the man who had called on the freedom riders to suspend their protest, who had commended the Albany, Georgia, police chief for his gentility in rounding up and jailing black marchers, and who had complained that King's Birmingham demonstrations were ill-timed and ill-advised."[14]

Thus, CRS did not intervene. Desegregation of St. Helena Parish schools was initiated in September without widespread violence. Hale Boggs was reelected to Congress in November.

CRS soon learned that "congressional interest" in a case often went with the territory. It learned, too, that Congress had to be treated with respect but not obeisance. Congressional inquiries were more frequent in the early years. They would often be triggered by local officeholders who did not like to see federal officials conferring with protest leaders—whom they saw as disreputable troublemakers. Fearing, often correctly, that conciliation might lead to change, they called on their congressman to halt what they saw as an unwarranted federal intrusion.

Sometimes by letter, occasionally by personal briefing, CRS would interpret its responsibility to the inquiring congressman. It pointed out that CRS intervention most likely would prove to be a benefit to his constituency, since unresolved conflicts usually led to greater disruption later. When congressional complaints about CRS went to the secretary of commerce or, later, to the attorney general, CRS would be asked to draft the reply in the name of the cabinet officer. Ultimately, CRS came to understand that in most cases the "congressional interest" was not a veiled threat but simply a form of constituent service, which could be satisfied by a serious response.

14. Ibid., 112.

Fire Prevention as Well as Firefighting

Besides fighting the fires of racial conflict in the localities where it occurred, the Community Relations Service developed a fire prevention program. From its earliest days it was apparent to CRS's leaders that the roots of racial animosity lay deep beneath the surface of American society. Turmoil could break forth at any time in any of a thousand localities. The CRS staff could address only the more troublesome threats. It made sense to augment the work of the conciliators by encouraging and assisting other agencies in their efforts to address racial conflicts and the social problems from which they stemmed.

Four support programs were developed to reach out to these other resources. One identified those services within the vast network of federal programs that might help alleviate community conflict. This federal liaison enabled CRS to alert civil rights enforcement officials to neglected violations. It could also encourage grant-giving agencies to direct their resources to specific communities where educational, job training, and employment benefits would help to facilitate the resolution of racial tension.

The second prevention activity reached out to national voluntary organizations. It was designed to assist these groups, whose local constituencies extended into thousands of communities, to maximize their support for civil rights programs. This network also identified local resources that could be brought to bear in specific situations.

A third national program was addressed to the creation and strengthening of local human relations commissions or other local biracial committees that helped communities better utilize their own resources for interracial communication and problem solving. With the help of the Advertising Council, CRS mounted a media campaign to "sell" the idea of human relations commissions to interested local jurisdictions. Then CRS made staff and consultants available to provide on-site assistance with problems of creation or operation of commissions.

The fourth firefighting national program was the NCC. Both President Johnson and LeRoy Collins saw CRS as an educational fountainhead that would reach out to opinion molders and community leaders across the nation to create a climate in which civil rights and racial amity would flourish. The National Citizens Committee for Community Relations was seen as a pillar of this prevention program—450 of America's most influential individuals personally enlisted by the president to give hands-on assistance when called upon. It was CRS's responsibility to provide staff services and program guidance.

In perhaps a score of instances individual NCC members were asked to undertake conflict resolution assignments when staff conciliators were not available. There was no clear consensus on the effectiveness of these performances. Some CRS staff members felt that, without adequate training or supervision by staff, volunteer conciliators presented more trouble and risk than advantage. In any event, for five years the roster of NCC members was to serve as a resource list upon which CRS could call in a variety of cases, large and small. How to use all that NCC horsepower effectively was the challenge. Collins and Harold Fleming both thought that the NCC's size made it unwieldy, but it certainly provided muscle on occasions when CRS was in need of some.[15]

Julius Manger, for example, as chairman of a major hotel chain, designed a program to upgrade the employment status of blacks throughout his organization. He then sent his design to the heads of five other hotel chains, asking them to consider undertaking similar programs. He received affirmative responses from the Hilton, Statler, Holiday Inn, Carling, and Pick hotel executives. Since these chains also were headed by members of the NCC, it may be assumed that their favorable response was generated not only out of respect for a fellow business leader but also by the force of the president's charge when he had met with them in the Rose Garden.

Donald McGannon, president of Westinghouse Broadcasting Network, headed NCC's Mass Media Committee. He used the good offices of his local stations, and his influence with other broadcasting executives, to help CRS organize the sponsorship of local media conferences on civil rights and race relations. The objective was for local media executives to get together with minority leaders in order to work out better ways to cover minority news and views and to overcome discrimination in the publishing and broadcasting industries. Other NCC members also lent their prestige to the sponsorship of these local conferences, which were held in more than twenty communities in 1965 and 1966. Programs that evolved from these groundbreaking meetings were part of a nationwide effort to drive Jim Crow out of journalism that will be described in Chapter Ten.

In some instances, individual NCC members, on their own initiative, undertook projects they felt were needed. For example, Norman Cahners, the publisher of a group of trade magazines, established the Business Press Advisory Council in an effort to insinuate civil rights awareness into the consciousness of American business executives. The council functioned as a cost-free syndicate of news and commentary on civil rights themes

15. Annual Report of the Community Relations Service, fiscal year 1965.

appealing to the interests of business, which was made available to business publications with a combined circulation of ten million.

Alabama NCC members Winton Blount, Milton Cummings, George Le Maistre, and Arthur Shores were instrumental in getting the powerhouses of Alabama industry to issue a pro–civil rights statement calling for change in the state's racial climate. The statement, signed by the State Chamber of Commerce, the Associated Industries of Alabama, and other important business groups, was run in all Alabama dailies, the *Wall Street Journal,* and *U.S. News and World Report.*

The three NCC members in the state of New Mexico persuaded the governor to join them in sponsoring a statewide conference on civil rights, from which emerged recommendations for the state to adopt a fair housing law and to establish a state human relations commission. And the Women's Division of the NCC convened regional seminars for hundreds of the leaders of women's organizations to enlist their support of the nation's civil rights goals.

One of the NCC's most ambitious undertakings was to call attention to the problem of putting the hard-core unemployed into jobs. In the mid-sixties the nation first became aware of the twin specters of structural unemployment and the growth of a permanent underclass of minority nonworkers. Technological advances were eradicating hundreds of thousands of low-paying industrial jobs. The result swelled the ranks of poorly educated black males who, it would appear, throughout their lives and the lives of their progeny, would never experience sustained and gratifying employment. It was known that they existed by the thousands in America's cities, but their exact number could only be guessed because they were no longer even counted among the unemployed. They were a large component of the social dynamite piling up in the minority ghettos. Some of these hard-core unemployed, not even ready for skills training, needed help with basic work habits that would enable them to find and to hold even unskilled jobs. A scattering of business organizations and companies were experimenting with special programs for this group, but the unique techniques for effectively working with them were still outside the ken of most American businesses.

To fill this void, CRS organized some of NCC's captains of industry into the Business and Industry Advisory Committee. One of this committee's major objectives was to stimulate the development of, and codify, the state of the art for putting the hard-core unemployed into jobs.

Under the chairmanship of Stanley Marcus, of the Neiman Marcus retailing giant, the advisory committee in June 1967 conducted a conference where industry heads and leading personnel and training specialists shared the sum total of America's extant experience in working with the hard-core unemployed. The book that emerged from the conference was a down-to-earth manual on how to find, understand, motivate, train, and profitably employ them.[16] Unfortunately, the long-term effectiveness of the project was significantly compromised. By the time the book was published, CRS's energies were being expended elsewhere, leaving scant resources for promotion, distribution, or follow-up programming. It would not be the last false start to be made by CRS, which, as a small, ambitious agency, had to guard against letting its reach exceed its grasp.

The National Citizens Committee for Community Relations, which had existed only on the authority of Lyndon Johnson's telegram of invitation to the Rose Garden meeting, expired the moment Johnson departed the White House. The demise of the NCC resulted from a number of causes, perhaps the strongest of which was ambivalence. CRS, never fully comfortable in its marriage with so potentially influential an adjunct, had used the NCC mostly as a roster of volunteers who felt duty bound to help because Lyndon Johnson had asked them to. The task of molding the group into an organization that would genuinely engage the interest of the men of affairs whose priorities lay elsewhere called for a price CRS was unwilling to pay. The small agency could ill afford the resources required. Nor did it dare to risk the independence of action that such an organization would have demanded. CRS made no effort to persuade John Mitchell, the incoming attorney general,[17] to retain or replace the NCC. It was assumed that the Nixon administration, with no legal obligation to continue it, would have no interest in the perpetuation of a group of 450 Johnson appointees. The CRS staff was reluctant to press the case, uncertain about what new problems might arise in relating to a replacement group whose mandate, authority, and selection would come from a new president.

The mixed feelings of the CRS staff also reflected philosophical differences over the balance of resources to be invested in local and national programs. For most of the life of the agency, the prevailing view would emphasize the local effort, which deployed most of the agency's meager staff resources at the points of conflict. In this view, national programs should be used mostly to develop sources of support for local service. Wholesale programming to strengthen the efforts other groups might de-

16. National Citizens Committee for Community Relations, *Putting the Hard-core Unemployed into Jobs.*

17. In January 1966, President Johnson had issued an executive order transferring CRS from the Department of Commerce to the Department of Justice.

liver to the point of conflict was seen as too diffuse to justify more than a minimal staff effort.

The Interplay of Conflict and Change in Mississippi

The mid-1960s brought dramatic transformations that revolutionized power relationships between whites and blacks in the South. Rapid, raucous, and violent confrontations in Mississippi over a five-year period produced wrenching changes from a closed, authoritarian system of white dominance to one permitting negotiated change. While precipitating incidents generally focused on the schools, voting rights, or abusive law enforcement, conciliators found that issues were interrelated, and at the heart of most confrontations was the disparity of status and the denial of dignity.

Limited by its mandate and resources, CRS could play no more than a bit part in this sweeping drama. Nevertheless, it did serve as a catalyst that sometimes could reduce the violence and help speed the accommodation to change. Its unique role permitted CRS to witness firsthand the behind-the-scenes interplay of activity at local, state, and federal levels that succeeded in bringing change about.

The rising assertiveness of black protest and the increase in federal attention set the stage for black militancy, which forced Mississippi whites to adjust their image of their Negro neighbors from punching bag to contender. The nation caught a glimpse of this transition at the Democratic National Convention at Atlantic City in the summer of 1964. There the interracial Mississippi Freedom Democratic Party (MFDP) was partially successful in its effort to unseat and replace the all-white party that had dominated the state since the Civil War. While the MFDP refused a compromise settlement in Atlantic City, it succeeded in permanently breaking the back of lily-white Democratic politics. CRS saw the workings of this kind of political, social, and economic reversal at the grass roots.

For years the great reserves of political strength and purchasing power possessed by blacks by virtue of their numbers had been rendered useless by a system of political, economic, and law enforcement controls. New federal civil rights laws, federally funded social benefit programs, and more attentive federal law enforcement provided the tools for liberating blacks' economic and political power. But the tools were meaningless until tested against bitter white resistance.

In the midsixties Negroes began to test and to utilize their new strength. Confrontations large and small broke out locally and statewide. One center of anti-Negro violence was southwestern Mississippi, where numerous bombings and church burnings marked the answer of the Ku Klux Klan to the Negro thrust for change. Natchez provides an example of the problem and of the contribution of federal conciliators toward a solution.

The first city to be built along the Mississippi River, Natchez had been the cultural and economic center of the state of Mississippi before the Civil War. But its development had languished in the ensuing hundred years. In 1964 it was known as a small city of pleasant homes. At the annual Natchez Pilgrimage in March, more than thirty well-preserved antebellum houses were opened to public view, providing a festive and lucrative tourist attraction. The economy was largely based on the surrounding cotton and timber industries and on river commerce. The biggest employer was the Armstrong Tire and Rubber plant. The population of twenty-four thousand was about evenly divided between blacks and whites. A downtown shopping area employed no blacks except in menial positions.

Behind the city's public face of gentility was a rough-and-tumble river town, known for years for gambling, prostitution, and the illegal sale and consumption of liquor. The Ku Klux Klan and the Association for the Preservation of the White Race were accepted social institutions. The local newspaper vigorously supported the Klan, some of whose members were reputed to come from some of the "better families." The Klan exerted significant influence in four surrounding Mississippi counties and enjoyed wide support across the river in neighboring Louisiana.

The acceleration of civil rights activity in the South in 1964, including the Mississippi Freedom Summer program, which drew hundreds of northern college students into the state, brought a quick response from the Klan and other lawless elements. Across the state from Natchez, in eastern Mississippi, this response led to the murders of three civil rights workers—Michael H. Schwerner, Andrew Goodman and James E. Chaney. In the southwestern corner it launched a wave of bombing and burning centered in Natchez and in McComb, sixty-five miles away.

The civil rights movement first became visible in Adams County when a freedom house was opened in Natchez in June 1964 next to a tavern and grocery operated by an interracial couple. Within two months, three black churches had been burned and an explosion and fire had destroyed the store and tavern next to the freedom house. In September the home of Mayor John Nosser was bombed at the same time that an explosion fifteen blocks away wrecked the driveway at the home of Willie Washington, a black contractor. It was the second attempt at Washington's house and the third bombing in eleven days on property owned by Nosser. Nosser attributed the attacks to his role as a peacemaker who had stepped on toes of both sides. He told the *New York Times,* "I don't believe it was done by colored people. I believe it was done by white people. But it could have been either side."[18] By February 1965, a United States Civil Rights Commission staff document reported seventeen acts of violence against blacks in Adams County in recent months. None of the cases had been solved.

In September 1965, George Metcalfe, president of the Natchez branch of the National Association for the Advancement of Colored People, presented a petition to officials, asking for desegregation of the public schools. A few days later, Metcalfe was seriously injured when his car exploded as he left work at Armstrong Tire.

Negro anger first vented itself in a statement of twelve demands that community leaders presented to city officials. Tension peaked when the demands were denied. A mass protest demonstration was planned. Governor Paul B. Johnson Jr., upon receiving reports that people were arming themselves, sent six hundred National Guard troops to police the city, because of "imminent danger of riots, mobs and breach of the peace." Black leaders, fearing violence in the possible use of the troops to suppress their protests, canceled the demonstration. Instead they launched a boycott of downtown businesses.

Charles Evers assumed leadership of the Natchez protest following the attempted murder of Metcalfe. In 1963 Evers had replaced his murdered brother, Medgar, as Mississippi state secretary of the NAACP. Under his guidance the boycott was applied relentlessly for three months. Demonstrations and counterdemonstrations created an atmosphere of impending violence. Describing the emotional climate of the city, the *New York Times* reported: "The attitude expressed to visitors most often by white leaders is bewilderment that 'our Negroes should be acting disagreeably.' They insist that except for a handful of 'extremists on both sides' the white people of Natchez are generous and reasonable and that the Negroes are happy and grateful."[19]

Jim Draper arrived in Natchez in early September, shortly after the troops had been withdrawn and as the boycott was taking hold. He walked into a budding confrontation. The main street was crowded with angry people, blacks at one end, whites at the other. He was known to the leadership of both groups from previous visits, and they accepted his presence, but, he thought, without visible enthusiasm. Nevertheless the blacks detailed "a man with a large pistol" as his informal bodyguard. Late in the day Draper participated in a meeting between Evers and some of the white

18. *New York Times,* September 26, 1964.
19. *New York Times,* September 5, 1965.

leaders that resolved the impasse of the moment and enabled both sides to withdraw their forces without injury.[20]

Over the ensuing weeks other impasses and tentative resolutions were to become characteristic. Draper spent much of his time as a message carrier between the groups and as a tester of trial balloons. He developed a respect for Evers as a man "totally without fear." But Draper was frustrated because he was unable to establish the kind of relationship of full and mutual trust that he enjoyed with most of the other civil rights leaders with whom he had worked. Evers conveyed a feeling that he knew where he was going and did not expect much help from the federal government.

The city's white population, on the other hand, appeared to welcome anything that would help get the matter settled. To them Draper tried to explain that the blacks' demands were no more than what federal law required. For that reason, if for no other, those demands inevitably would prevail. Yet he found the whites totally unyielding when it came to making major concessions. With the atmosphere charged by flaring tempers, Draper felt he was making little progress in helping the parties to resolve the substantive issues. He did believe, however, that his role as intermediary helped to avoid misunderstandings that would have led to greater violence, which neither side wanted.

A breakthrough came in mid-October, when Draper "discovered" Ben Callon. A full year of experience as the CRS's agent in Mississippi had taught Draper that there was no more effective way to influence events in the rural South than to find and activate the power elite. Every town seemed to have one—a behind-the-scenes figure (or group) who was generally not visible in the management of local affairs, but who exercised great influence when it came to issues of personal importance. Ben Callon was a planter with extensive interests in industry throughout the area. Although he served as attorney for Adams County, he generally held himself aloof from the clash and clamor of the local arena. A friend of Governor Johnson, he was known as "the governor's man" in southwest Mississippi.

Callon apparently found Draper a man with whom he could talk comfortably, and Draper never visited the city without calling on him. Their conversations were wide-ranging—on one occasion lasting for the better part of a day. Draper urged Callon to exert his potent influence to help in keeping the lid on Klan violence and in persuading the city leaders to accept a settlement that would be consistent with federal civil rights laws. He pointed particularly to the danger of a racial bloodbath, and to the possible federal intervention that might result. He noted the governor's

20. Draper Interview.

vulnerability to bad press if the Feds found it necessary to move in. While Callon made no promises, Draper observed afterward that he appeared more frequently to be in consultation with the mayor and other city officials, and it also appeared that word had gotten out to the Klan to back off.

In the meantime the black boycott of downtown merchants continued. Estimates of the loss to some businesses ran as high as 50 percent. Fear and anger were rampant in the business community. In early November a group of white merchants started a movement for a counterboycott. If the black buying strike was not called off, all employers in the county would be asked to fire all black employees, and housewives would be asked to fire their domestic help. The movement was derailed when it was presented to the Chamber of Commerce for endorsement. At a meeting attended by 175 members, the president of the chamber and Mayor Nosser successfully argued for delaying the reprisal pending consideration by the chamber's board following a meeting with black leaders.

A series of agreements was negotiated and as quickly abrogated. With each failure, the blacks raised the level of their demands. Finally, on December 3, a settlement was achieved. The mayor, the board of aldermen, and the city's business leaders accepted a comprehensive agreement embracing and going beyond the original twelve points that the blacks had demanded back in August. The agreement covered retail employment, police and other areas of public employment, hospital policies, school desegregation, access to public facilities, appointments to the school board and other public bodies, and street and sewer improvements in black neighborhoods. Twenty-three of the largest stores had already hired black clerks and cashiers. Their employees and those of the city were instructed to address blacks courteously. Demeaning salutations were banned. The stores complying with the agreement comprised only 20 percent of the retail establishments, but they employed the bulk of the workforce. The blacks would continue a selective buying program, patronizing these stores and picketing others.

In his remarks at the signing ceremony Evers emphasized the triumph of black economic power. He said that the NAACP had set out to make Natchez a whipping boy, and had won. He expressed the hope that the rest of Mississippi would "take heed."[21]

On the heels of the settlement, James Laue, CRS's research director, made an on-site evaluation of what was done by the federal conciliators— why, how, and to what effect. He concluded that "all whites interviewed had high praise for CRS's role in Natchez, and all but two Negroes had sim-

21. *New York Times,* December 4, 1965.

ilar feelings. . . . The Negroes who questioned our helpfulness said that CRS 'always wants to talk and bargain us out of our rights—to settle things too soon.'" The evaluation report went on: "Conciliators and Natchez residents agreed that the most effective things CRS did included: (a) constantly keeping communication open between disputants and acting as an honest broker; (b) educating white leaders to the conditions, grievances and settlement terms of the Negro community; (c) avoiding violence in specific situations; (d) setting a tone of rationality, openness and the need for decision which made it possible for factions to negotiate differences."[22]

Within weeks of the Natchez agreement, Evers and the NAACP started a boycott in Fayette, Mississippi, a town of eighteen hundred people twenty miles from Natchez, in Jefferson County. Four hundred blacks demonstrated in front of the Confederate monument, where Evers warned a watching group of about fifty whites, with shotguns prominently displayed in their pickup trucks, that violence would be met with violence. The *New York Times* reported his words: "We're tired of your bombings and beatings. We've talked with you and we've prayed for you, and now we're going to sit and wait for you."[23]

Growing more provocative, he said, "The Ku Klux Klan is nothing but a bunch of misfits. You don't have nothing and you ain't going to have nothing." He then launched into a forecast of the political future of the county, which was 75 percent black. A year before it had no registered black voters, but since a federal voting registrar had arrived, black voters had come to outnumber whites by two to one. Evers said, "We're going to replace everybody in the courthouse and everybody in the City Hall that's not right and vote in some decent white folks and some decent Negroes."[24]

It took six months for the boycott to topple white resistance in Fayette, but change, when it came, was as far-reaching as in Natchez. Retail stores were desegregated, as were parks and public buildings. The police force was integrated, the use of courtesy titles was pledged, and street improvements in black neighborhoods were agreed upon.

Evers's victory statement was more conciliatory than the one he issued in Natchez. He said, "No longer will there be talk of what's best for the Negro or what's best for the white. We'll now discuss what's best for Fayette and Jefferson County. We're going to start working for what's right."[25]

22. Staff Report, Community Relations Service, Office of Program Evaluation and Development.

23. *New York Times,* December 25, 1964.

24. Evers's words in launching the boycott were prophetic. He himself was to serve as mayor of Fayette from 1969 to 1989.

25. *New York Times,* June 10, 1966.

Mississippi continued to command special attention from CRS for the next few years. Local casework continued in the face of ever-present violence. Jim Draper, as the man in the middle, found himself on more than one occasion in the gun sights of desperate men. A black farmer, protecting his home one night against marauding whites, braced Draper with a shotgun until he could establish his bona fides and his reason for being there. In Grenada one night, two Klansmen, firing an automatic rifle, hunted him through the dark streets near a black church where he was expected for a meeting.[26]

Mississippi's poverty made the state heavily dependent on federal subsidies to assist agriculture and other programs. Thus, the federal government had been traditionally a passive collaborator in the antiblack discrimination that characterized the administration of those programs.

When new civil rights laws suddenly required federal programs to be administered with an evenhanded respect for blacks, and when antipoverty laws required that minorities participate in program management and decision making, the long-standing partnership between white state and federal officials came under heavy strain. Negro organizations were eager to participate in the direction and operation of new federally funded education and development programs. State and local officials and politicians were bitterly opposed. In Washington the Mississippi congressional delegation on the one hand and civil rights advocacy groups on the other pulled every string within reach. Special task forces were created whose reports were studied and debated in the Washington headquarters of the federal agencies trying to identify, sort out, and evaluate conflicting claims.

Among the protest groups whose struggles for power in Mississippi drew great attention in Washington were the Delta Ministry of the National Council of Churches and the Child Development Group of Mississippi (CDGM).

The Delta Ministry sought to provide emergency food relief to the poor and also to stimulate community and economic development programs operated by blacks. In the midsixties rapid improvement in farm mechanization was driving black farm families off the land by the hundreds. Assistance for some was provided in makeshift camps—tent cities—supported by the Delta Ministry. In January 1966, seven hundred representatives of these displaced and homeless families met at Mt. Beulah, Mississippi, to protest "no food, no jobs, no land." Those attending the meeting pondered "dramatic" strategies for drawing attention to their plight. Shortly thereafter, a group from the tent city at Tribbett took over part of a deactivated

26. Draper interview.

air force base at Greenville and demanded that it be used as a site for manpower training and other assistance programs. Federal troops were used to oust the "invaders."

Controversy also came to a boil over the funding of the CDGM to run Head Start and other preschool programs—an enterprise that at one time employed as many as two thousand formerly untrained people to serve eight thousand children in more than one hundred centers.

Reliable information from the scene of these and other struggles was a valued commodity to Washington decision makers. Direct access to grassroots data, and a short chain of command, made CRS a key player at sub-cabinet-level meetings about Mississippi, where the agency won respect for the accuracy and immediacy of its situational reports and its advocacy of rational change.[27]

(Almost) Ready for New Challenges

Even as the new federal conciliation workers were molding an organization and learning their craft, new storms of racial conflict were rising. Backlash to Negro gains was eroding the climate of civil rights support. The unity of the movement was fractured by the debate over whether integration or black militancy would yield greater equity for minorities. New opportunities for the poor to participate in developing and running antipoverty programs set the stage for clashes between minorities and city hall. And civil disorders in northern cities awakened the nation to the intensity of black rage smoldering in urban ghettos.

With more work than it could handle in the South alone, CRS, in its first year, tried to hold itself aloof from major involvement elsewhere. It began to look north in the latter half of 1964, but it would not be until 1965 that, under new leadership and with an experienced staff, it would be poised to provide service on a national basis.[28]

Experience in Mississippi and the other southern states had helped to develop the rudiments of the community conflict resolution process. Not only did conciliators have some sense of what to do and when to do it; they also had a better understanding of their own abilities and limitations.

27. This ability to impart to policy-level discussions data about the nitty-gritty details of daily life on city streets and at county crossroads was a major asset throughout CRS's experience. However, its counsel was sought less after the Johnson years, as other federal agencies became more confident in their own access to the currents of minority life.

28. See Chapter Four.

Late in 1965, following Jim Laue's evaluation of the Natchez case, a staff conference took place in Washington at which the techniques and approaches that CRS had learned to use in problem solving were reviewed. As Laue and his team recounted the process they had observed in dozens of cases and identified the discrete steps that had been taken, patterns began to emerge. The conciliators listened, some with the surprise of the man who discovered he had been speaking prose all his life. Laid out before them was a matrix of what to do and how to do it: how to enter a community, on request or on CRS's own motion; strategies for fact finding; when and how to use or avoid use of the media; how to level the playing field for negotiation between parties of disparate strength; when to involve third parties; when and how to call on other federal resources; tactics for using an "end run" to circumvent an impasse; when, where, and how to engage the power elite; how to move name-calling and harangue to genuine communication, to dialogue, to negotiation.

Yes, they had indeed done those things, not by chance or instinct or common sense alone, but thoughtfully, deliberately, in planned sequence. Whatever intuitive abilities they had originally brought to the job were now buttressed by learned behavior. No, it wasn't hard science; there were no sure prescriptions for every diagnosis, no pills that could guarantee cures. Nevertheless, they had begun to develop a distinct body of professional practice.

Half the communities served during CRS's first year were in just five southern states. Mississippi was the busiest theater of operations, with twenty-two locations receiving service. Alabama was second. While there was a core of similarity in problems and responses throughout the southern states, there were also distinctive differences. At the same time that CRS conciliators were finding their way and earning their spurs in Mississippi, others were dealing with different challenges in Alabama.

Three

Selma Blow by Blow

A Dissection of the Community Crisis
That Turned the Tide for Voting Rights

News about the civil rights protests in Selma, Alabama, and their brutal suppression blazed across America's front pages and television screens for more than two months in early 1965 and paved the way for passage of the Voting Rights Act of 1965.

Selma's place in civil rights history might have been no more distinguished than that of scores of county seats across the rural south where black residents were denied their rights, struggled for redress, and were abused for their struggle. The difference resulted from the interlocking roles of a handful of individuals—and the social forces they represented—whose work converged in Selma at propitious times.

Located on a pleasant bluff overlooking the Alabama River, Selma came into being early in the 1820s as a shipping and trading center for the developing cotton plantations. A major munitions manufacturing center during the Civil War, it was captured and burned by Union forces in 1865. A legacy of racial bitterness remained. In 1964 a hooded horseman, depicted on a road sign leading into Selma, welcomed the stranger in the name of the Ku Klux Klan.[1]

Dallas County, of which Selma was the county seat, had been the first county in Alabama to organize a Citizens Council to resist the Supreme Court's school desegregation decision in 1954. Ten years later that council, three thousand strong, was the largest in the state. The county sheriff, James Clark, who maintained a volunteer posse of more than one hundred white men, was noted for his readiness to help police racial demonstrations anywhere in the state.

1. Potomac Institute summary, July 21, 1964.

In the early 1960s, white Selma was peaceful and prosperous, with handsome neighborhoods, stately mansions, eighteen millionaires, a country club, and a growing class of business and industry executives. Black Selma, with as many people, was unpaved and underserved. Race relations were rigidly choreographed according to century-old patterns. Dominance and subordination were prescribed by color. Black deference to whites was the expected behavior. Segregation was absolute—in church, in school, in social and civic life.

The Conflict over Voting Rights

A small cadre of middle-class Negroes who were not dependent on whites for their livelihood composed the Dallas County Voters League (DVL)—the city's closest approach to a civil rights organization. The DVL worked to enlarge the number of registered black voters, which stood at about one hundred and fifty out of a total of fifteen thousand of voting age. They encouraged people to register, helped to prepare them for the test, and comforted the many who tried and failed to overcome the obstacle course designed by Alabama law and the Dallas County Board of Registrars that implemented it. Otherwise things were quiet on the civil rights front.

The tempo began to change in late 1962 when SNCC included Selma in its Voter Education Project.[2] Bernard Lafayette, a twenty-two-year-old divinity student, was assigned by SNCC to assist Selma's voter registration effort. Lafayette, like many other civil rights flag bearers, brought to his assignment more than courage and deep commitment. A veteran of the sit-ins and freedom rides, he had been schooled in the theory and practice of nonviolent civil disobedience. He knew the principles and tactics for building a mass movement to bring about peaceful social change.

The civil rights movement in general had been slow to give priority to voting rights. A year earlier, at the height of the turmoil of the lunch counter sit-ins and the freedom rides, Justice Department suggestions that the movement might better invest its energies in voting rights were greeted with suspicion. Militants saw that as a government ploy to quiet things down and slow the thrust for civil rights reform. For its part, the Kennedy

2. With the encouragement and influence of the Justice Department, an informal consortium of church groups and private foundations had put up $500,000 to create and support the Voter Education Project (VEP). VEP then became a vehicle through which SNCC, SCLC, CORE, and the NAACP would coordinate their distinctive efforts to educate and register potential voters.

administration did indeed wish to dispel the violence in the streets. At the same time it saw the Negro vote as the most efficient way to win civil rights progress across the board. The logic was simple: once—and wherever—Negroes gained political clout, they would more easily win other victories.

The Justice Department was winning voting rights cases in the courts, but without a definitive Supreme Court decision progress had to be forged on a case-by-case basis. This tedious process required that Negroes be encouraged, helped, and defended in their efforts to gain registration.

In Selma, Bernard Lafayette immediately reached out to the Negro school and college students. He helped them to identify and protest their grievances. There gradually developed a program of youth demonstrations, marches, and school boycotts. The authorities clamped down with arrests and suspensions. Fearful of economic and other reprisals, the adult black community only looked on at first. As law enforcement became more punitive with the use of clubs and cattle prods, adults became more supportive and established a bail fund.

Lafayette was ready for the next step so important to building a mass movement—the large public meeting. It was at the mass meeting that people could take strength from one another, exchange information, and receive inspiration, hope, and a sense of the movement's objectives and strategy. But so intimidating was the racial climate that no Negro church would make itself available for that purpose.

The Rubicon was crossed in May 1963 when Sam Boynton, the cofounder of the DVL, died after a debilitating illness. The memorial service in his honor at the Tabernacle Baptist Church was combined with a mass meeting in behalf of the cause to which he had been devoted—voting rights.

The sheriff and his men made a show of recording the license plate numbers of the cars in the parking lot. They next made themselves prominent in the hall. Their presence, meant to be intimidating, had the reverse effect. Somehow the events of the evening brought a sense of militancy and unity to the voting rights movement. Thereafter, the mass meeting became a fixture of community life in Selma.

On June 12, 1963, the night Medgar Evers was murdered in Mississippi, Bernard Lafayette was beaten by two white men who clubbed him with rifles. The rumor that the two events were linked by some antiblack conspiracy was never validated. Nevertheless, Lafayette insisted on wearing his blood-stained T-shirt for two weeks. It symbolized the outrage and danger that many of Selma's Negroes felt.[3]

3. J. L. Chestnut Jr. and Julia Cass, *Black in Selma: The Uncommon Life of J. L. Chestnut, Jr.*

The tension continued to escalate. A voting rights demonstration by high school students on September 23 resulted in hundreds of arrests. The sheriff's posse was assisted by fifty state troopers under the personal leadership of state commander Al Lingo. The confrontation made national headlines.

A fact-finding team sent by the National Council of Churches reported on October 1, 1963, that seventy-five demonstrators were still being held under harsh conditions at "Camp Selma," a nearby prison camp. The attitude of the city was expressed by Mayor John Heinz: "Selma does not intend to change its customs or way of life." "Many responsible white citizens," the report said, "are afraid to speak out openly."

When the Civil Rights Act was signed in July 1964, a number of Negroes tried to integrate Selma's movie theater and a few of the white eating places. Gangs of white toughs disputed their passage, and there were some arrests and minor injuries. Demonstrations followed.

To end the demonstrations, Circuit Judge James Hare issued an injunction banning meetings of more than three people, and Sheriff Clark was quick to enforce it.[4] More than four hundred people were jailed for civil rights protests in the fall of 1964. The Justice Department sought to have the injunction overturned in federal court, but it took six months for that to happen.

Selma and Dallas County were no strangers to federal civil rights officials. Since 1961, the Civil Rights Division of the Justice Department had been working a slow, tedious strategy to bring voting rights suits throughout the South. To do this meant finding Negroes who had tried to register and been rejected—and who could withstand intimidation and economic reprisal. John Doar, then assistant chief (later chief) of the Civil Rights Division, personally spent months on the byways of the rural South finding sturdy complainants around whom strong cases might be built. He also made countless court appearances in behalf of Negroes who sought to exercise their right to demonstrate in behalf of voting rights.[5] Selma became a primary focal point for Doar after he encountered Amelia and Sam Boynton, founders of the Dallas County Voters League. On the wall of their real estate office he found an "honor roll" in the form of a plaque with the names of Dallas County Negroes who had tried to register. It was a bonanza of potential plaintiffs.

4. According to J. L. Chestnut Jr., while Sheriff Clark served as the front man imposing uncompromising, brutal, and racist law enforcement, the power and direction behind the scenes came from Judge Hare.

5. Taylor Branch, *Parting the Waters: America in the King Years, 1954–63.*

In late December 1964, John Doar and Burke Marshall suggested to John Griffin, chief of the CRS conciliation staff, that CRS might have a role to play in Selma. SCLC had decided in November to make common cause with SNCC in pushing voter rights in Selma. Martin Luther King Jr. was scheduled to make his first appearance there shortly after New Year's Day. Tension was sure to rise.

Mac Secrest headed a CRS team that arrived in Selma on January 12, 1965. His primary mission was to make an on-site assessment in order to learn for himself what the problems were and whether they might be responsive to conciliation by CRS. The team spent two weeks meeting, listening, and researching. Its members spoke with scores of officials, community leaders, and private individuals—black and white. These encounters took place at all hours—sometimes in clear view and sometimes in out-of-the-way places to assure confidentiality.

When Leaders Fear to Talk

The CRS assessment found a bitterly divided community, unable to manage true communication between blacks and whites. Even among whites, the divisions ran deep between extremists and moderates. The inherited wealth and power of Dallas County's first families was being challenged by the urban-focused business community interested in expanding the local industrial base. The business community had recently succeeded in wresting political control from the old guard. Joe Smitherman, the new mayor, was widely assumed to be more tractable on racial issues than his immovable predecessor had been, despite his campaign pledge never to meet with an "outside agitator" or talk to any supporter of Dr. King.

The city police and the sheriff's office contended about how and by whom racial demonstrations were to be policed. J. Wilson Baker, a former police captain, had been enticed by Smitherman from a teaching post at the University of Alabama to fill the newly created city post of public safety director. While the sheriff held sway over the county and the courthouse where the voting registrars did business, Baker insisted on primacy in the city, including the streets around the courthouse where the demonstrations took place.

Although the moderate whites had just won political control, they were fearful of losing favor with a conservative electorate. Worried that racial progress might incite white ruffians to violence, none dared propose interracial dialogue. The chairman of the Selma Ministerial Association, widely respected for moral stature and civic leadership, told CRS that he was part of a group of white men who had been meeting informally in recent weeks to discuss racial problems. But he would not reveal the names of the other members. Negro leaders described him as "a good man with a weak stomach."

The Negro community had its own divisions—between the older, more timid, don't-rock-the-boat leadership and the more venturesome, younger leaders of the Dallas County Voters League. DVL and SCLC were sometimes at odds over the internal contradictions between local and national agendas. SNCC and SCLC, while pledged to cooperation, were nevertheless rivals as to leadership, organizational prominence, and, sometimes, tactics. Among the local blacks, Amelia Boynton was regarded as the leader of the militant faction. To whites, she was a stormy petrel. Some felt that because of the vigor of her protest leadership, they could not afford to be in contact with her.

Secrest had first learned of Mrs. Boynton when he had interviewed the owner of the IGA supermarket. The man had said that he once asked Mrs. Boynton to leave his store when she had "demanded" that he employ more Negroes because so many Negroes shopped there. He said he might have treated her differently if she had approached him in a different manner.

Frederick Douglas Reese, a young man who had succeeded Sam Boynton as president of the DVL, was also head of the Negro United Fund. He worked as a science teacher at Hudson High School. While he had the confidence of local Negroes, he also enjoyed the respect of many white leaders and was the primary local contact with SCLC.

Public Safety Commissioner J. Wilson Baker, while a man of contradictions, was clearly the strongest force for racial progress among the white leaders. He had been able to coalesce a majority of white support on the issue of law and order, which he used as a two-edged sword. On the one hand, he required Negroes to conduct their demonstrations in accordance with local law and court decisions. On the other, he sought to protect the integrity of legal demonstrations by keeping Sheriff Clark, as well as white troublemakers, from disrupting the demonstrations. In frequent confrontations with demonstrators he preferred to rely on negotiation and persuasion rather than police force.

Baker's approach was as much a product of power structure strategy as of the commissioner's innate style of law enforcement. The business community wanted to avoid bad publicity at all costs. Selma was on the brink of a major industrial expansion. Several large corporations were considering making major investments in Dallas County. It was hoped that others would follow. These companies, all sensitive to the new federal requirements for equal employment opportunity, might have second thoughts about locating in an area of racial turmoil where they could not be assured of a harmonious workforce.

Many of the business leaders looked on the actions of Sheriff Clark and Judge Hare as an invitation to disaster. They saw Clark as another "Bull" Connor.[6] Moreover, some believed that SCLC had deliberately come to Selma because it, too, saw Clark as someone who, if aroused, would propel Selma and the voting rights issue onto center stage nationally. Wilson Baker had to succeed in controlling the demonstrators with civility, lest his failure open the gate to Jim Clark's unbridled force.

Wilson Baker, when interviewed by Howell Raines ten years later, said that SCLC's strategy for the State of Alabama had been known by law enforcement agencies since August 1964, when they had obtained a secret planning blueprint.[7] Clark's propensity for offering his posse throughout the state to help suppress civil rights demonstrations had identified him to SCLC as the person to be confronted to assure a response that would attract national media attention.

As was true in so many other towns CRS had assessed, white leaders of Selma said they found it difficult to discern who were the Negroes' true leaders and what were their grievances. Yet Secrest, a stranger in town, already had a copy of a statement of Negro concerns, drafted three months earlier. Approved by the leading organizations, it was in the hands of a committee appointed to discuss it with white leaders if and when that became possible.

The Negroes' concerns included: (1) job opportunities and advancement, particularly as policemen, firemen, and retail clerks; (2) improved recreational facilities; (3) improved housing conditions, paved streets, and adequate sewage; (4) equal pay for equal work; (5) an end to mass arrests and police brutality; (6) the opportunity to join the sheriff's posse; (7) freedom to register and vote without fear of reprisal; (8) compliance with public accommodations provisions of the 1964 Civil Rights Act; (9) desegregation of public schools; (10) proper respect in addressing Negroes according to their titles; (11) participation in the decision-making process.

The statement of concerns of Selma's Negro community might have been a useful agenda for good-faith negotiation if there had been any response

6. Eugene Connor, a native of Selma, was police commissioner of Birmingham when the civil rights demonstrations took place there in 1963. Police use of clubs, cattle prods, fire hoses, and dogs to restrain demonstrators was widely reported through the nation's news and television cameras. The resulting national outrage helped to build the necessary support for passage of the Civil Rights Act of 1964.

7. Howell Raines, *My Soul Is Rested: Movement Days in the Deep South Remembered,* 197.

to it at the time it was written. In January, three months later, however, with the community united behind SNCC and SCLC leaders and their almost exclusive focus on the voting rights issue, it had been relegated to a back burner.

The first feeble effort by moderate whites to take a public position occurred after a group of business leaders met with Secrest. They had been considering whether or not to make a public statement favoring law and order, which would be seen as an endorsement of Baker's treatment of demonstrators and a repudiation of Clark's methods. Secrest offered some suggestions and encouraged the statement's prompt issuance. It appeared in the paper the next day.[8]

Secrest had an appointment to meet with Dr. King as soon as the SCLC leader arrived in town on January 17. It had to be canceled because of an incident in the lobby of the newly desegregated Albert Hotel, where King, upon his arrival, was attacked by a member of the National States Rights Party. Secrest and King did, however, have a lengthy phone conversation. King made it clear that while SCLC had a genuine interest in helping to resolve the grievances of Selma's Negroes, its primary objective was to highlight abuses in Selma in order to support its overall goal of securing voting rights throughout the state of Alabama.

Voting laws in Alabama were designed to look equal in principle but to be anti-Negro in application. Each county had a three-person board of registrars appointed by the governor and his designees, thus unaccountable to any local authority. Under state law the county board of registrars met at the county courthouse the first and third Mondays of each month to register voters. Few blacks surmounted the contrived procedures, particularly the infamous literacy test in which answers to esoteric questions were subjectively graded. In Dallas County, ten to twenty people were processed on each registration day, with most Negroes being rejected. The legitimacy of the literacy test had been called into question by the Civil Rights Act of 1960, but that didn't stop its use in Alabama. In Dallas County, where the DVL had succeeded in two years in doubling the number of Negro registrants to three hundred, there were more than fifteen thousand of voting age. At a rate of forty a month, it would take thirty-one years for all of those eligible to be processed. Blacks demanded an increased rate of processing and a fairer application of qualification criteria.

8. Secrest wondered whether his words had been a decisive influence behind the final decision to go public with the statement. Such second-guessing about the impact of CRS counsel on critical behavior would often bedevil the federal peacemakers.

The Civil Rights Act of 1960 provided for the federal courts to appoint voting referees who could register voters if it was established in court that the state maintained a pattern or practice to deny registration to qualified minorities. By seeking registration, even if rejected by the Dallas County Board of Registrars, Negro citizens were qualifying themselves to some day apply to the federal registrars.

This ultimately resulted in a fixed choreography on each semimonthly registration day. Hundreds of blacks would take their places in the prescribed lines, with each applicant accompanied by the registered voter required to vouch for him or her. Those in front would be processed, with most being rejected. The majority of those in line, who were not processed, would return another day. Almost nightly mass meetings at Brown's Chapel Church were designed to encourage more people to seek registration and to cheer the persistence of those who returned to the lines repeatedly to be processed.

January 17 was to be a day of portentous developments in Selma. SCLC, SNCC, and local demonstrators would be out in force to support voter registration and to desegregate restaurants and other public accommodations. Martin Luther King was to address a mass rally that evening. CRS had learned that George Lincoln Rockwell, head of the American Nazi Party, and J. B. Stoner of the National States Rights Party, as well as representatives of the Klan and other white supremacist groups, were coming to Selma to create disturbances. Selma's civic leaders saw the day as an attempt by King to draw national attention. They decided to respond with deliberate conflict avoidance.

The SCLC agenda, however, was to court conflict as a means of illuminating injustice. That night, at Brown's Chapel Church, King exhorted an audience of eight hundred to mount more and larger street demonstrations. "Continue to play Dallas County—creatively and non-violently," he said.[9]

The city of Selma, mostly in the form of Wilson Baker and his police force, disposed of the challenge to law and order posed by the white supremacists with reasonable dispatch. The National States Rights Party member who attacked King in the lobby of the Albert Hotel was jailed promptly and sentenced on the following day. Rockwell was promptly arrested for disturbing the peace when he started a harangue outside the mass meeting that evening. A rabble-rouser in blackface and flamboyant garb who sought to provoke Negroes integrating the restaurants was promptly incarcerated.

9. *New York Times,* January 22, 1965.

The Negroes' public accommodations challenges were not resisted, by and large, although there were isolated attacks by angry whites. Since the start of the year the restaurant owners, anticipating a federal court order requiring them to desegregate under the 1964 Civil Rights Act, were ready for the inevitable. They would accept desegregation calmly, confident that once Negroes had established the principle that they *could* eat where they chose, they would return to their more familiar surroundings. On January 17 the restaurant owners accepted Negro diners and distributed to their white patrons a printed note explaining that they were unwillingly complying with federal law.

While conflict avoidance was white Selma's response through most of the city that day, provocation and conflict broiled at the courthouse, where Sheriff Clark held sway. Negroes who marched downtown to register were directed to a rear door and forced to wait outside in a cordoned-off alley. They demanded use of the front door and courthouse corridors, which were accessible to white registrants. Sixty-seven were jailed, including Mrs. Boynton, whom Jim Clark personally seized by the back of the collar and propelled down the street for half a block in clear view of the nation's news cameras.[10]

By the end of January, with the detailed mosaic of his assessment pieced together, Secrest was ready to recommend a sustained CRS commitment to Selma—with the intent of conciliating the immediate crisis and also dealing with the long-range disputes over ongoing inequities. Both issues would require the establishment of genuine communication between Negroes and whites, and so Secrest set that as his first objective. In order to achieve it, the conciliation team would have to help the parties keep the conflict from escalating out of control. They would also try to build bridges of interracial communication in preparation for the time when they could be used for effective conciliation.

At the same time Secrest was troubled by a paradox. There would be times when CRS, in pursuit of its goals, might find itself working at cross-purposes with some of the civil rights agencies. The CRS objectives were to reduce conflict and to help resolve Negro grievances in Selma. How would that affect the SCLC objective of dramatizing the injustices in Selma in order to win support for strong federal voting rights legislation?

10. Five days later Clark was again pictured in the nation's newspapers, this time bringing his club down on the head of a woman struggling on the ground in the grip of three deputies. The incident occurred when Dr. King approached the registration line to converse with reporters. The sheriff took King by the arm and ordered him back to the curb. The woman, whom the authorities later said outweighed the 220-pound Clark, had left the line and punched the sheriff in the face.

SCLC's intention to draw national attention to Selma became even more pronounced on February 1. Instead of the usual small-group procession to the courthouse on registration day, King personally led a parade there, in clear violation of the city's parade ordinance. When Baker threatened him with arrest, he calmly continued the march. He and seven hundred demonstrators were arrested that day. In keeping with his plan, King refused to post bond and was kept in jail for five days; from there, he orchestrated continuing demonstrations.

King's arrest and the impact of his published "Letter from a Selma Jail" brought support from across the country. According to Juan Williams, King's letter, published as an ad in the *New York Times,* was drafted before his arrest. The strategy was modeled after his "Letter from a Birmingham Jail," which had achieved resounding public sympathy two years earlier.[11] In the ensuing days Selma was visited by two congressional delegations and a host of civil rights leaders. Malcolm X paid a visit and announced that if Dr. King's doctrine of nonviolence was not successful, others, preaching a different doctrine, might take his place. The arrests brought new life to the Selma campaign, which had begun to show signs of exhaustion and burnout.

Community tension waxed and waned repeatedly through February as new issues passed in and out of focus. On February 4, U.S. District Court Judge Daniel H. Thomas, ruling on a Justice Department suit, decreed that the Dallas County Board of Registrars must process one hundred applications each day that it was open, that it could no longer require a literacy test, and that it must cease rejecting Negro applicants on technicalities. Applicants who appeared to register but were not processed would be permitted to enter their names in an appearance book to prove they had made the effort. He further ruled that if all applicants were not processed by July, he would appoint a voting referee to do so.[12]

King immediately called for a respite in the demonstrations while SCLC "evaluated" the court order. The rumor spread that SCLC was rethinking its strategy. Maybe the Selma demonstrations had reached the point of diminishing returns. Could Selma better serve as headquarters for an accelerated campaign throughout the state? The city's white leaders tried to prevail on Sheriff Clark to adopt a low profile. Without provocation by the posse, perhaps the focus of national attention would move elsewhere.

The sheriff did not buy into that strategy. On February 8, the Reverend James Bevel, while leading a protest to the registrars' office, was shoved

11. Juan Williams, *Eyes on the Prize: America's Civil Rights Years, 1954–1965,* 261.
12. *New York Times,* February 4, 1965.

and repeatedly prodded with Sheriff Clark's billy club before being arrested. Sentenced to five days in jail, he developed a fever and was removed to a hospital, where a doctor later found him guarded and shackled to the bed.

In the midst of the turmoil, King flew to Washington for a long-sought meeting with President Johnson. The president then announced publicly that he would soon send to Congress a proposal for additional voter rights legislation. The announcement appeared to have no impact on developments in Selma.

The Buildup to Bloody Sunday

On February 10, Sheriff Clark and his posse rounded up 165 children and teenagers who were demonstrating at the courthouse. Under the guise of arrest, he herded them with clubs and cattle prods on a forced half-march-half-run for more than two miles into the countryside. While physical injuries were few and mild, the experience was traumatic for many of the younger children.

After that day, there was no longer any possibility of the protest running out of energy; it emerged that night with a full head of steam. Mass meetings overflowed two churches. New faces swelled the ranks of demonstrators. Negro teachers turned out en masse—a certain sign that the conservative segment of the community was moving into the protest ranks. Night marches and round-the-clock vigils at the courthouse were urged. SCLC planned for a demonstration so large as to dwarf all that had been held before. It would take place on the next registration day, Monday, February 15. King canceled a previously scheduled voters march in Birmingham so that civil rights leaders throughout the state would be freed up to rally in Selma.

In the midst of it all, there was a confusing development. On February 11, the day after the mass arrest of children, six hundred students boycotted school and demonstrated again at the courthouse, showing they had not been intimidated by the forced march of the previous day. Clark, whose men had made almost three thousand arrests in the six weeks since SCLC had started its campaign in early January, took no action against the students. People speculated about the sheriff's surprising restraint. That morning the *Selma Times-Journal,* in a front-page editorial, had called Clark to task for his excesses in marching the children. Observers wondered if city officials had at last been successful in reining him in.

On Monday, February 15, almost three thousand Negroes demonstrated for voting rights in Dallas County and two nearby counties. With a parade permit issued by Baker, King personally led a march to the courthouse in Selma, where twelve hundred people lined up single file to sign the appearance book, attesting to their intentions to register. By the end of the day 570 had signed, and 120 had actually been registered, 20 more than the minimum required by Judge Thomas's latest order.

On Tuesday, the sixteenth, an additional five hundred Negroes lined up to sign the appearance book. When the Reverend C. T. Vivian led a small group into the courthouse through a side door to take shelter from the rain, Clark's men sought to remove them with the usual prods of their billy clubs. Vivian confronted Clark, calling him a brute and comparing him to Hitler. Clark punched Vivian in the mouth, drawing blood. He then had him arrested.

Clark's abuse of Vivian had an incendiary effect on the Negroes of Selma, already enraged by the shooting of Jimmie Lee Jackson the night before in nearby Marion. There state troopers and white ruffians had attacked Negroes who were leaving a protest rally at a church. Jackson had been mortally wounded. (He died a few days later.)

At the mass meeting the next night King reported SCLC's decision to intensify the effort until voter registration could take place without a single hindrance and until Sheriff Clark was removed. King said that until the power structure saw to it that these things were done, there would be broader forms of civil disobedience. A consumer boycott of downtown merchants would be launched, and nighttime demonstrations were being considered.

Aided by the rising sense of crisis, Mac Secrest found himself finally able, in early February, to move forward in bringing about direct discussions between blacks and whites. On February 6 he arranged for a small group of white moderate leaders to meet in private with a biracial leadership team from CRS—Deputy Director Calvin Kytle and Assistant Director Roger Wilkins. The Washington officials appealed to pragmatism. Since the Negro vote would inevitably result from federal legislation, why not end the turmoil by speeding the registration process? Could the board of registrars be persuaded to seek an increase in the number of registration days per month and quicken the process of registration from one hundred per day? (Montgomery was now doing one hundred per hour.) They suggested other measures that whites might take. One was to build public sentiment for "law and order" to assure the security of peaceful demonstrations. Another was to continue to press for interracial negotiation at the earliest feasible time.

Building on the momentum of the meeting with Kytle and Wilkins, Secrest was able, a week later, to convene the first meeting of black and white leaders of Selma. For two and a half hours there was a full and frank exchange of views. Secrest felt that each group learned a lot about the motivation and goodwill of the other. He called it a good beginning toward *real* confrontation and *real* communication. But it was slow going; he was unable to get them to agree on a specific date for a second meeting. It would be up to CRS to continue to stoke that fire.[13]

As the tempo of the demonstrations rose, so did resentment in the white community. Smitherman and Baker grew more agitated. They informed Secrest that the threatened night marches were sure to bring violence. Adequate police protection for demonstrators from unruly whites was doubtful; the city budget was already stressed because of police overtime. Baker began to show signs of combat fatigue. He revealed his feelings to Secrest in a late-night conversation on February 18. Continuation of the demonstrations was an act of bad faith. He cited his behind-the-scenes efforts with the registrars and the court to improve registration procedures. He said that the Negro leaders knew that these moves reflected the mood and intention of the new city administration to be responsive to Negro demands. Moreover, Judge Thomas had promised to appoint federal registrars in July. That meant that by August 1 all who signed the registration book would be registered.

Baker warned of a developing mood of white backlash. After-dark protests would bring it to a head. Night marches were likely to result in bloodshed and death. He was unwilling to subject himself to further twenty-hour days or expose his men to bricks, bottles, Molotov cocktails, and stray bullets in order to protect people who were inciting to riot. He felt that Negroes should recognize that they had won a big victory in Selma. A cooling-off period was needed to enable local whites and blacks to repair relationships and then move forward.

In his deep despair Baker complained that even the white moderates who had supported his efforts were turning away. He felt isolated. As a result, he had begun to have thoughts of resigning as public safety commissioner.

Baker's fears of growing white bitterness were confirmed the next day in a front-page editorial in the *Selma Times-Journal*. It offered veiled warnings about the consequences of what it saw as SCLC's provocative behavior.

> This newspaper regards with mounting alarm . . . the failure of local Negro leadership to assert itself in demanding an immediate departure of outside forces which are now deliberately provoking the understanding and sympathy of all sound thinking citizens perilously near to the breaking point.

13. Secrest interview.

For almost a month of the most difficult adjustment since Reconstruction Days, Selma citizens have displayed a degree of restraint which has awed and confounded everyone who has sought to exploit our proud city. That our people are temperate and law abiding and can swallow with dignity any law dose regardless of how bitter its taste is no longer a matter of speculation but an established fact.

But how long Selmians and their elected officials are expected to endure continuing jabs at the sore spots of their injured sense of justice is already a point of serious consideration.

On Friday, February 19, Governor George C. Wallace ordered the state police to ban night marches in Marion and Selma, blaming the trouble on outside communist-inspired agitators.

SCLC conducted its first night march in Selma that night. Three hundred Negroes moved out, led by Rev. Hosea Williams. Wilson Baker, acting promptly in order to preempt action by the state police, halted the march. Williams was arrested but released once the marchers were dispersed.

Jim Laue joined the federal conciliation team in Selma on February 20. He was a sociologist whose Harvard doctoral dissertation was based on research he had conducted while serving as a volunteer field-worker for SCLC. He had strong personal ties to King and to many of the SCLC leaders. On his way to Selma he stopped off at Atlanta to speak with a trusted friend, SCLC's executive director, the Reverend Andrew Young. Young confirmed that SCLC would continue its efforts in Selma until the white community did something about Negro grievances, which, it would now be made clear, encompassed more than voting rights. From then on, the demands of the demonstrators would also include such local issues as the hiring of Negro police and firemen, the paving of streets and improving of other facilities in black neighborhoods, and the establishment of lines of communication between Selma's black and white leaders.[14]

On the twenty-first, Laue met with Baker, who reviewed the blacks' new list of demands. The public safety director explained why there was nothing to negotiate. Street paving in the black neighborhood would require an assessment on the property owners. Black owners wouldn't want that. Hiring Negro firemen was impossible because integrated living in such tight quarters would not be accepted. As to hiring Negro police officers, he had told Negro leaders he would accept applications but had received none. While the city had no money now for new positions, he hoped he might be able to hire both black and white officers soon. As for voting, that was controlled by court order and the city could do nothing about it.

14. James Laue, interview with the author.

On Sunday evening, February 21, more than a thousand people crowded into Brown's Chapel to cheer the announcement that the proposed boycott of Selma merchants was on. Governor Wallace's name was booed for his ban on night marches. Speakers noted that night marches were never banned when the Klan used them.

On Monday morning, the twenty-second, the air was heavy with tension. King and Young spoke at a mass meeting. Then two hundred and fifty Negroes, proceeding in the legally allowed groups of five, lined up at the courthouse—fifty who wanted to sign the appearance book at the courthouse door, the others farther back. Many whites gathered around. The town was buzzing with word of an earlier incident when a Negro had been beaten by a bat-wielding white. The state troopers and the sheriff's posse were present in force, but Wilson Baker was in control, directing the procession with a loudspeaker from his car. The crowd disbanded by the time the applicants had signed the book.

Fred Miller, a federal conciliator whose accent and manner permitted him to move easily in hostile white crowds, picked up a rumor of a possible attempt on King's life. Laue passed the word to Baker and Andrew Young.

That night King addressed a rally at Brown's Chapel. Enlarged protests were discussed. The Selma boycott would be extended to the buses. Plans were going forward for a major march from Selma to Montgomery to voice outrage at the shooting of Jimmie Lee Jackson and to protest Alabama's voting laws directly to Governor Wallace. Twilight marches were to begin the following evening. Scheduled to take place between 6:00 and 7:00 p.m., they would be timed to include schoolchildren and workers and yet not breach the ban against night marches.

There was talk of the danger. Dr. King told of a message he had received from a "high government official" warning him of an assassination plot. Young, referring to the whites lining the street outside, said, "It's going to be hell out there." He asked the crowd if any of them had ever been hit by a baseball bat when they were young. Many answered yes. Young responded: "That scar heals in six weeks, but scars of segregation never heal, so you be ready to march."

As King left the church at the end of the meeting, the street was filled with bystanders, most of the whites having come from a meeting of the Citizens Council, where Governor Ross Barnett of Mississippi had been the guest speaker. The city police were on hand. A detachment of Colonel Lingo's state troopers drove up and started questioning Dr. King. Wilson Baker, fearing that they might arrest King, and knowing the consequences of such a move, directed the troopers to move on. There was a verbal confrontation, and then the state forces withdrew.

The next morning Baker complained to Laue about Lingo. "If this goes on I'll probably be leading the night march myself next week." He said that he and Mayor Smitherman would be meeting with Governor Wallace that afternoon to personally protest the colonel's move and seek some restraint.[15] Baker then revealed the city's plan for dealing with the twilight marches so as to shield the marchers from confrontations with county and state law enforcement officers. The city police would arrest the marchers immediately, detain them without charges for a couple of hours, and then release them in small groups after all others had dispersed.

On Wednesday afternoon, about a hundred and fifty Negro teenagers started a march from the church to city hall. They were stopped by Baker two blocks short of their destination. They prayed, sang, and went back to the church. Baker felt that the meeting with Governor Wallace probably helped in keeping Clark and Lingo out of the way.

Meanwhile, behind the scenes, the federal effort to encourage negotiations between blacks and whites in Selma continued. On Tuesday morning, February 23, LeRoy Collins, the director of CRS, was scheduled to attend a meeting in Birmingham. Secrest and Laue saw this as another opportunity to further interracial dialogue. Collins invited Wilson Baker and Carl Morgan, president of the Selma City Council, to join him that evening for a meeting with Andrew Young of SCLC and F. D. Reese of the Dallas County Voters League.

The government representatives thought the discussion provided for a full and frank delineation of SCLC objectives and what might be expected of the city administration and influential whites in response. While no formal agreement emerged, there was an understanding on three specific points: (1) Effort would be made to persuade Judge Thomas to amend his order to require the board of registrars to process a minimum of three hundred to three hundred and fifty applications on each of the two days per month that the board was in session. (2) White leaders would make continuing efforts to support greater fairness in law enforcement and voting. (3) Biracial discussions would be undertaken on a regular basis.

While Young and Reese were unable to offer any guarantee of the cooling-off period requested by the whites, they indicated that a de facto truce might develop in the next two weeks. The movement and its leaders were exhausted, and several were in the hospital. Besides, energy had to be conserved for planning the march on Montgomery. Young said that plans for night marches were temporarily on hold.

The de facto cooling-off period Young had predicted did, indeed, begin

15. Ibid.

almost immediately. While King announced at one mass meeting, "We will win a voting bill on the streets of Selma," demonstrations were uneventful.

During the first week in March, protest activity was at low tide. SCLC made its plans for the march to Montgomery. SNCC tried to discourage the action, questioning whether the objective justified the danger. On March 6, the SNCC Executive Committee met in Atlanta and decided that it would not participate officially. However, individual SNCC members were free to do as they chose. John Lewis, SNCC's chairman, told the group, "I've been to Selma many, many times. I've been arrested there. I've been jailed there. . . . You decide what you want to do, but I'm going to march." Reflecting on that decision, Lewis wrote: "I couldn't imagine living with myself if the people of Selma had marched and I had not been with them."[16]

That day Governor Wallace declared that the march to Montgomery would not be allowed. Plans were made for a joint law enforcement operation to stop it. Sheriff Clark's posse and Colonel Lingo's state troopers would take their positions outside Selma on the far side of the Edmund Pettus Bridge. Wilson Baker threatened to resign rather than permit the Selma police to join them.

On Sunday, March 7, six hundred participants left the housing project playground near Brown's Chapel, walked six blocks through the streets of Selma, and crossed over the Edmund Pettus Bridge on their way to Montgomery. The leaders were John Lewis of SNCC and Hosea Williams of SCLC.[17]

As the demonstrators crested the bridge, they could see waiting for them a solid line of fifty state highway patrolmen about three hundred yards beyond the end of the span. The troopers stood shoulder to shoulder, with their hands in front of them gripping their batons. Dozens of posse members, many of them mounted, were grouped behind. More than a hundred white Alabamans had gathered to witness the action.

As the head of the column approached, Major John Cloud ordered the leaders to halt. They did so.

Hosea Williams called out: "May we have a word with the major?"

"There is no word to be had," came the reply.

Cloud then commanded the marchers to disperse within two minutes. When they failed to do so, came the further command: "Troopers, advance!"

16. Lewis, *Walking with the Wind: A Memoir of the Movement*, 320.
17. Ibid., 323–27. Dr. King felt committed to deliver the sermon at Ebenezer Baptist Church in Atlanta, from whose pulpit he had too long been absent. He entrusted guidance of the march to senior SCLC leaders Hosea Williams, Andrew Young, and James Bevel, who tossed coins to see which one would lead the march with Lewis.

With gas masks on and batons at the ready, the troopers formed a wedge that split the marchers to either side. There quickly followed a barrage of gas canisters, and then the charging posse using ropes and billy clubs. Eighty-four people were injured, seventeen requiring hospitalization. John Lewis suffered a fractured skull.[18]

Fred Miller, the CRS conciliator on the bridge at the time, later remembered it as the bloodiest event he had witnessed in nine years of trying to stave off racial conflict in the rural South. "I saw women beaten to the ground with billy clubs and then the state troopers and deputies would come up and threw tear gas canisters underneath them. They were out to beat heads, not keep order."[19]

Despite an agreement with Baker that state and county law enforcement would not pursue the demonstrators once they returned to Selma, the mounted posse followed the fleeing hundreds through the town to the doors of Brown's Chapel and to the stoops of the housing project. Blacks started to respond to the swinging clubs with bricks and bottles. Some emerged from their homes with firearms. Andrew Young moved through the angry blacks, appealing to them to forgo the use of force. According to Baker:

> And Congressman Young, he played such an important part of saving a bloodbath. He was just running wild up and down to these apartment units: "Get back into the house with this weapon. . . . We're not going to have any weapons out." Because I was there with him helping him, but I finally found out that would not do it, so I went to Jim Clark, the Sheriff, and told him, "Now, you get your cowboys, and you get 'em out of here, and you get 'em out of here now." . . . I finally told him in such a stern way that he did go get his men and get back out of there. I said, "now you are fixin' to cause a bloodbath, and there's gonna be a lot of us killed, too, and I mean get 'em out of here now." . . . We knew things were really fixing to pop.[20]

The Second Crossing

The following morning, SCLC headquarters in Atlanta advised Jim Laue that the organization was enraged at the federal government's slowness in responding to Sunday's carnage. It was insulting that the FBI said it was going to investigate to determine whether there was an excessive use of force by the posse and the state police; everyone had seen the brutality on television. There would be a second march the next day—this time to

18. Ibid.
19. *Atlanta Journal and Constitution Magazine,* May 12, 1974.
20. Raines, *My Soul Is Rested,* 203.

be led by King. Religious, civil rights, and civic leaders from all over the country were being asked to join. Already the response was massive. CRS got word to the Justice Department and the White House of the Negro determination to push on regardless of the consequences.

SCLC appealed to U.S. District Court Judge Frank Johnson for an order enjoining Governor Wallace from interfering with a march from Selma to Montgomery. The judge, on Tuesday morning, set a hearing on this motion for the following Thursday. But, fearing another bloody confrontation, he issued a temporary restraining order barring King and his followers from conducting a march until their petition could be heard in court. The civil rights forces called the judge's response an unconstitutional infringement of their First Amendment rights.

While the judge did not issue his restraining order until the morning of the second march, the leaders of the march expected it. It was a source of agonizing debate deep into Monday night. The federal courts had been a sturdy ally and protector in the fight for civil rights. The movement had never set itself against the federal courts. Could it afford to do so now? That night, at Brown's Chapel, Dr. King told the crowd, "We've gone too far to turn back now. We must let them know that nothing can stop us— not even death itself. We must be ready for a season of suffering."

Governor Wallace responded to these developments by stating that there would be no march on Tuesday. He dispatched one hundred state patrol cars to Selma to reinforce the troopers already there and indicated that there would be no change in police tactics.

On Monday and Tuesday a steady stream of vehicles passed over the Pettus Bridge into town, bearing four hundred and fifty dignitaries and other visitors from throughout the country. They were responding to King's invitation to join him in the second march. Troopers stopped every vehicle to inquire where people were coming from and going to and why.

On Monday evening, March 8, President Johnson summoned LeRoy Collins to the White House to tell him that Sunday's tragic bloodshed shamed the nation. His concern was compounded by the prospect that it might be repeated on Tuesday with even greater ferocity. He instructed Collins to go to Selma and make sure that didn't occur.

On Tuesday morning, Collins and Secrest boarded a White House Jet-star plane at Andrews Air Force Base outside Washington, arriving at Craig Air Force Base, near Selma, at 10:30 a.m. Fred Miller greeted them at the airport. The march was scheduled to step off in three hours.

The government's representatives met with Dr. King and other civil rights leaders at the home of Dr. Sullivan Jackson, a Selma dentist with whom King was staying. Collins told King of the president's concerns and asked him to consider what the consequences of the march might be. King replied that he had already wrestled with his conscience, but he must go forward, even if it meant that he would die on the streets of Alabama. Besides, the movement was determined. Not even Judge Johnson's order would hold the marchers back, and he would lose control if he refused to lead them. Further appeals by Collins were fruitless.[21]

CRS then raised the question of whether, after the march started, a way might be found to avoid violence. Secrest and Young stepped out of the room to consider options. Secrest asked what if the troopers physically barred the roadway? Would the nonviolent marchers seek to march over or through them? Young replied that they would not. What if Collins could get assurances from Clark and Lingo that the marchers would not be attacked if they halted when stopped, conducted their protest on the spot, and returned to the church? Would they do it? Young didn't answer. Instead the two returned to the other room to discuss with King and Collins the realistic options that would face the marchers once they had been stopped. After hearing the Young/Secrest formulation, King said that he would consider it but could not commit himself in advance to turning back after a successful crossing. "He wound up by saying he would do the best he could."[22] That was all the federal mediators needed.

Secrest and Collins excused themselves. Back in Miller's car they raced to Brown's Chapel Church, where they were sure to find Sheriff Clark monitoring the preparations for the march. Collins explained that he had reason to believe that Dr. King, a man committed to nonviolence, would stop when halted. He wanted assurance from Clark and Colonel Lingo that under those circumstances there would be no repetition of the use of force. Clark replied by inviting Collins and Secrest into his squad car. They drove over the Pettus Bridge on Highway 80 east to Colonel Lingo's command post in an automobile dealership down the road.

Lingo was hesitant and noncommittal. Collins repeated his message. The president of the United States personally wanted assurance that there would be no bloodshed. Finally Lingo stated that it was not his intention— unless it should prove necessary—to use force to halt the march or to break up a meeting or interfere with the protesters' right of assembly, petition, and prayer. CRS insisted that no time limit be placed on the highway assembly, and Lingo agreed.

21. Secrest interview.
22. LeRoy Collins, telephone interview with the author. Secrest's March 23, 1965, report of the events of that week describes the meeting between King and Collins as ending in an agreement that King would turn back if stopped and allowed a prayer ceremony.

Lingo interrupted the discussion several times to use the phone in another room. Secrest and Collins had no doubt he was talking to Governor Wallace and getting his approval.

They returned to Miller's car to find King. In the playground near the church, where the march was about to start, they advised him of Lingo's stated intentions. King made no commitment as to what he would do when stopped.

Fifteen hundred marchers, fearful but determined, set out on their trek to Montgomery, fifty miles away. The column, four abreast and more than a half-mile long, wound its way out of the Negro neighborhood and through downtown Selma—black citizens of Dallas County of all ages, and dignitaries of all colors from across the United States.

As they approached the bridge a black man, Stanley Fountain, chief deputy U.S. marshal for the Southern District of Alabama, advised Dr. King and the other march leaders that if they continued their march to Montgomery they would be in violation of a federal court order. The procession moved on.

The federal conciliators headed for the appointed place of confrontation. Lingo had said that he would position his men two or three miles beyond the point of Sunday's face-off so that the demonstrators could march that far. At the last minute he had changed his mind and placed the troopers exactly where they had been on Sunday.

Collins took a position where he could observe the developments and be clearly visible to both Lingo and King. He was still uncertain about how they would perform. The whole arrangement had been based on supposition. No formal agreement had been reached.

As the marchers approached, Major Cloud, as he had done on Sunday, announced over the bullhorn that the group would not be permitted to go further. Dr. King declared that they had the right to march to Montgomery to present their grievances to the governor.

Cloud replied: "We are here to see that this march will not continue. It would not be conducive to the safety of this group or the motoring public."

King then asked for and received permission for the group to pray. After the singing of "We Shall Overcome," four of the march leaders took turns in leading the group in prayer. The leaders then turned and started the column back across the bridge to Selma.

Just before the marchers turned back, Lingo made a surprise move. He ordered his troopers off the highway. The route to Montgomery was unobstructed. Unmindful of this development, the marchers turned around and headed back across the bridge. When Secrest later asked Lingo why he had withdrawn the troopers, the colonel told him that if the demonstrators wanted to go ahead and violate the federal court order, he didn't think it was his place to stop them.

At 6:00 p.m. Collins and his team met with King and other movement leaders at Dr. Jackson's house. The mood was one of relief and cordiality. The talk was of the plight of the Negro in Alabama and SCLC's future plans. It was obvious that it would soon be time to move on from Selma. Collins departed from Craig Air Force Base on an Air Force jet at 7:30 p.m., having fulfilled the president's assignment—to assure that there would be no bloodshed in Selma that day.

At 9:00 p.m. Secrest and Miller attended the session at Brown's Chapel Church. Dr. King declared to the crowd that their mass meeting on U.S. Highway 80 across the bridge from Selma was a great victory. He said he fully expected a favorable court decision voiding Governor Wallace's ban on a march to Montgomery. The march would be completed at that time.

Most of his listeners seemed both relieved and gratified by the developments. They had braved the storm fully prepared to be bloodied. They accepted King's view that the day had moved America a step closer to the ultimate victory. However, to others in the audience who felt that King had permitted himself to be turned back, the claim of victory had a hollow sound. Indeed, among militant blacks it was to remain a smear on King's reputation for years, and in some measure it reduced his influence upon them. In later years the event was to be cited in militant circles as reason to be guarded in working with CRS, which, they said, was sometimes more interested in compromise than in the assertion of principle.

In his notes summing up the contribution of CRS to the conflict avoidance that took place on March 9, Secrest acknowledged the importance of timing and the readiness of antagonists to find a way out. In Selma that Tuesday both the state of Alabama and SCLC wanted to avoid a repetition of "Bloody Sunday," but they were committed to a collision course. CRS provided them with a means of avoidance. March 9 was the time for CRS to play its crisis response role. It was clearly not a time for advancing the long-range conciliation effort started in January. That would have to be resumed later on.

A Crisis That Didn't Have to Happen

Selma's torment did not end with the crossing of the bridge. That same evening, Tuesday, March 9, three of the white ministers who had come to Selma to support the march were set upon by four whites, all with police records. James Reeb, a Unitarian minister from Boston, died of his injuries the next morning. That event refueled the fires of protest. Many of the visiting marchers stayed on. From around the country additional clerics and church members of all faiths converged on Selma to express their outrage.

On Wednesday the Selma City Council decreed that there would be no more marches or demonstrations. That afternoon a group set out from Brown's Chapel for the courthouse to lay a wreath in honor of Reeb. They had barely started when they were stopped by the city police led by Baker. Still seeking to avoid arrests, Baker had a rope drawn across the street, beyond which the demonstrators were forbidden to pass. Instead they congregated in the street in front of the church and there commenced an all-night vigil—which was to last for five days and bring Selma to the brink of another catastrophic explosion.

The white population of Selma, particularly its rowdy element, so long held in check by the city police, became increasingly contentious. Growing numbers gathered around the area of the vigil, which was now cordoned off by city, county, and state law enforcement authorities. The area along Sylvan Street between Brown's Chapel and the First Baptist Church became known as "the compound" and the boundary rope set up by Baker as "the Berlin Wall." People could leave individually, but not in groups.

The new developments rekindled President Johnson's concerns. He ordered LeRoy Collins back to Selma. John Perry, then serving as Collins's special assistant, made the trip with him. Years later he was to recall their late-night arrival at the compound:

> It had been raining; it was muddy and awful there, and the church which was the headquarters for the civil rights groups was there. Alabama and local county cops had circled this place, this church. And there they were facing inward—toward the vigil. And this nasty group of people were behind them, yelling taunts and racial epithets at us. I thought, "Why are you looking at us? We don't intend to harm anybody. The trouble is on the other side. Why don't you point your guns that way?"...A little later I went back out and stood with a few blacks and a few whites from New England, holding hands and singing. This black woman standing next to me cried out. It must have been a pellet gun, because a rifle bullet would have killed her. But it knocked out her bottom front two or three teeth and went under the tongue. She crumpled down, with blood pouring all over her. So I helped carry her in. There was this black doctor inside the church. He seemed exhausted. They stretched her out on a horsehair sofa, and the doctor started working on her.[23]

Tension mounted all day Thursday. The number of visiting protesters arriving in the compound grew larger, and the hostile crowds continued

23. Perry, telephone interview with the author.

to gather on the perimeter. At 10:00 p.m. Collins, Secrest, Miller, and Perry met with James Orange, the SCLC staff worker heading the vigil, and some of the SNCC staff. CRS asked whether, in view of the volatility that could turn to violence at any time, they should consider terminating the vigil. The civil rights workers replied that they wanted nothing more than their constitutional rights, and that it was the job of law enforcement not to contain them but to protect them in the exercise of those rights.

The federal conciliators then presented that view to Baker. They pointed out that the parade restraint was self-defeating, since it served to continue the confrontation and focus national attention on Selma. Why risk another outbreak of violence, when relief in the form of a court decision permitting the march to Montgomery was only days away? Baker said that the city council would be unrelenting in its parade ban. Secrest then raised a proposal already discussed with Orange. Would groups of five be permitted to move to the courthouse—as had been previously allowed for voter registration?

Baker said yes; although the mayor would probably be against such a move, he thought he could convince him to allow it. Thus, at 1:00 a.m., the government representatives left the compound with a feeling of progress. A demonstration would be allowed at the courthouse Friday, and the vigil would be disbanded.

On Friday morning Mayor Smitherman rejected Baker's agreement to permit the march to the courthouse. Tension on both sides of the "Berlin wall" mounted further. The corps of dignitaries was growing in status as well as in size. It now included prelates, labor leaders, and congressmen. On Saturday the ministers decided that they would no longer submit to the parade ban. More than a thousand confronted the police line. Unable to pass, they redeployed into smaller groups; they tried breaking out through the housing project; they tested other routes out of the compound—all to no avail.

On Monday morning, as King presided over what was expected to be a crucial mass meeting, Secrest and Baker entered into desperate council in Baker's squad car. They agreed to ask Justice Department attorneys to call Judge Thomas in Mobile to see if he would persuade Sheriff Clark and Mayor Smitherman to allow the march to the courthouse. The call resulted in a proposal that the march would be permitted, but only two abreast on the sidewalk. Demonstration leaders rejected the idea, insisting that they would march in the street. A second proposal was offered—three abreast on the sidewalk, five minutes of singing at the courthouse, a short prayer service, and a return to the church. This was also rejected.

Minutes before another unauthorized march was to start, Secrest himself called Judge Thomas, and again the judge called Sheriff Clark. Clark talked to Hosea Williams. The deal was struck. The formation would be three abreast, two on the sidewalk, one in the street.

The barriers were removed. At 5:00 p.m. a crowd now swollen to two thousand started out on the brief but solemn procession from the compound to the courthouse. A wreath was placed in memory of Reverend Reeb. Prayers were recited. There was one song. The group returned to the church. The entire event had taken less than an hour. The long vigil and confrontation were over.

That same evening, Monday, March 15, President Johnson addressed a joint session of Congress to seek enactment of the 1965 voting rights bill he was about to submit. It was the first time in nineteen years that a president had addressed a joint session to request domestic legislation.[24]

In one of the most stirring appeals of his presidency, Johnson said:

> At times history and fate meet at a single time in a single place to shape a turning point in man's unending search for freedom. So it was at Lexington and Concord. . . . So it was last week in Selma, Alabama. . . . What happened at Selma is part of a far larger movement which reaches into every state and section of America. It is the effort of American Negroes to secure for themselves the full blessings of American life. . . . Their cause must be our cause, too. Because it is not just Negroes, but really all of us who must overcome the crippling legacy of bigotry and injustice.
>   And we shall—overcome![25]

LeRoy Collins and his wife were guests of the president and Mrs. Johnson at dinner that evening and in the president's box in the House gallery when Johnson spoke. Dr. King had also been invited to sit with the presidential party but went to Selma instead to speak at funeral services for the Reverend Reeb.

The March to Montgomery

On Wednesday, March 17, Judge Johnson ruled that the march to Montgomery could go forward, enjoining any effort by the state to restrain it.

On Sunday, March 21, thirty-two hundred marchers left their Selma staging area, on the way to Montgomery at last. With that third and final

24. President Truman had appeared before a joint session in 1946 to seek authorization to seize the railroads in order to settle a labor dispute.
25. *New York Times,* March 16, 1965.

crossing of the bridge, Selma passed from the limelight of national attention. Remaining behind were the still unresolved problems of prejudice,
discrimination, and racial inequity.

President Johnson invited Governor Wallace to the White House to
make a personal, and what he thought was persuasive, plea that the governor assure the safety of the march. Wallace waited until he was back
in Alabama to advise Johnson that the state could not afford to provide
protection for the marchers. An enraged Johnson immediately invoked a
contingency plan federalizing the Alabama National Guard and also sending troops from the Second Infantry Division at Fort Benning, Georgia.

Johnson was not content to end his personal intervention there. Seeing
the success of his voting rights program now intertwined with the behavior and success of civil rights forces, he left no stone unturned in his efforts to guarantee a successful march.

The judge had ordered that only three hundred could continue the march
after the first night because the highway narrowed to two lanes. How, the
president asked, were the others to return safely to Selma? It turned out
that there weren't enough buses; a special train had to be ordered.

Johnson's belt-and-suspenders style of guarding against problems came
into full play. John Doar, as assistant attorney general for civil rights, had
overall responsibility for security and law enforcement. But the provost
marshal of the U.S. Army, a major general, was sent down to provide
oversight of the major general in charge of the guard. The president also
sent down Ramsey Clark, then deputy attorney general, to look over
Doar's shoulder. LBJ also called Burke Marshall out of retirement for a few
days and sent him to Selma, too, just to assure that everything went well.

Johnson instructed LeRoy Collins to use his conciliators to facilitate logistical arrangements and liaison with local authorities. CRS staff members made advance contact with mayors, sheriffs, and police chiefs along
the route, advising them of the federal government's interest in a trouble-
free operation and helping to plan for contingencies.[26]

The most intricate work was in Montgomery itself, where unrelenting
local demonstrations over the previous two weeks had already rubbed
black/white relationships raw. NCC member Winton Blount,[27] one of the
most influential men in the state, was asked to convene the leaders of the

26. This employment of federal conciliation teams to forestall problems on civil
rights marches was to become standard operating procedure in ensuing years. It was
used, for example, on the Poor Peoples Campaign in 1967, to escort "the longest
walk" of Native Americans from Sacramento to Washington, D.C., in 1978, and on
farmworker marches in California and Texas.

27. He was later appointed postmaster general by President Jimmy Carter.

power structure of Montgomery in his own home, to meet with the federal officials. To an audience that tendered only grudging cooperation, Collins, Doar, and Ramsey Clark gave evidence of the high priority the White House attached to the success of the march. Laue recalls Blount muttering about how none of this would be necessary "if not for the little Napoleon [Governor Wallace] up there on the hill." Following a two-hour discussion of Collins's appeal to reason and to regional pride, the leaders present agreed to do what was asked of them.

For all of the complexities, security arrangements proved to be adequate. Laue recalled:

> The Montgomery police department asked if I would get the march leaders to move King back in the line of march at a particular point going through a black area of Montgomery where there were three-to-five-story, old apartments on either side of a narrow street. They felt it would be awfully hard to secure that area against an assassination attempt. And so I proposed that to Andy Young and he took it back to the march leaders and they said, "No." They would not be intimidated by white racism and threats. Instead they decided to keep King in the front line of the march but ask all the black preachers from Montgomery to wear dark suits like King. Andy laughed, "They can't tell us apart anyway."[28]

Collins later was to pay a price for his role in facilitating the march. Truck-mounted news cameras were constantly focused on the head of the march column. One day they caught Collins and King walking along in earnest discussion. The next morning that picture was front-page news throughout Florida: "Ex-Governor leads civil rights march with King." Years later, when Collins was running for U.S. senator in Florida's Democratic primary, the picture was circulated across the state. Collins was convinced that it was responsible for his defeat.

By mid-April, CRS was back in Selma seeking to encourage the conciliatory efforts it had sought to nurture since early January. The boycott was still in place, but for the most part the days of mass meetings and protest demonstrations had passed. A three-judge federal court had found Sheriff Clark guilty of contempt, and the effectiveness of the posse had been reduced, strengthening Wilson Baker's authority for law enforcement in the city. White moderates were beginning to move a little more boldly.

By June a number of interracial dialogues had begun, although no major reforms had taken place. The mayor and city council began a series of weekly meetings with Negro leaders. The Selma Chamber of Commerce endorsed a statement on racial fairness drafted by the state chamber,

28. Laue interview.

which it had previously rejected. It persuaded the city council to do like-
wise. The statement was then reprinted in the *Times-Journal,* along with
signatures of endorsement of eleven hundred white Selma citizens.

Two powerful outside forces were offering financial incentives for interracial cooperation: the federal government and industry.

In the past, federal assistance programs for the poor had not been welcome. Negroes were denied help from the federal government's surplus
food program because the city and county had refused to provide the
necessary start-up funds. It remained for CRS, working with the Department of Agriculture and the Alabama Council on Human Relations, to
arrange for an alternate means of channeling surplus food to Selma's poor.
Now there was a change. Many of the new antipoverty programs, which
required interracial dialogue in planning and execution, offered funding
that white Selma found difficult to reject.

Selma's thrust to bring new industry to the area was encountering
difficulty because many of the major firms being courted were troubled
about making multi-million-dollar investments in unstable communities
plagued by racial turmoil. CRS, with the support of some of its NCC
members, helped to instill into these discussions an insistence on the
part of the companies that the city resolve its problems and offer a climate that would be congenial to equal employment policies.

To clear the way for federal programs, CRS also facilitated contact between Selma's leadership and the Washington officials who made the funding decisions. Mac Secrest recalled, in 1990, his arrangement for an interracial delegation from Selma to visit with several federal agencies in
Washington about pending and possible programs. He personally greeted
the members of the delegation when they arrived at Washington's National Airport and volunteered to drive them to their hotel. His station
wagon proved to be a little small for the size of the group. The solution
was found by having Mrs. Boynton sit on Mayor Smitherman's lap. Secrest
thought that the interracial communication in the station wagon was just
fine.

Four

Equality of Results

The Revised Civil Rights Agenda

By 1965, the Supreme Court and Congress had affirmed racial equality as a matter of law. But their efforts fell far short of building human equality into the American way of life. A second phase of the battle for civil rights was still to come. Lyndon Johnson identified this second phase as the battle for equality of results. The objectives of this battle would be harder to clarify, and even harder to attain. The struggle would lead the federal government's racial troubleshooters to take on assignments not previously conceived of either by them or by those had brought the Community Relations Service into being.

More Than One Kind of Justice

The achievement of equal rights under law had created a false expectation among many that somehow a more equal distribution of America's bounty would soon follow. As the realization dawned that the newly won right to dine where they pleased changed little for minority families struggling to put the daily meal on the table, the emphasis of the civil rights struggle changed from a fight for theoretical justice to a struggle for distributive justice. As minorities began to realize that the achievement of equality would have to be further deferred until new economic and social battles were won, new conflicts emerged.

In the second half of the sixties, the struggle to convert equal opportunities to equal outcomes became a crucial factor in shaping the nature of racial conflict. It sharpened the frustration that led to urban riots; it fractured the civil rights movement, bitterly dividing black power strategists from integrationists; it diluted white support for evolving civil rights objectives. It also explains, in part, the failure of the movement to catch hold in the North as it did in the South.

The thrust for equality of outcomes helped to shape the CRS program in the North and undergirded CRS's enlargement of its mandate beyond the conception of its creators—except, perhaps, for Lyndon Johnson, who had sounded the most persuasive articulation of the need for distributive justice. In his 1965 speech at Howard University he called for a second part to the battle for civil rights. The challenge, he said, was to move Negroes through "gateless poverty" compounded of the need for employment, education, housing, and health care. He indicated that only a comprehensive program addressed to all these inequities would do: "They are a seamless web. They cause each other. They result from each other. They reinforce each other. Much of the Negro community is buried under a blanket of history and circumstance. It is not a lasting solution to lift just one corner of that blanket. We must stand on all sides and raise the entire cover if we are to liberate our fellow citizens." He then pronounced a new civil rights goal: "This is the next and more profound stage of the battle for civil rights. We seek . . . not just equality as a right and a theory, but equality as a fact and as a result."

In redirecting the focus of national concern from legal equity to equality as a result, the president, for the first time, included the problems of northern communities in the federal government's civil rights agenda. The black ghettos of America's northern cities graphically illustrated the absence of distributive justice. Despite laws in many states that had guaranteed the full measure of civil rights, minority neighborhoods in the core of big cities were islands of desperate poverty, marked by poor income, education, health, and housing and high rates of crime. The new civil rights laws did not change anything in the ghettos. Long-suppressed feelings of deprivation crystallized into outbreaks of free-floating rage. This rage took visible form in 1964, when rioting in New York City, Rochester, New York, Philadelphia, and elsewhere started a spate of "long hot summers."

"Riot Prevention" in the Summer of 1965

In the spring of 1965, CRS, still less than a year old, and with a staff that had not yet reached fifty, was designated to spearhead a massive federal effort to reduce the risk of America's most vulnerable cities going up in flames. It required a quick turnabout for an agency whose focus had been southern and rural to gear up for conflict resolution and prevention in the urban North.

In 1965 the programs embraced within President Johnson's War on Poverty, which promised to produce better housing, jobs, and education for the poor, were just beginning to function. Federal administrators saw themselves as in a race against time. How could the new programs have an impact before the heat of another summer triggered a new wave of violence?

The problem was placed in the hands of the President's Council on Equal Opportunity, the cabinet-level committee established to coordinate the federal government's civil rights work. The chairman of the council was Vice President Hubert Humphrey. As the council struggled with the question of how to deal with its implicit assignment to keep the cities "cool," it found its answer in a proposal by CRS, which that agency had drafted in an effort to get the federal government to address civil rights problems in the North.

The CRS plan had been born out of the frustration of a few staff members who were troubled by the agency's preoccupation with civil rights problems in the South. Its adoption by the President's Council on Equal Opportunity resulted in Humphrey creating the Vice President's Summer Task Force on Urban Problems. Task force members included the secretaries of Labor and HEW, the attorney general, the director of the Office of Economic Opportunity, the administrator of the Housing and Home Finance Agency,[1] the chairman of the Civil Rights Commission, and the director of the Office of Emergency Planning. LeRoy Collins was named executive director of the task force, and CRS the coordinating agency. Day-to-day management was delegated to the thirty-three-year-old black assistant director of CRS, Roger Wilkins.[2]

Wilkins, who later succeeded Collins as director of CRS and who imparted to it much of the operating style and sense of mission that characterized it for many years, was at that time something of a reluctant dragon, not quite sure of the CRS mission or his own role in it. He had been practicing law in New York when he was recruited by Fowler Hamilton, the director of the U.S. Agency for International Development, to join him as special assistant. In that capacity, he was one of the highest ranking Ne-

---

1. This agency was the forerunner to the Department of Housing and Urban Development.
2. Janis and Samet interviews.

groes in the federal civil service. While not widely known on the national stage of civil rights, he had long since cut his eyeteeth in grassroots activity. He had been born and raised in an atmosphere of familiarity with racial and social issues. His father, who died when Roger was nine, had been a reporter and then business manager for a leading Negro newspaper, the *Kansas City Call*. His mother, a national board member of the YWCA, was prominent in that organization's civil rights efforts. His uncle was Roy Wilkins, the national executive secretary of the NAACP. So it was not surprising that the younger Wilkins would have worked in the NAACP youth movement in high school, or that he would have been president of the NAACP branch at the University of Michigan. While in law school in 1955, he interned with the NAACP Legal Defense and Education Fund, which was then wrapping up its winning efforts in the *Brown v. Board of Education* case. As a practicing lawyer in New York, he had volunteered as a tester to help in the enforcement of open housing, and he had begun to make his voice heard on the need to oppose civil rights abuses in the North.

When asked to be an assistant director of CRS, Wilkins had misgivings. As he later recalled: "I thought that the concept of a group of people in Washington who would fly around the country was not workable. But I thought about it. My final view was that, whatever you think of the legislation, when Congress gives you people and money to do something about civil rights, you damn well better go out and try to do something."

His first impressions of the agency brought him no reassurance. "I remember a staff meeting just about when I got there. September or October 1964. All these white guys were sitting there. And they were talking about how we, CRS, were going to fix Mississippi. And I went home and told my wife, 'What kind of crazy people have I gotten myself involved with?'"

Misgivings turned to resentment as Wilkins found himself without significant influence in the agency's inner council and uninvolved in the conciliation program in the South—in which he had little confidence. Wilkins recalled: "I never opposed the agency doing things in the South. I just didn't think the entire program should be involved hopping from one southern hot spot to another, and my view, which I expressed often, was that we really had to work on the big cities—mainly in the north—because more black people lived in one block in Harlem than there were in all of McComb, Mississippi."[3]

3. Roger Wilkins, interview with the author.

In response to his demands, Wilkins was given a specific, although vaguely defined, portfolio as head of a newly created Division of Community Action. He recruited Seymour Samet and Jay Janis as his earliest staff, and the three began to lay plans for a federal civil rights effort in the North.

What ultimately emerged was a rough design for a crash program to expedite the movement of the new federal antipoverty programs and resources to America's inner cities. The financial assistance would be coupled with community relations expertise to help local communities be more responsive to the civil rights needs of minorities.

Too new to the Washington scene to shrink from audacity, they proposed that tiny CRS spearhead a major coordination of the full phalanx of federal social benefit programs. The three then sought to trumpet their idea within the federal civil rights community. It was quickly seen as a possible response to the anxieties of the President's Council on Equal Opportunity about the prospects of a long, hot summer, and the Vice President's Summer Task Force on Urban Problems was created, with CRS at the tiller.

From a list of cities where racial tensions were high, eleven were selected to receive task force assistance. Mayors were invited by the vice president to come to Washington with their key lieutenants who would administer the various new and improved federal programs. The invitations were issued without publicity to avoid the possibility that Washington's concern about riots would be construed as criticism of the mayors or serve as a self-fulfilling prophecy. The city officials met directly with the federal decision makers who had sign-off authority on the big funding programs. They then and there debated and negotiated program proposals and modifications, thereby cutting many months from the program-approval process and expediting the flow of federal funds.

At the same time that it was coordinating these meetings, CRS scouted the nation for community relations specialists who could take on summer assignments as CRS conciliators resident in each of the target cities.

Two of the mayors, Samuel Yorty of Los Angeles and Richard Daley of Chicago, refused to participate in the project. The program went forward in New York, Newark, Rochester, Philadelphia, Detroit, Gary, San Francisco, Miami, and Oakland. Each of the participating cities went through the summer unscathed by outbreaks of racial violence. Riots did take place in Chicago and Los Angeles, the two cities that had refused the program. CRS and the members of the Summer Task Force savored the results with discreet silence. They knew that the emergency infusion of federal dollars and community relations sensitivity may have been a good first step, but it was far from being the answer to urban unrest.

CRS Moves North

The Summer Task Force experience convinced CRS that conciliators should not be concentrated in Washington but instead located closer to the action. It also demonstrated that CRS, working as program facilitator as well as conflict resolver, could do a better job in helping cities to address underlying problems. What happened in Rochester helped lead to that conclusion.

Rochester had been the second city to "blow" in the summer of 1964. It happened in late July, and CRS, still less than a month old, was totally consumed with problems in the South. Rochester was ignored. By October, however, the agency had had second thoughts, and Collins told the staff that CRS should move toward trouble rather than away from it. As a result, Mac Secrest was assigned to assess the situation in Rochester to determine what role, if any, CRS might play.

His recommendations were to put a consultant in Rochester for two months to help the city design a community relations plan and structure and to act as a liaison between Rochester and Washington to expedite the movement of federal programs to the city.[4] However, nothing was done about the report until Rochester was named a candidate city for the 1965 summer project.

My first field assignment, within weeks of joining the CRS staff in the early spring of 1965, was to check out Rochester, as well as Detroit, to help validate their inclusion in the final selection for the Summer Task Force project.[5]

On the plane to Rochester, I studied the report of Mac Secrest's earlier visit and a sheaf of newspaper clippings detailing the city's racial conflicts over the past year. It provided me with an overlarge list of people I ought to see, with some of whom I had already made appointments.

A key name on my list, and a new player at the table since Secrest's visit, was the Reverend Franklin Florence. He was the leader of a new and highly vociferous black protest organization that had put the old-line Negro organizations temporarily into the shadows. Following the latest trend in

4. Memorandum of October 19, 1964, from A. M. Secrest to Dr. John A. Griffin.
5. This was typical CRS on-the-job training for recruits—sink or swim on an assignment always beyond your previous experience. Since no one else had ever had such an assignment, mere survival made you an instant expert. In 1965 I was a veteran within the new and tiny profession of community relations workers, having served the American Jewish Committee for seventeen years. But my race relations experience, devoted largely to writing and research, plus volunteer experience in community organization and coalition building, was hardly the ideal preparation for assessing ghetto tensions or analyzing the ghetto–city hall relationships of America's central cities.

choosing an acronym to use as a name for a new social protest group, with the full name to be determined later, it was known as FIGHT, which would stand for Freedom, Integration, God, Honor, Today. FIGHT's militant posture, its protest demonstrations, and its provocative language appeared to have Rochester's establishment on edge. Clearly, it had helped to keep the question of racial disparities, and programs to remedy them, on the front page. I had been unable to reach the Reverend Florence by phone to set up an appointment in advance. Seeing him was high on my agenda.

It was standard operating procedure for CRS, on entering any city for the first time, to make an early call on the protest leaders. This approach was sometimes disconcerting to the city's power brokers, who often spoke of those leaders as "agitators" or, worse still, "outside agitators" or "rabble-rousers" and often "communists." CRS was to learn that a surprising number of public officials truly believed that the agitator rather than the grievance was the root of the protest. Only sometimes was CRS able to convince them that the unprotested grievance festers, while protest, by opening the wound, can lead to faster healing.

Getting to see the Reverend Florence was not easy. Telephone calls to possible contact people were fielded gingerly: they might or might not be able to reach him; he might or might not be able to call me back. Inquiries of other black leaders and at other agencies in the ghetto were equally frustrating. In midafternoon, at a neighborhood settlement house, a tall white man in his midtwenties pulled me aside and said, "Why do you want to see the Reverend Florence?" We spoke briefly and made a tentative appointment for my hotel room at midnight.

Shortly after twelve the young man appeared with the Reverend Florence. The minister did not respond to my greeting, nor did he remove his hat and coat or take the proffered chair. Offers of refreshment were declined. I was interviewed for a half hour by the younger man; at first I could induce no more than monosyllabic participation from Florence. When he finally spoke, Florence treated me to a variety of opinions about the possibility of my being a spy for the FBI, my choice of hotel, and my room on an upper floor, which permitted me to look down on the poor Negroes below. He then wanted my guarantee that Rochester would be included in the summer program. When I told him I could only make a recommendation, he asked me to pick up the phone at that moment and call my boss so that he could hear my recommendation. When I said that I would not report in that manner, at that time, he announced that he would call his good friend Congressman Adam Clayton Powell in the morning, who would jolly well make sure that Rochester got the program. Before leaving, he sat down and shared, in a limited way, some of the perceptions of Rochester's black leadership. When we parted he assured me that he either might or might not cooperate with the CRS summer representative. I was later to learn that there was nothing personal in Florence's in-your-face conversational style. The persona was part of his job description.[6]

The movement of FIGHT and the Reverend Florence to center stage was not a totally spontaneous phenomenon that emerged by chance from the riot of the previous summer. In fact, it was the enactment of a protest formula taking place in other cities as well. The master script had been written by the Industrial Areas Foundation (IAF). The foundation was the creation of a sociologist and self-styled "radical" turned community organizer named Saul Alinsky. The tall young man who brought Florence to my hotel room was on the IAF staff. He was assigned to Rochester because the Rochester Council of Ministers had contracted with Alinsky to build a militant protest movement that would help impel city leaders to initiate meaningful social change.

The Alinsky technique was to organize a power base around the community's most deeply felt grievances through methods that "rubbed salt into the wounds." Dramatization of the injustice through innovative and outrageous forms of protest built cohesion among the protesters at the same time that it created intolerable consternation within the community at large. With long-ignored injustices suddenly spotlighted, and then made difficult to preserve, it became easier for the city to introduce social change.[7] Church groups that sought Alinsky's assistance in the late sixties in order to create an imperative for social change may also have been moved by another theory. By channeling suppressed anger into organized protest, groups like FIGHT provided a safety valve for the inchoate rage that might otherwise break out into violence as it had the previous summer.

Sam Convissor was recruited to serve as the CRS field representative in Rochester for the summer of 1965. As a former press aide for mayor Hugh Addonizio of Newark, he understood the workings of city government and its nexus with the ghetto. His assignment was broad: to use his

6. While I did not know it at the time, I was one of the earliest targets of a process later to be described and named by Tom Wolfe in an essay called "Mau-Mauing the Flak-Catchers." He pictured it as the use of uncivil and even abusive conversation to intimidate and destabilize a government functionary, presumably to enhance one's negotiating posture.

7. The technique had originated in Alinsky's work in the Chicago slum known as Back of the Yards. This was the area behind the meatpacking plants inhabited by the plants' workers, largely Polish immigrants. Alinsky's teachings and his organizing skills were credited with getting the heretofore hapless workers to organize, to protest, and to sustain their efforts until change resulted. In the space of a few years the Back of the Yards saw far-reaching changes in social conditions.

ingenuity to help implement the two purposes of the task force. Those objectives were to speed the flow of federal funds coming from the new antipoverty programs and to help the city improve the climate of race relations. Convissor worked as a troubleshooter, mediating between federal and local officials, between public agencies and advocates of the poor people they served, between minority leaders and city hall. When red tape was the problem, he and his CRS counterparts in the other cities participating in the project learned that a phone call to task force headquarters could generate priority attention. When necessary, even the weight of the vice president's office was available to help break a logjam.

At the same time, Convissor worked to improve communication across racial lines and to draw attention to problems of intergroup friction that needed to be resolved. Working unobtrusively, he made contacts throughout the city, offering assistance where need and opportunity suggested. In many ways the job was made easier because Rochester was a city justifiably proud of its civic virtue. Its colleges, parks, and libraries were prized institutions. Eastman Kodak, Xerox, and other major corporations demanded and contributed to the city's problem-solving approach. To help school desegregation work, Rochester instituted the first magnet schools in the country. When it recognized, and decided to come to grips with, the problem of antagonism between its police and its minority community, it recruited Laplois (Lakey) Ashford, national youth director of the NAACP, as deputy public safety director.

An unanticipated dividend of Convissor's summer labors was the ghetto support activity his presence had catalyzed. In September, I attended a farewell luncheon for Convissor tendered by about fifty city and civic officials with whom he had worked. People rose, one by one, to testify how the federal government's demonstration of interest had energized them to direct their own programs more sharply to the unaddressed needs of the poor and minorities. Some indicated that thanks to Convissor they had begun, for the first time, to work with minority leaders, community aides, and public officials with whom they should have been collaborating in the past. Others said they were impressed that a federal agency working at the street level could get the immediate attention of decision makers in Washington.

CRS Joins the Department of Justice

Even as CRS's activity in southern hot spots and its leadership on the Summer Task Force on Urban Problems were embellishing its reputation within the federal government, other forces were at work to bring about what Collins would see as a clipping of the agency's wings. Following passage of the Voting Rights Act of 1965, discussions were initiated to bring about tighter coordination of the widely scattered responsibilities for federal civil rights activity. The coordinating efforts of the President's Council on Equal Opportunity, under Vice President Humphrey, were seen as inadequate. To many, the attorney general's office was the logical command post. A variety of options were proposed for CRS, ranging from making it an independent agency, to attaching it to the soon-to-be-formed Department of Housing and Urban Development, to attaching it directly to the White House, to making it a part of the Department of Justice.

Collins favored keeping CRS in Commerce, in the belief that it would continue to be most effective by energizing the business community to support civil rights compliance. Besides, Commerce, under Secretary Hodges, allowed CRS the full freedom of an independent agency in determining its own policies and programs. Humphrey was supportive. Burke Marshall, though out of government by the time the issue was joined, had always believed that CRS's freedom to negotiate might be dampened if the agency was placed within the Justice Department, which was seen as a coercive force.

Attorney General Nicholas Katzenbach and Assistant Attorney General John Doar, as well as key presidential aides such as Joe Califano, saw a need to make the attorney general the dominant figure overseeing the government's full civil rights effort. They mistrusted conciliated solutions that weren't bound to verdicts and court orders.[8] They questioned how the government could be conciliatory with respect to those things the Constitution required. They feared that CRS might pursue peace rather than justice.

Collins, Fleming, and Calvin Kytle, who served as acting director of CRS after Collins was elevated to undersecretary of commerce, saw the Katzenbach view as too legalistic. They felt he had no vision of the vast arena of controversy in which CRS operated—the arena that lay between a court decision on a specific case and the final achievement of social change consistent with the law. Wilkins called this the place "where the restructuring of society becomes a personal reality."[9]

Members of the civil rights community, still vaguely untrusting of the Justice Department, lobbied to keep CRS out of its control. But their own unresolved ambivalence about CRS robbed their efforts of vigor.

---

8. Katzenbach recalled that he and others had reservations about including the concept of conciliation in the civil rights law when it was being drafted.

9. Wilkins interview.

The determination of the Department of Justice to gain a measure of control over CRS was probably strengthened by its experience in Selma, where it had been disconcerted, at times, by CRS's independent role and informal problem-solving techniques. Katzenbach could still vaguely recall difficulties at Selma, when asked about it twenty-five years later: "One of the difficulties that at least John Doar felt was that Governor Collins would be heading down one track while he was heading down another. This did cause confusion. I remember during the demonstrations at Selma that was certainly John's view. He would say one thing and somebody from the Community Relations Service would say another. And he thought it was very confusing." Burke Marshall's recollection confirmed: "I guess that the Department of Justice thought that it should have control of the Community Relations Service in order to avoid whatever kind of confusion they had at Selma and other places."[10]

In January, Johnson submitted to Congress an executive resolution transferring CRS to the Justice Department, with the agency's director given the rank of an assistant attorney general. Whatever its motivation, the move, approved by Congress in April 1966, turned out to be the right one. Justice Department credentials commanded more respect and attention from local authorities than had those from Commerce, and the direct line to the attorney general amplified CRS's voice within the federal civil rights community. The fear that CRS might be subordinated to the Civil Rights Division was never borne out—perhaps because Ramsey Clark, as attorney general during the early years of the change, understood the importance of CRS's nonlawyerly role and established a pattern of according full respect to its equal status with the litigative divisions. The affiliation with Justice sometimes made it more difficult to explain the intermediary role to both sides, but the conciliators soon became adept at surmounting the problem.

President Johnson appointed Roger Wilkins to be director of CRS in January 1966. That event inaugurated a change in the direction of the agency that no one, including Wilkins himself, would have foreseen. By the end of Wilkins's term in January 1969, program emphases had shifted from South to North, from rural to urban, from firefighting to fire prevention. Recruitment of black staff members was accelerated; Hispanic recruitment was

---

10. Katzenbach and Marshall interviews. In a telephone interview on August 23, 1990, Doar could not recall any undue tension between CRD and CRS in Selma, nor any differences with Governor Collins related to the crossing of the Pettus Bridge. He noted that in general differences as to the priority to be given the litigative as opposed to the negotiated approach were not unhealthy, and the various attorneys general under whom he served supported each as circumstances indicated.

initiated. Most significant, the balance of program goals that had teetered between mere compliance with the law and wider objectives of social justice moved perceptibly toward justice.

These changes came about not only because Wilkins was adventurous and well connected. He offered a charismatic leadership that infused much of the staff with an almost arrogant sense of mission. But he also had the political savvy not to overstep the bounds of bureaucratic prudence.

Using the Shadow and Substance of Political Influence

Wilkins saw the director's influence within government as an important tool for advancing the CRS program, which needed all the support it could get from other federal agencies. He saw the exploitation of the prestige of his position of director as a deliberate strategy for leveraging the strength of a small agency. A close personal friendship with Ramsey Clark, who was confirmed as attorney general in March 1967, gave Wilkins and the CRS running room to test some innovative approaches.

The two men first came together in the aftermath of the Watts riot in Los Angeles, when Clark, as deputy attorney general, headed the federal team looking into the disorders and planning the scope of Washington's relief effort. Wilkins and Collins had gone on-site as Lyndon Johnson's first representatives while the fires were still burning, and Wilkins stayed on with Clark and provided valuable liaison with the black community.

Later, after Clark had succeeded Katzenbach as attorney general, his understanding of the social dynamite that had led to the Watts explosion helped him to see the good sense in the CRS analysis that without evidence of the government's pursuit of justice for minorities, racial conflict would remain endemic in the urban ghettos. Writing in 1970, Clark enlarged on this precept, observing, "There will be no social stability if major segments of society are excluded from the mainstream and millions go on living in poverty." He concluded that "the long history of mankind says you will have neither order nor justice unless you have both."[11]

CRS's influence among other agencies of government was also enhanced by the close relationship between Clark and Wilkins. In Wilkins's words: "If we couldn't get the cooperation we needed from the Department of Labor, I'd call Ramsey and ask him to call [Secretary of Labor Willard] Wirtz. And it would get done."[12]

11. Clark, *Crime in America: Observations on Its Nature, Causes, Prevention, and Control*, 345.
12. Wilkins interview.

The respect for Wilkins within the government was also enhanced by the fact that the president had personally presided at the White House ceremony at which he was sworn in as director of CRS—an honor rarely accorded to one of subcabinet rank. Johnson's selection of Wilkins, with Clark's vigorous support, was not hurt by the fact that Wilkins was the nephew of Roy Wilkins, who was reputed to have ready access to the Oval Office and for whom Johnson had a warm regard. Johnson may also have had a more pragmatic reason for the appointment. In later years Wilkins speculated: "Johnson needed to have visible black executives in his administration. He felt he needed it politically, and he needed it in his heart. He, as a human being, needed to feel—needed to know—that he had given significant responsibility to black people. So that in the beginning gave me access to a lot."

Nor did Wilkins have any problems—or illusions—in accepting the luster that rubbed off from his uncle's good name. As he later recalled, "The fact that I was Roy's nephew was not unhelpful. Two guys named Wilkins— one's a prominent guy, so be nice to the kid. That's the way a lot of people viewed it."

He also made use of the small network of blacks within the federal government's leadership ranks. Lacking access to the "old boys' network," they developed a "new boys' network." Wilkins remembered that this group included Lisle Carter, an assistant secretary of HEW; Ed Sylvester, head of the Office of Contract Compliance in the Department of Labor; and Carl Holman, deputy staff director of the U.S. Commission on Civil Rights. To that select group Wilkins added "a person who was outside that group only because she was not in the government, Marian Wright Edelman." Reflecting on the effectiveness of networking, Wilkins said, "Those contacts just magnified the reach and the impact of CRS. Lisle and Carl and Ed and I magnified each other. One of us would go to a meeting at the White House; we'd all know about it. That was enormously helpful."[13]

Responding to Racial Conflict in the North

As CRS conciliators hurtled from crisis to crisis, priorities were often determined by the volatility and visibility of the confrontations. Minority protest and white resistance set the stage for some of the most visible and most volatile. In many localities, it was the NAACP, or the local ministerial association, that organized the outcry for change. The Urban League,

13. Ibid.

SNCC, and CORE also generated activity that would determine where CRS would go. In the South, the major advocate for change in the most publicized protests had been SCLC. For a time that group also served as a lightning rod in the North—although the outcomes were different.

CRS mediated between Dr. Martin Luther King Jr. and Chicago's Mayor Richard Daley when King first tested SCLC's wings in the North. CRS tried to supply a conciliating presence in Memphis, where SCLC was supporting the sanitation workers' strike, and CRS was with Dr. King at his death on the balcony of the Lorraine Motel. CRS worked in cities around the country to help repair the ruptured fabric of race relations following the riots that marked King's death, and they accompanied the mule trains when his inheritors brought the Poor Peoples Campaign to its summer encampment at Resurrection City on the Mall in Washington, D.C.

The voting rights victory won on the streets of Selma was the high-water mark of the SCLC's politics of provocation through peaceful protest. The Voting Rights Act of 1965 toppled the last great barrier to full achievement of theoretical justice in the South. But the achievement of distributive justice—attaining the power and the wherewithal to enjoy the full benefit of the rights they had won—still lay beyond the reach of the minority poor in many parts of the country. For this fight the battlefield would have to include the North, where prejudice and discrimination were deeply entrenched in practice, if not in law.

When SCLC turned north, it deliberately looked for the toughest target so that a victory would open the way for significant change and sensitize the nation to the need to do battle against racial discrimination and poverty in the North. The target was housing discrimination in Chicago. The strategy was the same as in Selma—to provoke a brutal response that would outrage the nation. In place of Sheriff Jim Clark and his posse, the foil would be the residents of the lily-white working-class neighborhoods of Chicago and the adjacent city of Cicero.

A coalition of Chicago civil rights organizations had already initiated vigorous protests, focused mainly on discrimination in the schools. CRS had been helpful in brokering a meeting between the protest leaders and the city's powerful mayor, Richard Daley. The mayor was totally resistant to the coalition's demands. Its alliance with King galvanized the movement and brought additional thousands to the protest marches, which now focused on desegregated housing in Chicago and its suburbs. Angry white residents responded with a level of rage and verbal violence that the veteran civil rights workers found as frightening as any they had encountered in the South. Only the massed strength of Chicago's police department prevented the bloodbath many feared.

The Chicago real estate industry was not about to make any moves toward open housing, and the city's power structure, including the mayor, while discommoded, was not about to apply the pressure required for change.

CRS conciliators Sam Dennis and Phil Mason, who had been monitoring the situation from the start, were joined by Jim Laue when SCLC entered the fray. The three endeavored to work with all parties to keep open the channels for negotiation.

Despite the attention the marches had received, SCLC leaders felt they had not been able to generate the overwhelming outpouring they had expected from the ghetto. The response of the national media had been less than spectacular. Fund-raising and participation from around the country were not encouraging. King and his strategists considered escalating their gamble by calling for a national infusion of protesters to lay siege to the city. In the face of serious doubt as to the possible success of such an effort, it was never tried. Jim Laue saw in this and other signs evidence that an exhausted SCLC leadership was looking for a strategy to enable it to declare a victory and go home.

At length SCLC decided to play a trump card. It planned for a major march in the neighboring city of Cicero, a lily-white working-class community with a reputation for violent resistance to any Negro incursion. The threat brought the desired result. With the mayor's support, the Chicago power structure convened a summit conference at which the leaders of the real estate industry met face-to-face with the protest leaders in the presence of the mayor and the kingpins of the city's business, religious, and civic institutions. Within two weeks, an agreement was worked out. The housing industry and relevant city agencies offered to improve compliance with open-housing laws and regulations, and religious and civic leaders undertook to develop education programs in support of open occupancy policies. While the agreement lacked the guarantees and performance deadlines that the protesters would have liked, pledges were made for a good-faith effort, in exchange for which SCLC and the civil rights coalition suspended the marches for an unspecified period.

While the settlement was hailed by many as a victory, the Chicago adventure had fallen far short of the hopes of King and his associates. Despite SCLC's best efforts, it had failed to galvanize either significant outrage among Chicago's blacks or an outpouring of support from around the nation. As a pilot program to chart the way for cracking racial poverty and injustice in the North, it had shown them that this was not the way to go.

The importance of the settlement lay less in Chicago than in its confirmation of the expectation of many that segregation in the North was not likely to yield to the methods of the movement that had prevailed in the South. To those who had come to expect that SCLC would produce block-buster breakthroughs for social justice, it was a disappointing venture.

Jim Laue, reflecting years later on what turned King back from Chicago, pinpointed three contributing factors. One was the disciplined control of the city by an old-fashioned political boss strongly allied both to the ethnic neighborhoods as well as to much of the leadership of Negro political and civic organizations. The second factor was the reduced financial support coming from the liberal sources that had passionately put their money into the civil rights struggle in the South. The third was the difference in the immediacy of the issues. As Laue explained: "Gandhi used to say that 'soul force' is used most effectively when there is a direct correspondence between means and ends. When you're sitting in on a lunch counter stool, the means are the ends; the behavior of your protest is precisely the behavior you wish to be guaranteed by law. When you want open housing, on the other hand, there's no direct connection between picketing and marching and living in peace in a nonsegregated neighborhood."[14]

The Poor Peoples Campaign

By 1967 the civil rights movement's mighty engine for waging war on injustice through the power of peaceful mass protest lay idle. The legislative victories required to assure equal rights under law had been won. But the triumph offered no satisfaction without follow-on progress toward distributive justice. The fact that SCLC's effort to crank up the war machine to battle for equal housing in Chicago had an ambiguous outcome did not deter King and his associates from seeing the future of the civil rights movement as tied to the struggle for a better life for America's impoverished millions.

The new objective would be to mobilize a mass protest of the poor in order to awaken the American conscience to economic injustice. SCLC's leaders envisioned a rough parallel to the successful strategy of the past: consciousness-raising to ready the nation for legislative change. To dramatize the issue there would be a great convergence of the nation's poor upon Washington and a continuing encampment on the Mall—at the center of the seat of government. The purpose would be to provide a background drumbeat for an intensive lobbying effort with Congress and the Executive Branch agencies.

14. Laue interview.

CRS was not alone in seeing this as a high-risk venture. The federal government at its highest levels had serious concerns. Officials understood that in order for SCLC to find the encampment useful, the encampment would have to be visible, provocative—even abrasive. The potential for disorder seemed monumental. Violence, whether stemming from aroused whites, from undisciplined minority members swept up in the campaign, or from overstressed agents of law enforcement, could result in a bloodbath. Fear of riots on the streets of Washington or police violence might shame the nation and be a major setback in progress toward social change: There could easily be spillover to other cities.[15]

The fact that Martin Luther King Jr. would be the presiding figure of this mass lobbying effort offered some reassurance that it would not get out of hand. Nevertheless, chaos and disaster could result from any failure in planning or administering the logistics of the envisioned gigantic tent city. Food, water, housing, public safety, and health services would need to be provided and maintained without breakdown. CRS advocated full support and close coordination by all relevant city and federal agencies.

Under the attentive eye of the attorney general—and the less apparent but no less attentive eye of the White House—the federal apparatus answered the call. With the city government of Washington carrying the burden of responsibility, more than twenty local and federal agencies formed a coordinating mechanism to provide SCLC with logistical assistance and to keep the effort of building and managing a new city in the heart of the nation's capital from going awry. CRS was given the job of "coordinating community relations." This meant monitoring the interface between SCLC and all of the participating agencies in order to anticipate problems, make sure that little went wrong, and that what did go wrong was promptly remedied. For example, Wilkins flew to Miami in January, and to Atlanta in March, to personally sit down with King to stress the need for advance planning and arrangements, such as obtaining the dozens of permits that would be required to plant a new city in the middle of Washington, D.C. And when unrelenting rain converted the encampment on the Mall to a wallow of mud, CRS called on the U.S. Public Health Service to assure the necessary safeguards against the outbreak of disease.

15. Those with an eye for history remembered the disastrous results of a comparable bivouac of the poor on Washington's Anacostia Flats in 1932. There thousands of unemployed veterans of World War I moved in for an indeterminate stay in order to lobby for the immediate payment of war bonuses. On orders of the president, the veterans were forceably evicted by army troops led by Chief-of-Staff Douglas MacArthur. The harsh tactics left a legacy of bitterness around the country for many years.

Planning strategies for the Poor Peoples Campaign had been well under way by early April 1968, when everything came to a screeching halt with the murder of Dr. Martin Luther King Jr.

In late March, the thirteen hundred sanitation workers of the city of Memphis, mostly black, were six weeks into a strike for union recognition and economic gains. Mass demonstrations supported by the black community were encountering stubborn resistance. Tensions were high. Against the advice of his staff, already overwhelmed by preparations for the Poor Peoples Campaign, King accepted an invitation to speak before a Memphis rally, where his presence seemed to reinvigorate the movement. He returned on April 1 to lead a march of sanitation workers and their supporters. A number of people broke away from the march and started breaking windows and looting. "Many stores along the march route were damaged, 280 people were arrested, 60 people were injured, and a black sixteen-year-old boy was killed by police gunfire."[16]

King was upset that a demonstration under his leadership had erupted in disorder. He and his colleagues immediately understood that it had been a mistake to participate in a display of this size without the careful planning, training, and management of SCLC organizers. King decided he would lead another march—this one with proper SCLC guidance. The date chosen was April 8. He and a cadre of aides returned to Memphis on April 3. He died on April 4.

Jim Laue had joined the CRS team that was trying to conciliate the Memphis controversy, in order to be available for planning discussions with SCLC leaders about the Poor Peoples Campaign, now only weeks away. He shared a room at the Lorraine Motel with Andrew Young. The adjacent room was shared by King and Ralph Abernathy. On April 4 Laue was in his room listening to the six o'clock news.

The sound of the fatal shot brought him to the balcony door to see the civil rights leader fallen. Others were calling for aid. He rushed back for towels and blankets, feeling as he did so that it was already too late to provide comfort.

Unable to reach Roger Wilkins in his office or at home, Laue called the attorney general to advise him of King's death. Ramsey Clark made immediate arrangements to fly to Memphis, asking Laue to arrange for him to meet with SCLC leaders to express the federal government's concern and offer its assistance.[17] When Wilkins learned of King's death, he

---

16. Henry Hampton and Steve Fayer, *Voices of Freedom: An Oral History of the Civil Rights Movement from the 1950s through the 1980s.*
17. Laue interview.

moved to augment the CRS team in Memphis and Atlanta so that it could bolster SCLC in making necessary arrangements with the authorities in both cities and for the funeral.

Anticipating the wave of outrage that might engulf America's black communities, CRS took what it feared might be futile measures to help communities deter the onrushing hurricane and alleviate the consequences. In Memphis, CRS arranged for the attorney general to meet with King's followers and the strikers on the one hand and the mayor and public safety director on the other to help maintain a climate of calm. CRS conciliators throughout the country were kept informed of developments in Memphis so that they might be able to dispel rumors as they met with law enforcement and civil rights officials working to relieve tensions. Their efforts proved to be weak sandbags against the mounting tidal wave of riots that broke out around the country.

Within a month of King's funeral, and with ghettos still smoldering, nine caravans bearing representatives of the nation's poor left their various points of origin for a labyrinthine journey to the encampment at Washington, D.C. Accompanying the two caravans that started from Marks, Mississippi, was a symbolic mule train with blue-denimed attendants, which SCLC had made emblematic of black rural poverty. Each of the nine caravans had a CRS team charged with negotiating the travelers' safe passage through what at times would be unsympathetic-to-hostile country. This meant monitoring SCLC's efforts to obtain campsites, route permits, health care, and provisions all along the line of march and improvising ways to forestall disaster. It meant meeting with city policy makers, peace officers, and news reporters to help them understand that the caravan following half a day behind was a group of determined Americans seeking to peacefully petition their government, and not some ragtag rabble bent on trouble.

It was clear from the outset that the CRS role would be one of clearing minefields. Trouble started immediately in Marks, Mississippi. Seven SCLC organizers were arrested, and students and teachers were suspended for their recruiting activities. Conflict spiraled upward with a school boycott, followed by threats of teachers being fired. CRS helped to negotiate a solution—official closure of schools for a few days until the caravans got started, with classes to be made up at the end of the year.

Fear of police overreaction was heightened after a police official from Virginia started a rumor in advance of the caravan reaching Selma, Alabama, that the marchers were armed and prone to violence. To ease that concern, CRS thereafter arranged for each police jurisdiction to reassure itself by having its own scout join the caravan two stops before the scheduled arrival in each city. The outcome was unanimous praise from all the southern caravans for police cooperation en route.

Near Cincinnati, rival participating youth gangs threatened to disrupt the caravan. CRS's recommendations about giving the youth groups specific responsibilities resolved the problem. In Detroit, CRS met with SCLC leaders and the mayor to conciliate police brutality allegations. In Seattle, police refused to allow caravan buses to park at the scheduled staging area, threatening confusion and possible disorder at the very start of the march. CRS, enlisting the assistance of the U.S. attorney and the U.S. marshal, arranged for the police to cover the parking meters. When ideological and personal differences between leaders of the western caravan seemed likely to split the marchers into two groups proceeding separately across the country, CRS took on a mediation role that enabled the caravan to continue as a united group.

The riots following King's assassination, and the determination of King's successors to carry on with plans for the Poor Peoples Campaign without the stabilizing power of King's personality added to the government's anxiety that misfortune might befall the project.

The nine caravans converged on Washington in mid-May, creating Resurrection City, an instant community of tents and plywood shacks that was built to house fifteen hundred but at times sheltered as many as seven thousand.[18] The residents were enrolled for an imprecisely programmed season of petition and protest. With the cooperation of the National Park Service, the city government and the city's churches, and other public and private agencies, SCLC was able to accomplish the logistical miracle of organizing, housing, feeding, and entertaining the residents of the tent city and moving them about the city by the hundreds for demonstrations at the Capitol, the White House, and dozens of federal agencies, all the while maintaining an orderly community.

The lobbying efforts scored few victories. Among the many poverty-related issues that the campaign raised with the leaders of government, the greatest energy came to focus on hunger. New reports of starvation in the rural South added fuel to the effort. Immediate relief in the form of liberalizing the food stamp program was totally rejected by the Agriculture Department. Efforts in Congress got little support. The SCLC push appeared to be a total failure. Behind the scenes, Roger Wilkins and Ramsey Clark tried to generate an end run through the White House. With the support of Sergeant Shriver, who headed the administration's anti-

18. Andrew Young, *An Easy Burden: The Civil Rights Movement and the Transformation of America,* 483.

poverty program, and Joe Califano, the president's chief aide on domestic programs, the proposal was taken to President Johnson. He liked it well enough to explore funding possibilities with Wilbur Mills, chairman of the House Ways and Means Committee. Mills advised that in view of the extraordinary efforts required to win the recently adopted emergency appropriation for the war in Vietnam, the proposal would be a nonstarter.

In Resurrection City, enthusiasm was wearing down. As platoons of new residents replaced the old, as boredom set in, as sweltering heat and drenching rains and muddy streets made life difficult to bear, tempers wore thin, group cohesion became less effective, and codes of behavior became less binding. The tendency toward disorder became less responsive to the moral influence of camp leaders and more demanding of police presence.

The CRS job of making sure that nothing bad happened became increasingly difficult. Demands intensified for close liaison with SCLC and camp leaders, for troubleshooting problems with the police, for arranging the quick resolution of logistical breakdowns, and for conciliating and avoiding conflicts on the streets.

As the weeks wore on, and with the lobbying effort showing few results and community control becoming increasingly difficult, there was mounting discord within the SCLC leadership. While the prospect of closing the encampment when its park permit expired on June 23 was not unwelcome, there was fear that it held the danger of dismounting a tiger.

Antagonism was rising between police and residents of the camp. There were rumors of residents secreting firearms, and that a hard-core remnant might refuse to leave. A midnight incident of rock and bottle throwing drew a tear-gas response from the U.S. Park Police. The Justice Department was fearful that the closing of the camp might end in violence. The CRS priority became to encourage SCLC's effort to generate strategies to assure a nonviolent withdrawal and to encourage leaders of law enforcement in their plans to assure restraint in the use of force.

On June 24, Ralph Abernathy led about two hundred and fifty residents to a final appeal for economic justice before their prearranged arrest on the Capitol grounds. A half hour after their departure from Resurrection City, Roger Wilkins and other observers accompanied the police, who made a sweep of the tent city, arresting the fewer than a hundred remaining residents. There were no more than a handful of reports of disorderly resistance and forceable arrests. Disorders in Washington, D.C., that night were suppressed by a curfew order and an overwhelming presence of law enforcement personnel.

The ending of the Poor Peoples Campaign with hardly a whimper signaled the end of formal efforts within the civil rights movement to devise a grand strategy for winning distributive justice. Equality of results would continue to be the elusive objective of the second phase of the battle for civil rights, but the engagements increasingly would be fought on smaller battlefields and by local troops. CRS would continue to adapt its strategies to match the evolving struggle.

Preemptive Problem Solving—A New Agenda for CRS

The volcanic intensity of summer riots in 1965, 1966, and 1967 caused American leaders to recognize the depth of Negro rage in the central cities. To CRS's leadership the riots were a reaction to racial inequity and injustice beyond the healing reach of civil rights laws. The persistence of inequity and indignity was the demon that had to be exorcised.

As his term moved toward 1968, its final year, Wilkins still found himself unable to define the CRS program to his own satisfaction. He felt that under LeRoy Collins, CRS had rocketed from crisis to crisis, driven by objectives that were always in flux. For all the hundreds of instances of CRS intervention in local conflicts, despite the scores of settlements negotiated to resolve minority protests of unfairness in the schools, on the job, and in the justice system, the total impact seemed transitory and far short of the fundamental change required to help set America straight. He had a gut feeling that CRS would be more effective in dealing with racial conflict if its primary concern was social justice rather than group relationships. Conflict resolution struck him as too opportunistic, lacking precise goals and objectives. Limited to a peacekeeping role, CRS could only respond to situations of other people's making, never initiating programs of its own. More troubling was the fact that peacekeeping was more likely to focus on symptoms than on root causes. It influenced change only at the margins, not at the core of the American dilemma. To play a role of consequence CRS would have to find a way to make its own direct contribution to speeding minority progress from equal opportunity to equal achievement.

Mounting such a new program faced two formidable obstacles: first, neither the Justice Department, nor the administration's budget watchdogs, nor the congressional appropriations committees would approve enlargement of the CRS program beyond its Title X mandate to prevent and resolve conflict; second, a new CRS program would need to fill a role that did not duplicate what other federal agencies were already doing.

With the aid of CRS Deputy Director George Culberson, Wilkins first set about inventing the new CRS role by launching a program planning process that, for a federal agency, was a unique adventure in participatory democracy. Every member of the professional staff was assigned to a task force for researching issues and developing options. The entire professional staff reviewed proposals in vigorous, often clamorous debate.

George Culberson, who had succeeded John Griffin as CRS associate director for compliance in the summer of 1965 before becoming deputy director in January 1966, was one of the acknowledged deans of the community relations profession. A onetime high school principal in Pittsburgh, he served as the first executive director of that city's pioneering Human Relations Commission. He was a founder and early president of the National Association of Human Relations Officials. In the early sixties he headed the Air Force Office of Contract Compliance, which he then staffed with community relations professionals, some of whom subsequently followed him to CRS.

Wilkins and Culberson complemented each other. Wilkins saw in the older man a pragmatic idealist who had learned to navigate the shoals of political infighting on both the local and the national scene. Culberson was trained to provide administrative and technical oversight to a field staff that was still learning its profession, an area in which Wilkins's interest lay in outcomes rather than in details. Above all, Culberson understood and accepted the critical function of any second in command—to leave to his chief those tasks most suited to the director's skills and predilections and to faithfully perform all others.

The program that emerged was one by which CRS would provide technical assistance at the grassroots level that other federal agencies could not reach, supporting minority self-help endeavors leading to "empowerment" of the minority community. This assistance would be provided in five areas: economic development, education, housing, mass communication, and administration of justice.

With a program design in place, a rationale had to be developed to make it square with the congressional mandate of helping communities to overcome disputes, disagreements, and difficulties. Title X had said nothing about community empowerment, and minority assistance programs were already addressed by the War on Poverty.

The rationale that developed was rooted in what CRS had learned about the causes of urban riots. Its line of reasoning was tailored to exploit the high priority that successive national administrations attached to riot prevention. Consistent with the recently published report of the National

Advisory Commission on Civil Disorders, chaired by Governor Otto Kerner of Illinois, the theory held that a basic contribution to civil disorder was not poverty alone but the concurrent alienation of the minority poor. Alienation was a product of the indignity of being discounted: of being ignored in the decision-making processes that govern daily life, and being denied participation in the management of the institutions that shape your community. The best way to overcome alienation would be to give minorities a stake in society by maximizing their participation in, and control of, the institutions that influenced their destiny.

That line of reasoning proved to be persuasive. To Attorney General Ramsey Clark, who approved the program in the waning months of his incumbency, it squared with his own thesis that America could not guarantee either justice or order without having both. To the incoming Nixon administration, as represented by Richard Kleindienst, who as deputy to Attorney General John Mitchell gave oversight to the CRS program, it was a pragmatic approach to ghetto problems. As a result, budget increase followed budget increase for four years as CRS retrained its staff, added experts and consultants in each of the five fields of technical assistance, opened offices in forty-four cities, and deployed a staff of 323 (up from about 150 in 1968).

From 1969 to 1973, CRS applied only about a quarter of its resources to conflict resolution. Three-quarters of its capacity was dedicated to the new conflict prevention program. The mission was to help in the creation and strengthening of minority institutions and the strengthening of minority influence in majority enterprises. Some called it minority empowerment. This endeavor was largely catalytic: brokering alliances between Party A and Party B, with Party A being a minority entity familiar with a specific need but short on expertise and financial resources and Party B being a white institution (corporation, foundation, university) capable of supplying both. The objectives of these alliances—some of which were successful and some of which never left the ground—covered a wide range of institutions and activities. These included: minority economic development corporations, ghetto credit unions, tenant management associations, housing cooperatives, and public housing security agencies. Some community groups were schooled in federal communications law. They learned how to challenge the licenses of radio and television stations when they came up for periodic renewal required by the Federal Communications Commission and use this as a weapon to influence better minority employment and programming arrangements. Minority consortiums found technical assistance to help them bid on television cable franchises. Minority groups began to challenge and change the nature of police practices. The result was a strengthening of minority police officer associations, community support of police minority recruitment programs, special minority training for police promotional exams, and community challenges to culturally biased civil service examinations.

CRS's role in these empowerment ventures varied from that of a major player at a program's conception and community organization stages to short-term assistance at critical junctures in order to facilitate federal funding, circumvent political roadblocks, and conciliate quarrels within the sponsoring community. A sampling of the outcomes that the preventive program yielded in the half year prior to its sudden termination in 1973 includes:

—The Georgia Association of Police Community Relations Officers was formed to bring police and minority citizens together in training workshops around the state.

—A program in Raleigh to train minority community members to relate more effectively with the education establishment received help in organizing and obtaining funds.

—Minority businessmen in four Alabama cities received a shot in the arm via technical assistance provided by business development organizations established with federal funds.

—In Birmingham, Huntsville, and Mobile, technical aid was provided in the critical areas of loan packaging, contract procurement, and management skill development.

—An industrial park in Tuskegee, funded by the Economic Development Administration, was expected eventually to provide four thousand jobs.

—Latinos in Chicago, who formed the Latin Communications Junta to press for the employment of Hispanics by the media, began to see the first fruits of their effort.

—The sixty members of Detroit's minority Metropolitan Contractors' Association found new doors open to them when a Small Business Administration set-aside program made it possible for them to bid on $2 million worth of contracts for the rehabilitation of properties repossessed by the Department of Housing and Urban Development.

—Puerto Ricans in Connecticut, troubled by miscarriages of justice resulting from language difficulties, were successful in getting interpreters to work in the courts of Hartford, New Haven, and Bridgeport.

—Hispanics in Rochester, New York, formed the Ibero-American Action League, which received the support necessary to plan the development of a $4 million low- and moderate-income housing project.

—Public housing residents in Buffalo formed the Buffalo Tenants Organization to share some responsibility and decision making with management.

—Third-year law students at Texas Southern University Law School, the second largest minority law school in the country, gained new opportunities to intern in the offices of the U.S. attorney, the city attorney, and the district attorney.

—Youth Service Bureaus were organized in Denver to serve as central referral agencies to assist minority youth beginning to encounter trouble with the law.

—A minority land development corporation in Pittsburgh won initial HUD funding to plan development of a new commercial-residential development.

—A group of ex-prisoners in Philadelphia developed a program to provide postrelease services to newly discharged inmates.

—Eighteen hundred minority neighborhood residents arrested in Pittsburgh benefited from the bail reform activities of the newly developed minority-sponsored Community Release Agency.

—Black and Chicano community groups in Fresno effectively utilized the HEW civil rights compliance process to oppose discriminatory practices of the local school board.

—Minority residents of San Bernardino formed a community development corporation that started to revitalize their neighborhood by rehabilitating sixty-four units of abandoned housing owned by the Veterans Administration.

—Native American organizations in Seattle established a migrant housing facility to supply social services and temporary housing for seasonally unemployed migrant workers.

—Local parent advisory committees, required by law to advise school districts with respect to the use of Title I funds for educationally disadvantaged children, but untrained as to their responsibilities, were helped by a network of state advisory councils to become more effective advocates of their children's interests.[19]

In mid-1973, with the nation's fear of ghetto violence reduced to a distant memory, and with CRS defenders John Mitchell and Richard Kleindienst occupied with Watergate problems, the Bureau of the Budget prevailed in its long-term opposition to the preventive program and brought it to an end. The budget analysts, always troubled by CRS's inability to quantify its outputs in conventional terms, or to prove that its preventive programs lowered the risks of riots, recommended that CRS reduce its

19. Drawn from CRS Annual Report, 1973.

staff by two-thirds, abandon its program of crisis prevention, and limit its work to responding to racial crises after they arose.

The rationale offered by the budget cutters was a simplistic one—that the CRS programs directed toward such things as housing, education, and economic development were already within the purview of other agencies of government. They failed to recognize that only CRS utilized the unique approach of helping individual local groups find the skills, resources, and levers of power to make decisions and keep control within their own communities.

The abandonment of the CRS experiment was probably inevitable. The idea of fostering minority community empowerment as a means of overcoming alienation and alleviating discord may have been well conceived, but the resources available to it were too puny to help achieve major social change. If the intent and drive that motivated the CRS program could have been transferred, along with the components of the program, to the relevant major departments of government, a significant outcome may have resulted. But the nation was a far distance away from accepting the notion of minority empowerment as an appropriate function of the federal government—and Lyndon Johnson, who might have understood it, was long gone.

Five

When Cities Erupt

Preceding chapters have looked chronologically at many of the issues and events that shaped the first decade of the Community Relations Service. Succeeding chapters, taking a longitudinal approach, will trace specific aspects of racial conflict in America, as seen through the eyes of the Community Relations Service. This chapter will focus on the climate of rage and violence that influenced the events of that time, concentrating on the inner-city riots—how they came about, what happened, how they were controlled, and what their consequences were in terms of America's struggle for a more equal society.

The Changing Characteristics of Black-White Relations

By 1964, civil rights advocates and scholars were increasingly aware that the passage of civil rights laws was no more than a first step toward the achievement of equal status for blacks. To many, equality under the law would be a hoax if it did not lead to changes in the second-class status that Negroes experienced in their daily lives. Without major changes in policies and massive investment in programs for education, employment, housing, and intergroup understanding, the civil rights revolution would prove to have been a ship with no cargo. While President Johnson's new War on Poverty was seen by whites as a generous commitment to improving the lives of disadvantaged people, black leaders saw no evidence that the government had either an understanding of the size of the investment required or the will to make the effort. Many sensed, too, that white supporters of the movement did not have the heart for the long and greater struggle ahead. Already these ideas were being translated into social action by so-called extremists who advocated that blacks go it alone. Black separatism, black nationalism, black power became symbols around which many would rally in the years ahead. The issue of whether the struggle for equality should continue on the road to integration or branch off on the path toward black self-determination would, in the next few years, fracture the civil rights coalition and lessen the vigor of white support for civil rights.

In 1964 Arnold M. Rose, one of Americas's leading race relations scholars, who had been Gunnar Myrdal's collaborator in writing *An American Dilemma,* sounded a warning: "It is not certain yet that the conflict has been won. All vigorous protest movements generate new forces that hamper the achievement of the movement's goals. One is the reaction, or 'backlash.' Social changes and efforts to achieve social changes run up against both concrete vested interests that are hurt by the changes and a general anxiety that is stimulated by the rapid change itself. The full dimensions of the reaction cannot be assessed yet, but certainly one can expect that the conflict between the Negro protest and its reaction will generate more violence."[1]

A nationwide poll in April 1964 showed that 70 percent of Americans favored passage of the Civil Rights Act. But many were anxious and even fearful about the changes that would result. How would a new level of racial equality impact their personal lives? Moreover, millions in the South and many in the North were still uncompromising opponents of civil rights. That same spring, Alabama's governor, George C. Wallace, the leading spokesman for racial segregation, won at least 25 percent of the vote in the Democratic presidential primaries in three *nonsouthern* states. He came within 5 percent of winning a majority in Maryland. In 1963 and 1964 more than half a dozen *nonsouthern* cities and states conducted referendums in which the voters turned back civil rights legislation in housing or public accommodations.

Black activists pointed out that even some civil rights allies were quick to resist new arrangements that called for sharing power and authority. A new breeding ground for racial confrontations came into being in August 1964 with the signing of the new federal antipoverty law. This legislation, which would soon provide new resources and means for attacking the social and economic deprivation of the poor, also provided new avenues for minority residents to challenge traditional approaches to allocating social welfare benefits. One component of the War on Poverty, known as the

---

1. Rose, "Foreword," *Annals of the American Academy of Political and Social Science* 357 (January 1965): ix.

Community Action Program, was to emphasize "maximum feasible participation of the poor" in planning and administering many of the local programs. Organizing and training impoverished residents to participate in
the design and administration of programs would prove to be a source of
conflict with local officials and established agencies.

Harris Wofford, a White House adviser on civil rights in the Kennedy
years, wrote:

> The principle of the anti-poverty program, and particularly its community
> action program, to encourage maximum feasible participation of the poor
> was an open invitation to conflict—between city hall and the advocates of
> the poor, between local government and privately funded philanthropic
> agencies, and between competing racial minorities. . . . Johnson had been
> forewarned by his advisors about the political risk, but he said in his mem-
> oirs that such democratic processes—by giving minorities a stake in pro-
> grams affecting them, were necessary to overcome apathy. He wrote: "I re-
> alized that a program as massive as the one we were contemplating might
> shake up many institutions, but I decided that some shaking up might be
> needed to get a bold new program moving. I thought that local governments
> had to be challenged to be awakened."[2]

Some analysts saw the antipoverty program, coming on top of civil
rights progress in the South, as contributing to a further rise in Negro expectations and a consequent increase in the level of frustration within the
ghettos. The lag time between the delivery of programs and the achievement of change brought additional frustration.

The Urban Riots Begin

On July 16, two weeks after the president had signed the Civil Rights
Act of 1964, there were riots in New York City. It all started outside a ju-
nior high school in summer session when the superintendent of a nearby
building sprayed water on three boys. In the escalating disorder, which
ultimately became a battle between police and three hundred bottle-
throwing youths, an off-duty policeman shot and killed a fifteen-year-old
black boy who allegedly had threatened him with a knife.

The killing enraged the Negro community. Two days later, at the end of a
Harlem rally protesting antiblack violence in Mississippi, rioting broke out.
The looting, vandalism, and police confrontations lasted several days. Before they ended, a similar disturbance took place in the Bedford-Stuyvesant
area, a black neighborhood in New York's borough of Brooklyn.

2. Harris Wofford, *Of Kennedys and Kings,* 464.

A week later an outbreak in Rochester, New York, required the National Guard to restore order. By the end of August there had been widespread disorders in Jersey City, Elizabeth, and Paterson, New Jersey; in Philadelphia; and in the Chicago suburb of Dixmoor.[3] The nation recognized with alarm that the discontent of its ghettos had begun to erupt with cataclysmic force and the outbreaks threatened to be pandemic.

In answer to the question of why, spokesmen from across the spectrum of social analysis were quick to point out that civil rights progress had not changed anything in the Negro ghettos of the big cities where the pain of poverty and the insult of prejudice were a daily assault on black dignity. The civil rights victories had given false hope of change but were really irrelevant to ghetto life. During the ten years of favorable court decisions and federal legislation since 1954, the gap between blacks and whites in income, in employment, and in education had increased. Lack of progress in the face of elevated expectations was certain to heighten frustration.

Many activists and social analysts chose to describe the urban violence of this period as "rebellions" rather than "race riots." They saw it as a thrust for equality and revolt against oppression, akin to the violent protests of the prerevolution American colonists. The criminal connotations of the word *riot* were too dismissive of the true significance of the outbreaks. The words *race riot* historically applied to pitched battles between Negroes and whites, or white assaults upon blacks. These disorders were different. According to the National Advisory Commission on Civil Disorders, "The civil disorders of 1967 involved Negroes acting against local symbols of white American society, authority and property in Negro neighborhoods—rather than against white persons."[4]

As the "long hot summers" became a feature of American life, the infant Community Relations Service, overwhelmed by its assignment to ease racial violence in the South, wanted no part of them. But it soon became apparent that, ready or not, the nation's designated race relations troubleshooters would have to play a hand.

The Inferno Close Up

Often the first CRS view of a riot was from the sky—a conciliator's sighting of the smoke or flames from still-burning neighborhoods, depending on whether it was day or night and on how soon he had been able to get

3. Lucy S. Davidowicz, "Civil Rights and Intergroup Tensions," 186.
4. *Report of the National Advisory Commission on Civil Disorders,* 110.

a plane from wherever he was when news of the outbreak reached him with his assignment. Sometimes it was sooner, when violence erupted in a city where a conciliator lived or happened to be working on another case. In the summer of 1966, Roger Wilkins was meeting with the CRS executive staff in Washington when an emergency call came in from Christopher Mould, a conciliator on assignment in Chicago. Wilkins switched the call to a speaker phone, so that the group could hear Mould's report from a phone booth at an intersection where mob violence was mounting. The call terminated abruptly as Mould announced his departure, to the sounds of the booth being uprooted around him.

The efforts and effectiveness of the Community Relations Service varied from city to city. Opportunities to be useful depended on unfolding events, relationships, and community dynamics. When it came to CRS helping a city deal with outbreaks of civil disorder, there were three stages for possible assistance—before, during, and after. During those peak years of racial ferment there was little that CRS or anyone could do to prevent a riot.[5] Whether CRS assistance in stimulating programs for summer youth employment, for better police-community relations, and for improved communication across the racial divide could make that much of a difference was anybody's guess. During the riot control phase there were limited opportunities for a conciliator to be useful. Mayors or police chiefs were most likely to accept or call upon CRS assistance in situations related to the involvement of the minority community's leadership. Such assistance included consultation as to the wisdom and conditions of a curfew, using minority volunteers to discourage violence, or avoiding harsh conditions of arrest and confinement. Sometimes the opportunity for a CRS contribution while the violence was raging was zero despite days of watchful waiting. Often the most useful assistance came at the end of the disturbance, to help resolve grievances, speed emergency repair programs involving federal assistance, and develop programs to repair fractured relations between racial groups.

In 1966, CRS representative Milton Lewis, tied up with problems in East St. Louis, could not get into Omaha until July 7, three days after a three-day period of rioting had begun. There his most significant effort in the short run was to help overcome factionalism among minority organizations,

5. In later years CRS developed a program of risk analysis that identified those cities where racial tensions were critically high and where a blunder might trigger an outbreak of civil disorder. Conciliators tried to work with mayors and police officials in such cities to lower the risk levels. The extent to which these efforts helped to reduce the number and intensity of urban outbreaks, like any "nonevent," could never be measured.

so that they could more coherently negotiate their grievances with city hall. Over the longer term, CRS worked closely with the mayor to help the city gain access to federal funding programs that addressed problems that had contributed to racial tensions.

Typical of CRS's experience with riots was its involvement with the civil disturbance in Buffalo in 1967. Starting early in the year the assigned conciliation specialist made regular visits about twice a month to deal with a number of conflict situations. Staying two or three days each time, he had begun to gain the confidence of a number of black and white leaders. In early May he reported mounting tension among youth in the ghetto. Problems included gang activity, a lack of recreational facilities, a lack of employment opportunities, and poor police-community relations. Tension was also rising about the organizational activities of BUILD.[6] He tried unsuccessfully to get city officials to meet with minority leaders, especially the militants. He perceived more readiness on the part of the mayor than of members of the city council. He also tried, unsuccessfully, to get the police department and the Human Relations Commission to apply for funds from the federal Office of Law Enforcement Assistance (OLEA) for a police-community relations program. Early in June the conciliator was able to get the mayor and city leaders to sit down with Buffalo's media executives and CRS's media experts to discuss how the media might improve the way they handled stories of racial tension. There were also discussions on improving police-media cooperation.[7]

When civil disorder broke out on June 27, CRS sent in an interracial conciliation team. The Negro conciliator met with militant ghetto leaders and discussed the demands they would like to place before the city's government and business leaders. The white conciliator, in the meantime, worked on those same public officials and business leaders to interpret ghetto perceptions and to prepare them to sit down with minority representatives to negotiate the demands likely to come before them. With the cooperation of the U.S. attorney, CRS also consulted with police officials on tactical approaches for restoring law and order while minimizing provocative moves that would impede their efforts.

6. BUILD was similar to the FIGHT organization in Rochester, described in Chapter 4.

7. Buffalo was one of only a half-dozen cities where CRS was successful in spreading the practice, originated in Chicago, under which all the media agreed to a thirty- or sixty-minute moratorium on reporting news of disorders, to allow time for verification of information and thus avoid false or misleading statements that would inflame the situation.

In the immediate wake of the disturbance, CRS huddled with state and local officials on the failure of the business community's program to generate summer employment for youth. The resulting change put greater responsibility for job creation and recruitment on the State Employment Office and on local Negro organizations. At the same time, CRS staff in Washington met with other agencies on ways to improve the relevant federal programs in Buffalo, particularly those bearing on employment and job training.

Omaha and Buffalo were just two of more than two hundred communities that were reported to have civil disturbances in the summer of 1967. The National Commission on Civil Disorders acknowledged 164, which it grouped in categories of intensity. Eight "major" disorders were marked by many fires and by intensive looting lasting more than two days, with sizable crowds, requiring use of National Guard or federal forces. Thirty-three "serious" disorders were characterized by isolated looting, some fires and rock throwing, between one and two days of violence, and the use of state police. Of those classified as "minor" disturbances, many would not likely have received national attention if occurring singly.[8]

A Senate investigating committee that examined seventy-five disturbances in sixty-seven cities reported a total of eighty-three deaths and 1,897 injuries. All the deaths had occurred in only twelve of the disturbances.

The worst of the riots came in July, when first Newark and then Detroit erupted in massive looting, uncontrollable fires, and many deaths. In Newark the carnage claimed twenty-three lives; in Detroit, forty-three. Restoration of order in Newark required the National Guard in addition to the full resources of the city and state police. In Detroit, police and the National Guard proved insufficient, and U.S. Army troops were deployed. Property damage in Detroit amounted to $40 million. About seven thousand people were arrested.

In Detroit the triggering incident was a Saturday night police raid of an after-hours bar and social club in the heart of the downtown Negro business district, a neighborhood known for high crime, substandard housing, and tensions over alleged police brutality. The United Community Civic League was the last of these five so-called blind pigs targeted by the vice squad that evening.[9] The 3:30 a.m. raid found an unexpectedly large party honoring some recently returned Vietnam veterans, and eighty-two

8. *Report of the National Commission on Civil Disorders,* 113.
9. Blind pigs, or places selling illegal intoxicants, had existed in Detroit since the end of Prohibition.

were arrested. The July 22 night was hot, and people were still on the street. In the hour it took to transport those arrested, a group of about two hundred gathered. Rumors spread that police had used excessive force in the raid. At about 5:00 a.m. Sunday morning, as the last of the group was being taken away, a soda bottle broke a police car window. A trash can smashed through a plate-glass storefront. A youth cried out, "We're going to have a riot." Vandalism began to spread. The violence commission reported, "A spirit of carefree nihilism was taking hold."[10] The police response, at first permissive because of insufficient personnel on duty, became increasingly harsh.

Mob violence escalated with arson and assaults on the responding firefighters. Again and again firemen had to abandon a fire scene in a hailstorm of rocks and bottles. Reports of snipers, valid in a few cases, were grossly magnified, leading to overreaction by the police and the National Guard troops with which they were reinforced. Undisciplined gunfire by police and the unseasoned and poorly trained guardsmen against inappropriate targets (including at least two instances of fire from tank-mounted machine guns) caused many of the deaths. Exaggeration and rumor contributed to the fear and rage on both sides.

CRS took on a new role in Detroit as part of the federal team dispatched by the president to advise him on the validity of exercising his constitutional authority to deploy U.S. Army troops in response to a state's request for help in quelling an insurrection beyond its ability to control. Authority for the president to make federal forces available to help states overcome domestic violence is rooted in Article 4, Section 4, of the Constitution, with guidelines for its use governed by an act of Congress passed in 1792. The reluctance of the government to deploy the army against Americans has led to great restraint in its use. Governors have requested such support less than a dozen times, most notably in labor disputes, and requests have been denied in instances where the grounds were deemed to be insufficient.

Just before midnight on July 23, Attorney General Ramsey Clark received at his home the first of several phone calls from Mayor Jerome P. Cavanagh of Detroit and Governor George Romney of Michigan, expressing their concern over rising violence and the possible need for federal assistance. The attorney general promptly alerted the secretary of the army, Stanley Resor. Clark advised President Johnson of the situation at about 3:00 a.m. Calls from the army to the Michigan National Guard indicated the guard's assessment that it would be able to handle the situation. Two thou-

10. *Report of the National Advisory Commission on Civil Disorders,* 86, 4.

sand guardsmen were in the area and another three thousand would be there by noon.[11] By 6:00 a.m. the army was prepared to move five thousand paratroopers from Fort Bragg, North Carolina, and Fort Campbell, Kentucky, to reach Selfridge Air Base by noon, whence they could readily be deployed to nearby Detroit.

Several conversations ensued between Romney and Clark, in which the attorney general sought to make clear that federal troops could not be committed without a written request from the governor stating that there was an insurrection that the totally committed law enforcement resources of the state could not control. Shortly before noon, the president received a request for federal troops from the governor. Although the message lacked the specific assurance that state forces were unable to control the disorder, President Johnson authorized the movement of troops to Selfridge and asked Cyrus Vance, the former undersecretary of defense, to take charge of the federal operation in Detroit and to ascertain that the situation on the ground met the constitutional and legislative requirements for the deployment of troops. Vance immediately left for Selfridge on a military plane, with a special Department of Justice team consisting of Warren Christopher, deputy attorney general; John Doar, assistant attorney general for civil rights; and Roger Wilkins, director of the Community Relations Service.

The team met with the governor and mayor, police and military commanders, and leaders of the minority community and toured the riot area. The level of riot incidents had abated since the previous day. The governor said he was reluctant to declare a state of insurrection because of a fear that insurance claims might thereby be invalidated.

Vance recommended the deployment of state police and National Guard units that had not yet been committed to riot duties. He later ordered army troops moved to the city's fairgrounds so as to be instantly available for street duty if needed. The incidents of disorder increased rapidly during the evening despite the full commitment of city and state law enforcement resources. Shortly before 11:30 p.m., Cyrus Vance reported to the president. On the team's recommendation, Johnson then signed the proclamation and executive order authorizing the use of federal troops and federalizing the National Guard.

As the soldiers took over, the violence receded. Analysts attributed the troops' effectiveness to a number of factors. They were deployed in large

11. Details derived from "Final Report of Cyrus R. Vance, Special Assistant to the Secretary of Defense, Concerning the Detroit Riots July 23 through August 2, 1967," copy in author's collection.

numbers and moved in with a professional, no-nonsense bearing. At the same time, the army was seen as a not-unfriendly presence, since a significant proportion of the troops were black (unlike the police and the guard); since many ghetto residents had seen service; and because the troops appeared initially with guns unloaded. The soldiers were quick to establish civil relations with the residents, and in some instances lent a hand in the cleanup process.

The Washington team continued to provide federal oversight in the following days during which the massive and disciplined presence of the army helped to bring the disorders under control, and as federal efforts to provide disaster relief and support rebuilding efforts got under way.

For Roger Wilkins, this was his second presidential assignment to the heart of the volcano. He had been sent to Watts to assist first LeRoy Collins and then Ramsey Clark in assessing the federal government's role in damage control and repair following the violence there. One of his major concerns was with police behavior and the overreadiness of law enforcement to use deadly force in time of riot.[12]

In Watts, where police had a reputation for abuse of minorities, he had found himself a near-victim. He and John Perry were returning to their hotel from dinner. Perry, who was driving the rental car, was white. He had been special assistant to Collins when Collins was director of CRS and had gone with him to be associate undersecretary of the Commerce Department when Collins became undersecretary.[13] A police car pulled them over after following them for several blocks. Two white officers approached, one on either side, with guns drawn. Perry was taken to the back of the car; Wilkins was spreadeagled across the hood and patted down to the accompaniment of a stream of anti-Negro invective. Only after Perry had established his identity did the police seek Wilkins's credentials. The incident ended with apologies and an explanation that there was a lookout for an interracial pair who had just pulled off a robbery nearby. From inside sources, Wilkins later learned two bits of relevant information: no such robbery had been reported, and the officer who had held the gun to his head had killed a minority resident with a shotgun just a few days before.

Detroit presented Wilkins with a sense of déjà vu. On one occasion, while patrolling the city with Vance and Christopher, Wilkins was seated behind the Negro driver. Whenever they were stopped by either police or National Guard personnel, officers approaching from the left did so with

12. Wilkins interview.
13. Perry interview.

guns drawn and, on one occasion, with the muzzle placed at Wilkins's neck. When the approach was from the right side, it was accompanied by, "May I help you, sir?" Wilkins hoped that the lesson was not lost on his companions.

At other times it was even scarier. Familiar with reports as to the over-zealousness of the National Guard and the state police, Wilkins ventured forth with some trepidation on his nightly patrols to take a reading of the level of activity in the curfew area. At one time a guard convoy passed him, made a tire-squealing U-turn, raced up beside him, and ordered the car over at gunpoint. They stopped a car behind him, too, screaming, "Out of the car! Out of the car!" Remembering Watts, Wilkins was quick to emerge from the car with hands raised, shouting over and over, "Department of Justice! Department of Justice!" As an uncertain guardsman approached, he told him in which pocket to find his U.S. Government credentials.

Under Wilkins's watchful eye the soldiers then queried the terrified black parents and children of the other car that had been stopped. The man turned out to be a night shift employee of one of the auto companies, with a special pass to be out after curfew. His family had picked him up to drive him home. As he left the scene, Wilkins thought about the growing number of reports of people killed and wounded by the unseasoned and poorly trained National Guard and wondered about the terror felt by the family he had just observed, and all those others stopped by the guard without a federal official looking on.[14]

Legacy of the Kerner Commission

On July 27, even before orders had been given to remove the para-troopers from a calmed but still smoldering Detroit, President Johnson announced the creation of the National Advisory Commission on Civil Disorders, chaired by Otto Kerner. Its assignment was to investigate the recent riots and come up with answers to three questions. What happened? Why? What could be done to keep it from happening again?

The president's demands were both wide-ranging and specific. As to the causes of the riot, he wanted to know, on the one hand, the extent to which they might have been planned and, on the other, the extent to which they might have been generated by economic and social deprivation. He inquired as to the role of the police—their training, equipment, and per-formance. He wanted to know why some cities "blew" and others didn't,

14. Wilkins interview.

why some people rioted and others did not. He asked for recommendations for better controlling outbreaks of violence and also for eliminating
the causes.

The eleven prominent committee members selected by Johnson were
criticized by some minority advocates as being too establishment oriented
to have a real understanding of the way things were in the ghetto. The
group was a balanced one, varying in social outlook from the president of
the American Federation of Labor to the president of Litton Industries.
Nevertheless, even its liberal members, such as Mayor John Lindsay of
New York and Roy Wilkins of the NAACP, were seen as too mainstream.

As things turned out, the mainstream reputation of the commission
was its greatest strength in gaining acceptance for the bombshell of a report it submitted seven months later. The report was a blunt indictment
of American society for the squalor and despair that festered in its slums.
It appealed for a range of corrective programs that would, if adopted, tax
the nation's resources beyond all previous conceptions.

It was clear that the commission had been shocked by what its studies
had brought forth and wanted to sound an alarm loud enough to inspire
a national effort to reverse what it saw as a catastrophic trend that was
moving the nation "toward two societies, one black, one white—separate
and unequal." In its introduction, the commission's report declared: "Segregation and poverty have created in the racial ghetto a destructive environment totally unknown to most white Americans. . . . What white
Americans have never fully understood—but what the Negro can never
forget—is that white society is deeply implicated in the ghetto. White institutions created it. White institutions maintain it, and white society con-
dones it."[15]

The report documented how the cities shortchanged minorities on the
delivery of public services (for example, by providing grossly inadequate
teachers) and compromised their dignity and physical security (for example, by providing their police with great discretion but little guidance as
to interrogation techniques and the use of deadly force). The documentation of inadequacy and degradation extended to the areas of housing,
health, welfare, and employment, among others. The report presented
"after-action" accounts of twenty-four of the larger disorders, including the
social climate in which they were incubated, the triggering incidents (generally involving the police), tactics and strategies for control, and the training, equipment, supervision, and performance of the law enforcement

15. *Report of the National Advisory Commission on Civil Disorders*, 1, 2.

agencies involved. For years it would be referred to as a baseline from which progress, or the lack thereof, could be measured.

Commenting on the nature of its recommendations, the commission warned: "These programs will require unprecedented levels of funding and performance, but they neither probe deeper nor demand more than the problems which called them forth. There can be no higher priority for national action and no higher claim on the nation's conscience."[16]

For years after, CRS representatives, when consulted by municipal officials on the level of interracial stress in their cities and how to relieve it, would refer to the Kerner report as a possible point of departure for self-examination and program ideas.

Concern as to the Use of Federal Troops

The frequency of incidents of civil disorder in the sixties encouraged the various administrations in the Justice Department to do two things. First, they examined the constitutional and legislative provisions by which states could request the help of the army to quell a disorder that the state could not control, and they established a written history of such requests. Second, they developed procedures that would permit a swift response to any future requests. The cooperation and coordination among the White House, the Justice Department, and the Pentagon had been demonstrated in the response to the Detroit blowup. Yet that episode was immediately clouded by political recriminations. Governor Romney, a leading contender for the Republican presidential nomination a year away, charged that President Johnson, against whom he expected to be running in 1968, had deliberately delayed committing federal troops in order to exact from Romney the public admission that he was unable to control an insurrection in his state.

The Nixon administration's Department of Justice set up its own standard operating procedures to assure that if the president should ever have to make such a decision, it would be well-informed, consistent with constitutional and statutory requirements, and permissive of a prompt response. A keystone of the procedures was the creation of a Civil Disturbance Task Force composed of senior officials of the relevant divisions within the Department of Justice to compose teams that would, on an instant's notice, fly to a beleaguered community to perform the functions

16. Ibid., 2.

that the Vance team had undertaken in Detroit. I was assigned to one of five teams that were organized, briefed, given guidance manuals, and instructed to stand by. My team was called upon just once—to monitor and advise on the need for military intervention in New Haven, Connecticut, on the occasion of the massive 1970 May Day rally planned in support of Black Panthers on trial for murder.

A year earlier, fourteen Panthers had been arrested and charged with the murder in New Haven of fellow Panther Alex Rackley. Among them was Bobby Seale, national chairman of the Black Panthers, who was accused of giving the order. Seale was not only well known among blacks nationwide but was also a celebrated figure among left-wing organizations. His fame had resulted from his participation as a leader of protest demonstrations at the Democratic Convention in 1968 and his subsequent appearance in the highly publicized trial of the "Chicago eight," at which he had been bound and gagged on the judge's order.

Widespread media attention had been drawn to the overly long and allegedly harsh conditions of pretrial detention for those accused in the New Haven trial. The American Civil Liberties Union had appealed the conditions of detention in federal court. A coalition of fourteen mostly white organizations had been formed to raise funds and public sympathy. The New Haven Panther Defense Committee planned a massive protest rally for May Day 1970. Special efforts were made to draw upon the activist student population along the entire East Coast to protest the unfairness of the trial. Fifty thousand attendees were expected to jam the two-block New Haven Green, an area in the center of the city bounded on one side by the courthouse and on the other by Yale University. There was fear that unlawful acts of protest, police confrontations, and incitement of the local black community (involved in civil disturbances in 1967 and 1968) might generate a riot beyond the capability of city and state law enforcement to control.

The governor had already responded favorably to the city's request for National Guard support. To save time in case the state should ask the president for federal troops, army units were prepositioned at an airbase in nearby Massachusetts. The Department of Justice team was on hand to assess the situation and advise the president as to whether the circumstances justified deployment of the army, and whether the legal and constitutional requirements had been met.

The leader of the team was Assistant Attorney General William Ruckelshaus, who carried the task force title of senior civilian representative. The other members included, among others, John Dean, special assistant to the attorney general, and James Turner, senior attorney (and sometimes acting assistant attorney general) for the Civil Rights Division.

My role was to provide liaison with the local black community and with voluntary civic organizations. Fortunately, Joshua Liburd and Jack Middleton were on hand to help. A conciliation specialist stationed in CRS's New England regional office in Boston, Liburd covered New Haven on a regular basis. He was well informed and highly regarded by both the black community and city hall. Middleton was the executive of the Office of Urban Affairs of the Archdiocese of Hartford, a service organization that sought to further programs reflecting the common interests of the civil rights community and the New Haven business and civic leaders. A seasoned community relations professional, Middleton had taken CRS training on setting up and running a rumor control center in a time of racial crisis. In collaboration with Phil Runner, executive director of the New Haven Council of Churches, he had set up a community-based rumor control and information center specifically for the upcoming protest demonstration. The rumor control center worked closely with police and other city information sources. It was staffed by volunteers from the Yale Divinity School. It was a textbook example of how a private agency should go about organizing and managing a rumor control center.[17]

From Liburd, I learned that the leaders of New Haven's black community were a sophisticated group vigorously opposed to efforts to involve community residents in the protest, which they saw as a distracting outside political event unrelated to their own programs of civil rights and social reform. They had made a particular effort to discourage black youths from participating in protest activities that might unnecessarily involve them in hostile encounters with police. Special events for young people had been planned to keep them within their own community during the May Day weekend. The black community also had organized its own rumor control center, which was more likely to have the trust of the minority community than would Middleton's. The two centers would be linked.

James Ahern, New Haven's chief of police, had, for a brief time, been a police-community relations consultant for CRS. His presence as chief of police, I knew, gave reasonable assurance that the police response to the demonstrators would be at a high professional level.

As I participated in the task force reconnaissance by mingling in the gathering crowd on its first day of assembly, there was little evidence of the deeply imbedded bitterness that had exploded in the minority ghetto riots; nor were there visible signs of the level of political outrage and emotional

17. CRS subsequently asked Middleton to convert his design into a manual, which served as a model for rumor control centers across the country for many years. Rumor control centers played a vital role in limiting chaos during civil disorders.

anger that had been ignited in the riots at the Democratic convention in Chicago in 1968. The climate seemed to be marked more by intellectual rage than emotional stress. Conversations in the crowd were punctuated by references to ideological conflicts that had factionalized left-wing splinter groups of the thirties and forties. There were more white faces than black.

Actual participation in the demonstration turned out to be closer to fifteen thousand than the estimated fifty thousand. Only at one point, when a police confrontation led to a questionable use of tear gas, did there appear to be an awakening of mass anger. The mood was quickly dispelled, however, thanks to the hospitality of Yale University, whose campus bordering the New Haven Green was open to the crowd as an ample area of refuge. At a later time, when National Guardsmen who had been stationed on the next block became a visible presence, the crowd began to stir with hostility. A cautionary word to police commanders promptly led to the guard being withdrawn from sight. A later disturbance was resolved by the demonstrators' own "self-marshals," Yale students who had volunteered and been trained for the job. That evening, a sound-and-light show on the Yale campus helped further deescalate tensions.

The demonstration ended with the weekend. The prepositioned federal troops returned to their home station, and the Civil Disturbance Task Force went back to Washington.

Black Power

Black rage, as demonstrated in the urban riots, undoubtedly generated a reciprocal anger on the part of many whites and led to the phenomenon of white backlash in some quarters. But it also had a far greater impact in impressing America's political leaders with the urgency of the need for ghetto reform. Some black leaders, convinced that the persuasion and negotiation of the civil rights coalition could never provide the white power structure with the imperative to invest the enormous resources that would be required to effect meaningful change in the lives of the deeply disadvantaged, believed that playing the violence card would help provide that imperative. They learned to manipulate the symbols of violence to magnify the impact of violence.

The Black Panthers were quick to use the attention-getting value of news photos of black protesters carrying rifles. The "Black Power" slogan, first made a public battle cry by Stokely Carmichael, proved to have a magical power to alarm, regardless of the varied meanings intended by the thousands of speakers who gave voice to it. H. Rap Brown, who succeeded Carmichael as leader of the Student Nonviolent Coordinating Committee, magnified his notoriety with "Burn, Baby, Burn!" The firestorms that consumed black neighborhoods did not require the help of Brown to get started. Whether some of the later ones burned hotter because of incendiary slogans is hard to know. But there was no doubt that they were attention getters.

"Black Power" first sounded in the nation's ear in the wake of the wounding of James Meredith. Meredith, who had made history in 1962 by being the first black to attend the University of Mississippi,[18] set out to do it a second time by demonstrating in 1966 that a single black man could march for civil rights unarmed and unprotected from one end of Mississippi to the other. It was a solo operation, without the support of any of the organized civil rights community. He was severely wounded by three shotgun blasts in June.

Three civil rights organizations seized the fallen banner, instantly mobilizing marchers to take his place. CORE, SNCC, and SCLC muted their growing institutional and ideological differences in united determination to show that the time had passed when Mississippi roads could be denied to blacks. The rallies, marches, meetings, and demonstrations along the way drew support from local populations despite the absence of any clear unity of purpose among the leaders, all of which was amply reported by a sizable press entourage.

SNCC, which had evolved since 1964 from an organization that welcomed white volunteers to one that now believed that blacks needed to rely on their own resources, was deeply involved in efforts to build political power in Mississippi jurisdictions where blacks were in the majority. The march provided the group with new audiences among which to pursue that program. Stokely Carmichael, the recently elected national president of SNCC and a vigorous speaker, sounded the political control note from every platform along the route of march. In Greenwood, Mississippi, on the evening of June 16, an angry Carmichael, just out on bail from an earlier arrest for helping to erect a tent against police orders, first sounded the words that were to preoccupy and confound the civil rights debate for the next several years—black power!

18. Meredith did so with the help of a federal court order, weeks of negotiation by the attorney general and his chief lieutenants, the personal intercession of the president of the United States, and in the face of two thousand raging Mississippians who killed two people, wounded twenty-four U.S. marshals, and were finally held at bay by twenty-two thousand U.S. troops. An army detachment, never smaller than five hundred, remained at Ole Miss for the two full academic years he attended.

To a very responsive audience he said: "We're asking Negroes not to go to Vietnam but to stay in Greenwood and fight. We need black power. What do we want?" The answer came thundering back: "Black power!"

Carmichael continued: "If they put one more of us in jail, we're not going to pay a bond to get out. We're going up there and get him out ourselves. Black power!"

Came the reverberating echo: "Black power!"

The speaker went on. "You can't depend on the march here in Greenwood. You must build a power base . . . the power has got to get you a black sheriff. . . . White people aren't going to do it for you . . . you have to stop being ashamed of being black and don't try to be white. . . . Now that doesn't mean to be anti-white . . . but get the nappiest-headed black man with the broadest nose and the thickest lips and make him sheriff!"

Following the speech, Paul Good, a writer for the *Nation,* first asked the question that would beguile the country. In his August 8 article he reported: "But what did it all mean exactly? Storm courthouses? Run over whites? After the shouting died, Carmichael and I talked quietly together. 'When I talk about going to the court house,' he said, 'it's an allusion. Negroes understand me. But whites get nervous when we don't keep talking about brotherly love. They need reassurance. But we're not about to divert our energies to give it to them.'"[19]

The "Black Power" chorus became the hallmark of all of Carmichael's remaining speeches on the march across Mississippi. The news reporters made sure that it captured the nation's attention.

After the march was done, the words echoed and reechoed—in the mouths of other rally speakers, in the columns of the news analysts, in the manifestos of a wide spectrum of organizations, and from the speeches of the president of the United States. Some sought to explain it—each with his or her own definition. Others left it to the audiences to make their own interpretations.

Black civil rights organizations were among the most concerned—especially the old-line civil rights groups that still saw integration as the only reliable highway to equality. Fearful that the impact of "black power" on white allies would shatter old coalitions and dry up funding sources, they were quick to allay fears and give assurances that the goal of integration was still intact.

In October, leaders of seven civil rights organizations—including Whitney Young of the National Urban League, Roy Wilkins of the NAACP, and A. Philip Randolph of the Brotherhood of Sleeping Car Porters, felt it

19. Good, "A White Look at Black Power."

necessary to take a full-page ad in the *New York Times* to clarify to the nation that the old civil rights movement was still the real civil rights movement and had nothing to do with black separatism, urban rioting, or black power. The ad said, in part:

> There is nothing new about these principles (upon which the civil rights movement rests). What is new are the conditions which compel us to re-state them—not the least of which is their abandonment by some individu-als and groups whose positions are nevertheless frequently interpreted as representing the civil rights movement.
> I. We are committed to the attainment of racial justice by the demo-cratic process . . .
> II. We repudiate any strategies of violence, reprisal or vigilantism, and we condemn both rioting and the demagoguery that feeds it . . .
> III. We are committed to integration, by which we mean an end to every barrier which segregation and other forms of discrimination have raised against the enjoyment by Negro Americans of their human and constitu-tional rights.

The ad then said that "society cannot perpetuate discrimination against Negroes and then blame the victims or their leaders for the outbursts of those who have been made desperate." Pointing to all who did not throw rocks and to the Negroes serving in Vietnam, the ad went on: "It is a cruel and bitter abuse to judge the worth of these larger numbers, the overwhelming preponderance of the Negro population, by the misdeeds of a few."[20]

Absent from the list of signatories were the leaders of SNCC and CORE, whose nonagreement with the statement was assumed, and Martin Luther King, whose reasons were unexplained.

Bayard Rustin, whose advocacy of coalition politics as the only way by which Negroes could make any significant social and economic progress had led him to sign the ad of the old-line civil rights leaders, nevertheless sought to create understanding for the origins and necessity of the cry for black power. In *Commentary,* he took issue with the president, the vice president, and all others who described black power as racism in reverse. He wrote:

> There is all the difference in the world between saying, "If you don't want me, I don't want you" (which is what some proponents of "black power" have in effect been saying) and the statement, "Whatever you do, I don't want you" (which is what racism declares). It is, in other words, both absurd and immoral to equate the despairing response of the victim with the con-temptuous assertion of the oppressor. It would, moreover, be tragic if white

20. *New York Times,* October 14, 1966.

liberals allowed verbal hostility on the part of Negroes to drive them out of the movement or to curtail their support for civil rights. The issue was injustice before "black power" became popular, and the issue is still injustice.[21]

Martin Luther King took a conciliatory tone. He wrote: "Black Power, in its broad and positive meaning, is a call to black people to amass the political and economic strength to achieve their legitimate goals. No one can deny that the Negro is in dire need of this kind of legitimate power.... Power, properly understood, is the ability to achieve purpose. It is the strength required to bring about social, political or economic changes. In this sense power is not only desirable but necessary to bring about the demands of love and justice."[22]

If the interpretations of "Black Power" were many and varied, "Burn, Baby, Burn," the signature slogan employed by H. Rap Brown, Carmichael's successor as chairman of SNCC, was far less equivocal. It may have first come into prominence in Cambridge, Maryland, where Brown had spoken and where a civil disturbance had resulted in extensive burning in the Negro area of the city. Many observers believed the damage would have been far less extensive if the fire department had not stood idly by, watching the conflagration rage. Units of the Maryland National Guard were deployed to restore order.

The state of Maryland charged Brown with inciting to riot in Cambridge. He was arrested by the FBI on July 26 at National Airport in Washington and taken to the federal courthouse in Alexandria, Virginia, where his lawyer, William Kunstler, got him released at 4:00 p.m. on the basis of a defective federal warrant. He was then rearrested on the steps of the courthouse by the Alexandria police. Following a scuffle with Brown's supporters outraged by the second arrest, he was jailed at the police station, which faced an all-Negro public housing project. A crowd of about two hundred gathered, including blacks and nearby white residents. "The potential for a racial incident was high, fed by general uneasiness about riot rumors, the incendiary nature of Brown's message, the nervous anticipation of the crowd, and the lack of experience of the Alexandria police in handling such situations."[23]

A CRS biracial team consisting of James Laue and John Gibson arrived at the jail in time to learn from Kunstler that an extradition hearing had been set for late August and that Brown would be released on $10,000 bail

21. Rustin, "Black Power and Coalition Politics."
22. King, *Where Do We Go from Here: Chaos or Community,* 42.
23. CRS draft report on conciliation activities.

as soon as the money could be raised—perhaps as late as midnight. For six hours, tensions among the crowd of four hundred rose and fell as the comings and goings of police units and the media generated interest or anxiety. Rumors circulated among Negroes on one side of the jail and whites on the other. Gibson and Laue continually circulated in the black and white crowds respectively, trying to lighten the atmosphere by providing up-to-date information and carrying messages to the police. Gibson worked with an SNCC representative to encourage the clearing away of the pop bottles that had begun to accumulate. The CRS team was able to satisfy the police that the crowd was not hostile; it just wanted to see Brown released. The revised police strategy based on that understanding was to avoid needlessly provocative activity—such as gunning motorcycle engines as a means of crowd restraint. When Laue pointed out to the police inspector that whites were permitted to circulate up to the police station steps on their side, while blacks were cordoned off some distance away, the police changed to a policy of exercising equal restraint against both groups.

Arrangements were endangered when the justice of the peace, whose presence would be necessary at the presentation of the bond, threatened to leave if the bondsman did not appear by midnight. CRS prevailed upon him to wait. CRS discussed with the police and the SNCC representatives the wisdom of a speedy departure when Brown was released, as opposed to holding a press conference on the jailhouse steps, as the reporters were demanding. SNCC representatives decided to defer the press conference until the next day. The release was finally worked out at about 1:00 a.m. Following a brief wave to the crowd, Brown was ushered by his associates into a waiting automobile. Gibson assured the crowd that Brown would return the next day to thank them for their support (which he did).

As the crowd started to disperse, slowly but peacefully, the CRS conciliators suggested to the police supervisors that hastening its departure with roaring motorcycles was likely to be a needless irritant. The motorcycles were withdrawn, and the crowd dispersed at its own pace.

Two days later, addressing supporters in a church in Washington, D.C., on July 28, Brown told the cheering crowd that the nation was on the verge of a black revolution that would "make the Viet Cong look like Sunday school teachers." He was also quoted as saying, "We will take an eye for an eye, a life for a life." He suggested that Negroes should "do more shooting than looting" when they riot. He referred to the stomping and shooting death of a policeman in Plainfield, New Jersey, as a beautiful example of black people controlling their community. Despite Brown's verbal violence, United Press International reported there were no incidents following the rally and that only four uniformed policemen, all Negro, were assigned to the event.[24]

In Washington, D.C., in the summer of 1967, in the midst of a national epidemic of urban riots, a bravura performance of the "Burn, Baby, Burn" harangue passed almost without notice. In contrast, Washington did "blow" eight months later when the triggering incident was the murder of Martin Luther King Jr.

The urban riots and the verbal violence that accompanied the riots generated two conflicting reactions among those who influenced public policy within the majority community. On the one hand were those whose response tended toward the encouragement of backlash. In May 1967 the Sunday edition of the *New York Times,* under the headline "Rifle Club Urges Antiriot Posses," reported that the National Rifle Association's magazine had advised its eight hundred thousand readers to form posses as the best defense against urban rioters and suggested that the best weapon for household defense was the twelve-gauge shotgun, although "there is a good deal to be said for a sledge or ax handle." During that period a variety of sheriffs and police chiefs were quoted as promising their constituents that "when the looting starts the shooting starts." During the week of the Detroit riots, California Governor Ronald Reagan called the disturbances "riots of the law breakers and the mad dogs against the people." Former President Eisenhower, in an article in *Reader's Digest,* spoke of rioters attacking the police "with animal ferocity."

Other public leaders, however, while they were attentive to the need to restore and maintain public order and justly prosecute the malefactors, were able to see beyond the crimes of looting and torching to the misery and degradation of ghetto life that had caused and fueled the uprisings.

President Johnson, in an address to the nation on July 27, 1967, announcing the creation of the Kerner Commission, said, "The only genuine, long range solution for what has happened lies in an attack—mounted at every level—upon the conditions that breed despair and violence. . . . We should attack these conditions—not because we are frightened by conflict, but because we are fired by conscience. We should attack them because there is simply no other way to achieve a decent and orderly society in America."[25]

Eight months later, in its comprehensive report on what happened, why, and what could be done to prevent it from happening again, the

24. UPI teletype report, July 28, 1967.
25. *Report of the National Advisory Commission on Civil Disorders,* xv.

Kerner Commission said, "To continue our present course will involve the continuing polarization of the American community and, ultimately, the destruction of basic democratic vales. . . . The alternative will require a commitment to national action—compassionate, massive and sustained . . . hard choices must be made, and, if necessary, new taxes enacted."[26] The commission's findings were an educational eye-opener for millions of Americans as to the true nature of the racial divide that was wounding the nation. The commission's recommendations were a blueprint for massive reform of America's economic and social structure, some of which actually took place as a result of the commission's impact.

While those who opposed civil rights were quick to label the riots as part and parcel of the civil rights movement, leaders of the movement took pains to distinguish the two. Although they identified riots as the consequence of oppression, they disavowed them as a means for achieving equality. But history has affirmed that riots were a powerful attention grabber that demanded a new intensity of response at the highest levels. The impact of the civil disorders was also to heighten the American public's understanding of the depth of the deprivation and degradation in the urban ghettos and to bring greater priority to the need to overcome the deficits in social and economic justice.

Not only President Johnson and his riot commission were moved to actions beyond what the civil rights movement had been able to generate. The role of the riots as an agent for change among a broad segment of the population was illustrated by the reaction of *Newsweek* magazine, which on the cover of its November 20, 1967, issue depicted two powerful black hands, one open in supplication, the other a clenched fist. The headline for the issue was: "The Negro in America—What Must Be Done."

Introducing a special twenty-two-page section, the magazine's editor, Osborn Elliott, described it as the culmination of the magazine's "most ambitious editorial project," involving editors, writers, and reporters touring the country, interviewing experts, and reporting on the subject for two months. As a result of what they learned, Elliott stated: "Newsweek deliberately departs from its traditional method of covering the news. In the 22-page section that follows there is analysis aplenty—but this time there is advocacy as well. The reason for this marked change of approach is that the editors have come to believe that at this particular time, on this particular subject, they could not limit their journalistic responsibility or their responsibility as citizens by simply reporting. . . . In part we were led to this approach by the events of last summer, when ghetto streets exploded in

26. Ibid., 1.

violence . . . and America was brought face to face with its central racial dilemma."[27]

There followed a detailed report of the anguish and anger *Newsweek*'s researchers had found in the ghettos, and page after page of recommendations for changes that needed to be made by government and other mainstream institutions in American society. According to Elliott, the editors concluded that the crisis required "a mobilization of the nation's moral, spiritual and physical resources . . . and strong and unflinching political leadership from the top."

How much good resulted in the long run from the increased attention stimulated by the riots is still in question. Certainly the federal government did not generate the enormous monetary investment that the Kerner Commission and civil rights advocates had indicated would be necessary to heal the social and economic sickness of the cities. Nevertheless, advocates of the disadvantaged continued for years to cite the danger of "long, hot summers" in order to resist efforts to trim the budgets of social programs. Some believed that fear of riots may have been an unacknowledged ghost at the conference tables of the decision makers, helping to tip the scales in favor of progress or, at least, to moderate cutbacks.

27. *Newsweek,* November 20, 1967, p. 32.

Six

Police-Minority Relations

A Lightning Rod for Racial Conflagration

"In most American cities, policemen and poor Negroes live in what can only be described as intermittent warfare. Hostility abounds on both sides," wrote U.S. District Court Judge George Edwards in 1968. The former police commissioner of Detroit went on: "all too often, police tend to act like an army of occupation."[1]

In the period from 1964 to 1989, CRS conciliators helped to resolve thousands of conflicts between minorities and police. While serious problems remained, a sea change of improvement occurred in the relationship Edwards had depicted. An examination of the origins, extent, and amelioration of the violence between police and racial minorities will delineate the unique role of the Community Relations Service among the many social forces that helped to bring about the change.

A Too Familiar Story

On New Year's Eve 1974, two large lumberyards in Port Arthur, Texas, went up in flames. The event followed a rally by three hundred blacks protesting the killing of a twenty-two-year-old unarmed black man who was shot in the back by a white police officer. The victim was fleeing jail following his arrest for a misdemeanor.

City hall and police headquarters had been immediately targeted for protest. Demands for dismissal of the police chief and four officers were

1. Edwards, *The Police on the Urban Frontier: A Guide to Community Understanding*, 24, 27.

placed before the mayor and city council. The mayor rejected the request pending the action of a grand jury. The grand jury found that the police officers had not violated the Texas criminal code.

Anger mounted on both sides of the color line. A protester's house was set afire; downtown stores suffered $5,000 worth of damage; unoccupied units of a predominately black housing complex were firebombed; seventy-five blacks and whites engaged in a pitched battle at the local high school.

At the CRS Regional headquarters in Dallas, Gustavo Gaynett read about the Port Arthur difficulties in the newspaper, made some phone calls, and packed his bags. It was part of his job as a conciliation specialist to monitor his assigned territory, to identify communities in conflict, to assess the need for CRS help, and to recommend a suitable form of assistance.[2]

Port Arthur's upheaval was a sad but familiar story to Gaynett. Among the thousands of conflicts CRS had encountered in its ten-year history, no scenario was more common than this one: an unarmed young black man shot in the back by a white officer; a violent response and organized protest from the minority community; rejection of demands by the local authorities; escalation of tension and stalemate.[3]

In the eyes of racial minorities across America, agents of law enforcement exerted unfair and heavy-handed control over their comings and goings, with little respect for their rights as Americans or their dignity as human beings. The crowning indignity—seen as the ultimate act of disdain—was the use of deadly force by the police. The outrage was magnified because the criminal justice system appeared rarely to punish the offending officer. Blacks throughout America saw due process of law as a step-by-step ritual of cover-up. Investigations were cut-and-dried exercises by brother officers. Whether conducted by the killer's commanding officer or by the police department's internal affairs bureau, the examination of the facts almost invariably produced a recommendation for the finding of justifiable homicide. Prosecutors, who worked daily as crime-fighting partners of the police, were unenthusiastic in presenting such matters to a grand jury or in pursuing a jury trial. Members of the juries, for their part,

---

2. A onetime official with the United Automobile Workers, Gaynett was one of the growing number of Hispanic conciliators who began to bolster the CRS ranks following Ben Holman's appointment as director in 1969. Determined to overcome the CRS shortage of "brown" conciliators, Holman had adopted a time-tested method for breaking new ground in minority recruitment; he gave hiring authority to a Hispanic. With Gilbert Pompa as assistant director for conciliation, a wealth of talented Hispanic applicants were identified over the next few years and hired in all parts of the country.

3. Community Relations Service, U.S Department of Justice, *Police Use of Deadly Force: A Conciliation Handbook for Citizens and Police,* 1.

were reluctant to indict or to convict members of "the thin blue line" that stood between them and the predators of the criminal world.

The fragility of relations between minorities and the police became evident to the American people when studies showed that many of the urban riots of the late sixties were triggered by police actions. As the most visible representatives of the white-dominated society that exercised authority in minority neighborhoods, police had to bear the brunt of minority resentment for the failures of other institutions whose ministrations did little to diminish the harshness of life in America's ghettos and barrios. The police, for their part no less prejudiced than the society from which they were drawn, were often less than punctilious in respecting the rights and dignity of the minority poor.

Deep-seated mistrust and antagonism between police and racial minorities were inevitable in a society where century-old norms requiring minorities to be kept in their place were being challenged by newly defined national goals of equal standing before the law. The police were totally unprepared by training or indoctrination to meet America's requirements for its peace officers in the last half of the twentieth century.

In the minds of many blacks, police attitudes were monstrous. "Why Cops Kill Blacks" was the banner headline, in one-inch type, across the front page of the *New York Amsterdam News,* America's largest weekly black newspaper, on December 17, 1977. It quoted the views of a foremost Negro psychiatrist, Alvin Pouissant, professor at the Harvard University Medical School: "They [the police] see blacks as subhuman and it doesn't take them much to kill. So far as they are concerned they are not killing human beings. . . . Most white cops are angry at blacks, are paranoid and full of hate. . . . These types of killings go on every day because white cops are not convicted. It almost seems like they have license to kill and, of course, they always have an all-white jury." These views had wide believability in the Negro community.

Police-Community Relations

CRS's earliest cases in the South required the agency to work with police in three types of situations: to encourage police protection of minorities against unlawful harassment, to encourage police protection for lawful protest, and to discourage police violence against civil rights protesters.

But it was not long before conciliators encountered cases growing out of the pervasive prejudice and discrimination within police departments themselves. Employment discrimination was rampant in every aspect from recruitment to training, assignment, and promotion. Police behavior was characterized by abusive treatment of minority residents that ranged from second-class service, to calculated discourtesy, to verbal and physical abuse. Complaint systems were inhospitable to minority grievances. In community after community, almost without exception, CRS witnessed deeply embittered minorities who felt degraded by their encounters with the police.

Bitterness between police and racial and ethnic minorities predated the civil rights struggle; it was rooted in American history and the sociology of class difference. The immigrant poor who crowded the urban slums produced more than their fair share of street crime and unmannerly behavior, inconveniencing and threatening middle- and upper-class lifestyles. For the police, maintaining the peace also meant keeping the poor "in their place." Not surprisingly, the poor tended to perceive the police as defending the property and physical security of the well-to-do, while being indifferent to the property and security of the poor. For the poor who were black, the police image was even more harsh. For hundreds of years it was the white peace officer who enforced the subordinated status of blacks in the South, and the migrations of millions of blacks to northern cities after the two World Wars brought that deeply ingrained fear of police to northern cities. The peaceful protest and civil disobedience of the civil rights era, which often pitted police against minorities, contributed to the historical antagonism.

Discriminatory police practices were not only undemocratic; they were also counterproductive. One of the most critical tools in law enforcement is community cooperation; yet in the areas where the incidence of street crime was the highest, where community self-interest would logically have been expected to produce the highest level of citizen cooperation, police tactics seemed stubbornly designed to alienate the community. As a result, public administration experts trying to modernize police management made common cause with civil rights advocates in pressing for a variety of reforms of police behavior. Their concerns were to become linked under the name *police-community relations*. The movement was to gain energy following the urban riots of the midsixties. While the exhaustive studies that had followed these riots tracked the root causes to racial inequities in education, jobs, economics, housing, health, and so forth, they also established that most of the disturbances had been triggered by police encounters with minority residents. That fact served as a powerful attention getter in local and national halls of power and brought greater priority to police programs that impacted on minority relationships.

Organized efforts to reform unprofessional and discriminatory police behavior, and to dispel the mistrust and antagonism between police and racial minorities, were born in the late fifties and early sixties. In 1955 the School of Police Administration and Public Safety at Michigan State University, in collaboration with the National Conference of Christians and Jews, conducted the first of what was to be an annual National Institute on Police and Community Relations. An avant-garde of police executives met with sociologists and leaders of community and minority organizations to define and debate the problems of police-citizen interactions in a time of social ferment and change and to find solutions. A literature began to develop, and a handful of progressive law enforcement agencies began to undertake programs.

In 1960 the St. Louis police department inaugurated the nation's first police-community relations unit. San Francisco followed in 1961. A scattering of communities experimented with improving communications channels by, for example, creating community advisory groups that met periodically with police either at departmental or precinct levels. Faltering efforts were initiated to recruit more minority officers. Special training programs on police-community relations were developed for the rank and file. By 1965 a full-time national center had been established at Michigan State to be a fountainhead of research, training, and publication. The International Association of Chiefs of Police (IACP) had begun to provide leadership and training in the area.

The bulk of the police profession, however, was resistant to progress, sometimes concealing from public scrutiny a pattern of practice that differed widely from the idealized standards police statesmen were trying to advance, sometimes merely going through the motions of reform. Patrick V. Murphy, an up-from-the-ranks New York City police commissioner, once recalled a convocation of New York City police where an earlier commissioner was introducing new regulations on police-community relations to his troops. Subordinate commanders seated on the platform behind him openly gestured their contempt for his message. In 1961 *Time Magazine* reported a meeting of the Houston Police Department at which Dr. Melvyn Sikes, a black CRS conciliator called in to help the department with its race relations, was introduced by the chief as "another one of those sobsister, slobbering sociologists."[4]

The disparity between standards and practice was most visible in the inner city and other impoverished areas where residents lacked the power

---

4. Sikes, telephone interview with the author.

to demand respect for their constitutional rights. However, as the civil rights movement infused minority communities with the courage to protest, issues of police behavior were joined in a raucous public clamor nationwide. The police, circling the wagons in a classic defensive posture, admitted no wrong, uncritically defended their miscreants, and vilified their detractors. In the minds of the minority community, this hard-shell response only served to confirm every charge against the police.

While a few of CRS's neophyte conciliators had a background in law enforcement, many had to learn on the job. Lack of experience in a technical field, such as education or police work, sometimes placed the early CRS conciliators at a disadvantage. Moreover, they often found that school superintendents or police chiefs whose organizations were in trouble tended to have a built-in resistance to accepting help from an outsider, much more so when the outsider was not a brother professional who understood the problems of the trade. To minimize this disadvantage, CRS early on recruited technical specialists to support the conflict resolution teams.

Dante Andreotti, who joined CRS in 1966 as the agency's first specialist in the administration of justice, trained the conciliators in police-community relations matters and supported their casework either on site or with daily phone consultations. He provided access to research findings, funding sources, and a wide range of experts, as needed. He was soon joined by Robert Lamb Jr., who later succeeded him as head of that office. Andreotti and Lamb were pioneers who had already made a mark in the shaping of police-community relations practice in America.

Andreotti, as a San Francisco police district commander, had been chosen in 1961 to organize and command the city's police-community relations unit, the second in the nation.[5] A no-nonsense street policeman who had worked himself up the ladder to the highest civil service grade of lieutenant, he wondered why he had been chosen for this job for which he had previously exhibited no special interest. He later thought it might have been because of his reputation as a fair man, who in twenty-one years of service had never found it necessary to draw his gun to effect an arrest. He grew into his new position through on-the-job training. From minority leaders and activists to whom he reached out, he learned about the problems of the inner city and the negative impact of police encounters on minority life. His first move to modify the image of the police as an oppressive force in the ghetto was to use his unit as a part-time job-finding agency for ex-convicts. His newly developing awareness made him understand that

5. "A Strong Police Command Vital to Avert More City Violence," *Washington Post*, June 30, 1966.

rehabilitation was a meaningless concept in a system where nothing but a dead end awaited the ex-offender. While Andreotti increasingly became an advocate for the ghetto poor, he found that his effectiveness in overcoming antagonism between the department and the community was limited. The respect won by his unit among minorities did not automatically rub off on a whole department that was resistant to change. At the same time, in the eyes of Andreotti's detractors, his unit's advocacy of minority issues tended to alienate it from the rest of the force.

Lamb was a police captain commanding Atlantic City's police-community relations unit when recruited by CRS in 1967. Having been raised in a household resistant to the indignities of being black in America (his father had been a supporter of the Back to Africa movement of Marcus Garvey in the twenties), he had entered into police work aware of the contradictory demands that would be made on him by the police culture on the one hand and his identification with the black community on the other. The challenge had helped him to develop a capacity for strategic thinking—finding ways to work for productive outcomes in a resistant environment.

With Andreotti and Lamb to coordinate backup, CRS's conflict resolution services could offer more comprehensive solutions to more deeply rooted police-community problems. Program tools and models were compiled as a resource to make available to any troubled department the experience of other police agencies in dealing with similar situations. Funding sources were identified to permit the development of new programs that otherwise might not have been affordable. A panel of outstanding police experts from around the nation was enlisted to be available as case consultants, to provide analysis and recommendations whatever the problem. Lee Brown, later to serve as the top law enforcement officer in Atlanta, Houston, and New York before being appointed coordinator of antidrug programs in the Clinton White House, served as a CRS consultant for more than twenty years.

A critical word in the lexicon of the first CRS conciliators was *credibility*. You couldn't be effective without credibility—credibility with the civil rights community, credibility with the activists, credibility with the police chief, the school board, the business community. For many conciliators, developing effective working relationships with police chiefs was the most difficult, except for the few who were at home in the police environment from previous experience. Among their other contributions, Andreotti and Lamb and their string of police consultants were essential for imparting credibility to the full CRS team with which they worked.

Of course the best credibility builder of all was a successful earlier case. The CRS vision of a successful case—as it would impact on the police chief—

followed this sort of scenario: The chief goes home to seven o'clock dinner for the first time in weeks, knowing that the streets are clear of protesters and no one has been hurt. Over dinner he reflects on tomorrow's follow-up activities: (1) breakfast with the leading black activist (with whom he is now on a first-name basis), who last month was calling for his resignation; (2) a 2:00 p.m. appointment with the consultant who is flying in from Washington to help draft proposals for federal grants for a new minority recruitment program and a cross-cultural sensitivity training program; and (3) an evening meeting with the Black Ministerial Association and the chairman of the city council's finance committee about getting the black community to support a tax referendum that would give the police the first cost-of-living increase in three years. While somewhat idealized, and certainly not invariable, such outcomes of CRS cases—and even lesser achievements—soon resolved the conciliator's credibility problem with the chief.

By the early seventies, conflicts involving police were the most common problem drawing CRS services. A number of factors contributed to this development. One was CRS's track record. In 1966 two-thirds of CRS cases were "alerted" (brought to the agency's attention) through the scanning of newspapers. By 1970 two-thirds were alerted as a result of previous cases, with requests mostly coming from public officials (police, schools, mayor's offices) and minority organizations.

A second factor was a growing awareness among leaders of local government that minority complaints about offensive treatment at the hands of police were legitimate. This new awareness was supported by the findings of the President's Commission on Law Enforcement and Administration of Justice. The commission had been created by President Johnson in 1965 to conduct a comprehensive study of America's justice system and recommend improvements. Chaired by Nicholas deB. Katzenbach, it enlisted hundreds of the nation's foremost scholars and practicing lawmen to examine current practice, identify and debate the issues, and formulate recommendations. Its report, issued in 1967,[6] documented widespread shortcomings regarding police-minority relationships, pointing out that these relations had a direct effect on police operations: "Poor police-community relations adversely affect the ability of the police to prevent crime and apprehend criminals. People hostile to the police are not so likely to report violations of the law, even when they are the victims. They

6. President's Commission on Law Enforcement and Administration of Justice, *Commission Report: The Challenge of Crime in a Free Society.* Citations attributed to the Crime Commission are drawn from chapter 6, "The Police and the Community," of *Task Force Report: The Police.*

are even less likely to report suspicious persons or incidents, to testify as witnesses voluntarily, or to come forward and provide information."[7]

Hundreds of illustrations drawn from scores of commission studies recorded an overall pattern of police abuse of the rights of minority citizens. A few examples:

> In one commission study observations were made in several cities of several hundred routine contacts between police and citizens . . . 15 percent of the interrogations began with a brusque or nasty command like "Come 'ere, punk," or "get your *** over here, pork chop." . . . Discriminatory statements, in particular, produce both anger and strong counter-prejudice among minority groups. The use of racial epithets such as "nigger," "coon," "boy" and "pancho" appears to be widespread, even though their use is condemned by responsible police administrators.[8]

Aggressive preventive patrol was a term that embraced a variety of police practices, some of doubtful legality, that had become common all over the country as standard methods of crime fighting. The simple "stop" for purposes of field interrogation was a common form of harassment, sometimes but not necessarily accompanied by the "frisk." Frequently used to discourage minorities from being where they were not wanted, stop-and-frisk was often applied without even the pretext of being related to a crime. In 1965, in San Diego, written reports were made of two hundred thousand stops, and it was thought that a similar number were unrecorded.[9]

Another dubious practice was the arrest on suspicion, or "for investigation." In Detroit, in the ten years from 1947 through 1956, more than thirty-three thousand arrests were made for suspicion, of which only sixty-five hundred resulted in criminal charges. Suspects were held an average of three days before release or arraignment.[10] The FBI's Uniform Crime Reports for 1965 recorded more than seventy-six thousand arrests for suspicion. In cities where arrest for suspicion was not permitted, minor crimes such as vagrancy or drunkenness were used instead.

The commission also cited the use of firearms by police as often unnecessary. The report expressed alarm at the small number of police departments that provided adequate instruction on when the weapon should be fired. It cited a Michigan State study of forty-nine police departments in Michigan, of which twenty-seven had no firearms policies.

7. *Task Force Report,* 144.
8. Ibid., 180.
9. Ibid., 184.
10. Ibid., 186.

Another powerful force speeding the transformation of police management in the United States was the creation by Congress of the Law Enforcement Assistance Administration (LEAA) to provide federal funding of programs that would enhance the quality of local law enforcement. Although LEAA was originally accused by community groups of being excessively devoted to hardware, it became a significant source for funding local programs to improve police management and police-community relations. Close cooperation between CRS and LEAA at times proved to be a useful means for effectively allocating funding.

Conference of Chiefs

In the early years of the Johnson administration the Justice Department acknowledged a responsibility to help local police agencies correct the deteriorating relationships between police and the minority communities. One of the first steps was for the attorney general to convene a conference of police chiefs to discuss approaches to the problem. The department saw this as a matter of some delicacy. The term *police-community relations* was already in disrepute in some police circles, where it was seen as a device for tying the hands of law enforcement that had been foisted upon the police by the "do-gooders." To minimize the resistance of chiefs, the subject was cast in terms of current management problems in policing. The IACP was given the contract to design and conduct the conference.

At the 1965 conference the civil rights/community relations content had been minimal. In 1966 a larger, but still cautious, dose of attention to inner-city problems was planned. CRS, newly arrived at the Department of Justice, participated on the periphery of the planning group. However, it made some slight contributions through its direct but informal advisory role to Attorney General Ramsey Clark. From the outset, the planners rejected the CRS proposal to include Negro experts among the speakers and resource participants. It was too early, the planners thought, to expect police chiefs to tolerate, much less respect, expertise from that source. It was only after great resistance, and on the attorney general's insistence, that they agreed to one black speaker, Assistant Attorney General Roger Wilkins, the director of CRS.[11]

---

11. The IACP was to come a long way in the acceptance of blacks, although it took many years to do it. Lee Brown, a black police consultant for CRS beginning in 1968, served as president of the IACP from 1991 to 1993.

At least one brave and innovative step was taken by the 1966 planners. They arranged for half a dozen social scientists, rather than police chiefs, to lead the small group discussions. This would be necessary because the thrust of the conference would be the exploration—in a confidential peer-to-peer setting—of the delicate subject of on-the-job stress and its impact on the chief's role. The intent was to use that discussion as an opening to a subsequent parallel discussion of the impact of urban stress on residents of the inner city.

CRS insisted that without the presence of blacks to provide a grounding in reality, that discussion, filtered only through the eyes of the commiserating chiefs, might well take on an Alice in Wonderland quality that would rob it of all value. The conference planners would not accept Negro participation. They finally agreed to a compromise. The six social scientists, none of whom were familiar with ghetto life, would be turned over to CRS for one day of intense training in the realities of police-minority interactions in urban America before they served as discussion leaders.

As faculty for the training, CRS selected three Washington, D.C., black activists known to be police irritants. One was Marion Barry, the Washington director of the Student Nonviolent Coordinating Committee (SNCC), who was then leader of a popular motivational movement of ghetto youth. He frequently ran street dances without permits, thereby exciting police surveillance and arrests on slight pretexts. The second was a woman named Willie Hardy. She was an advocate for the poor with a reputation as a thorn in the sides of the district's social service agencies. The third was James Lee, whose inner-city laundromat had become an informal community center and gathering place, and whose back lot had become an uneasy frontier between "hanging out" black men and patrolling police.[12]

The 1966 conference of chiefs was the last of its type under the direct sponsorship of the attorney general, although the Justice Department was to continue its gentle persuasion of police executives through other means—among them being the carrot of grants from the Law Enforcement Assistance Administration and the much-less-frequent stick of prosecution by the Civil Rights Division.

12. With the coming of home rule to the District of Columbia, Barry was to enjoy a long career in elective office, including as president of the board of education, mayor, and member of the city council. Hardy, chagrined that blacks were barred from the chiefs' conference, presented herself at the Airlie House Conference Center outside Washington, D.C., on the opening night and demanded to be heard. Two husky chiefs, at either elbow, escorted her from the premises. Hardy was subsequently to serve many years as chair of the Public Safety Committee of the D.C. City Council.

A far more insistent and effective engine of change was the angry protests of aggrieved minority groups in towns and cities across the country. CRS played its part by helping the antagonists to settle their differences. As the conciliators became increasingly effective, they were better able to move settlements toward long-range solutions rather than just temporary accommodations. The racial conflagration in Port Arthur, Texas, was a case in point.

Port Arthur

Port Arthur's city manager, George Dibrell, knew his city was badly in need of help but saw no clear path to finding that help until Gus Gaynett called and offered him the assistance of the Community Relations Service. In their first meeting, Dibrell was chary about a program that seemed to be an unlikely activity for the federal government. But after learning of CRS's work in other cases, he was ready to listen further. He was particularly impressed by Gaynett's suggestion, confirming his own findings, that the source of difficulty lay deeper than the current shooting incident. Writing later in *The Police Chief,* Dibrell recalled: "The black man's death turned out to be the tip of the iceberg as black citizens brought into the open a number of other community grievances that had been simmering beneath the surface . . . old prejudices resurfaced."[13]

After meeting with the principal antagonists and others in both the black and white communities, Gaynett found the conflict to be typical of scores of community crises that had proved to be responsive to CRS assistance. Moreover, he saw the potential for going beyond the mere resolution of the current impasse to seeking long-range solutions of underlying problems. In a recent enlargement of its operations, CRS had begun to offer formal mediation in lieu of conciliation in appropriate cases where the parties were willing to invest the time to get at root causes.[14] After city officials and black leaders agreed to try mediation, Robert Greenwald, a seasoned CRS mediator, was introduced into the situation.

13. Dibrell, "Mediation in Civil Rights Issues: The Port Arthur Experience," *Police Chief,* November 1976, 80.

14. In general, CRS construed conciliation as embracing any problem-solving mechanism, or combination of techniques, that enabled the antagonists to work out their differences so as to lessen discord and increase racial harmony. Mediation, on the other hand, followed the strict choreography of formal across-the-table give-and-take, presided over by a neutral third party, and focused on specific predefined issues, with the intention of reaching a formal signed agreement.

As with many mediation cases, weeks were consumed in getting the parties to agree on the issues, to develop sufficient confidence in the mediator, and to accept the rules of engagement he set forth, such as pledging to avoid provocative acts during the mediation period, to leave all media contact to the mediator, and to strive to build self-enforcement mechanisms into the agreement.

Four issues were decided upon for negotiation: use of deadly force; arrest and detention procedures; improved minority recruitment; and the development of a police-community relations program. Agreement was reached on all four issues, but it took thirteen negotiating sessions lasting into August, eight months following the precipitating incident.

Problems arose even before the first formal issue could be debated. The mayor would not permit any elected official to represent the city on the negotiating team, a position the minority representatives strongly opposed but ultimately went along with.

At the first session, Greenwald put the negotiators to work learning what American law and police science regarded as the state of the art in guiding police officers as to when to shoot. He had deliberately armed himself with material from sources the negotiators were likely to respect. The IACP, in a joint project with the Texas Criminal Justice Division, was developing a model policy on that subject. It placed more restraint on the police officer than did the Texas criminal code, and no city had yet adopted it. In studying the proposed state policy, the two negotiating teams learned that Port Arthur was typical of most Texas cities with respect to codifying when to shoot, but it was lagging far behind the state of the art.

While most authorities believed that the state law on police use of deadly force provided only a bottom line below which municipalities could not sink, the Port Arthur city attorney, who was a member of the negotiating team, asserted that the city could neither fall below nor rise above the state standard, thus making the issue nonnegotiable. His position, however, proved to be malleable as the negotiations proceeded.

Written instructions for officers with respect to arresting and detaining prisoners were sparse. For example, Port Arthur had no written guidelines whatsoever for when to use the stop-and-frisk policy. The chief of police fought against any such guidance being put down on paper. After he was voted down, the issue moved to whether guidance should be in the form of guidelines, which were not necessarily binding, or regulations, which were inviolable and called for disciplinary action against officers who violated them. The final agreement came to rest on written guidelines.

In launching discussion of the police department's arrest and detention procedures, the minority negotiating team, with Greenwald's guidance, prepared a list of a dozen questions, which were answered and debated in turn. The questions were designed so that recommendations might flow directly from the discussion they engendered. They included: "What provisions are there to minimize the necessity for arrest in favor of other alternatives (warnings, summons to appear in lieu of arrest etc.)?" "What precise policies are now in effect which guide officers in stop and search procedures? Has there been any attempt made to make known these procedures to the community at large, and especially the black community?" "What steps can be taken to reduce the likelihood of provocation or confrontation during interrogation or when arrests are made? Are there special procedures in effect regarding search and/or arrest of female suspects and do they adequately safeguard against violation of reasonable standards?"

The problem of recruiting minority officers was defined early on. The city's civil service director, a member of the city's negotiating team, spoke of the difficulty of persuading blacks to apply. "We have had very few minorities that would even come in and take the test," he said, attributing disinterest to the monthly salary of $759, which could not compete with the starting wages in local industry. This analysis was challenged by the Reverend Ransom Howard, who headed the delegation from the black community. Asserting that the issue ran deeper than money, he said, "Blacks have never got any respect." He recalled the words of a black officer who had resigned from the police force because of constant references to "nigger this and nigger that and boy this and boy that."[15]

Negotiators almost tumbled in midstream as they confronted the reality that even if they were to agree on a minority recruitment campaign, and even if it were to be successful, it would do no more than find, persuade, and prepare blacks to apply. It could not assure their appointment. It was always possible that criteria based on test scores and other factors might fill all vacancies in the training academy with whites who attained higher ratings. Even assuming black applicants entered the academy, there were no guarantees they would graduate.

The two members of the Civil Service Commission on the negotiating committee differed as to how much creative zeal could be used in bending the rules far enough to bring better racial balance to the police department in view of the fact that the state, not the city, presided over the civil service examination and selection system.[16]

Such problems were not new or unique to Port Arthur. So many com-

15. *Houston Post*, August 2, 1975.
16. Ibid.

munities faced similar complexities that the Law Enforcement Assistance Administration had established a special program at the Marquette University Law School to provide technical assistance to police departments in need. Greenwald had arranged for a team of experts from Marquette to study the minority recruitment problem in Port Arthur and to help the city build a program to overcome the problems. The negotiators decided to go ahead and utilize that technical assistance to develop a program.

To overcome the growing antagonism between police and the minority community, the mediating team had accepted the need for a police-community relations program. To help the negotiators decide what kind of a program was needed, Greenwald again had a team of experts to offer. The National Association of Police Community Relations Officers (NAPCRO) was the professional association for police-community relations practitioners. CRS had helped bring it into being several years earlier, to provide status, support, and increased technical proficiency to members of the budding profession. It included some of the best police-community relations people in the country. NAPCRO also was funded by the Law Enforcement Assistance Administration to help cities needing assistance with their police-community relations. The association currently was funded to offer assistance grants for pilot projects in ten cities. Greenwald served as a catalyst to bring NAPCRO assistance to Port Arthur. The two people whom NAPCRO assigned to Port Arthur were among the most experienced in the field. One was Robert Barton, the civilian head of the St. Louis Police Department's community relations unit, the first in the nation. The other was Major Leroy Swift, the commanding officer of the patrol division of the Kansas City, Missouri, police department. After Barton and Swift had reviewed the situation with the mediation committee, both sides agreed to recommend that the city council make a formal request to be designated a NAPCRO project city. This would entail a study of the attitudes of police and citizens toward one another, design of a community relations program to improve relationships, and technical assistance to the police-community relations unit that the police force would select.

Five months and thirteen negotiating sessions after the mediation process had begun, the city council enacted the four recommendations that composed the negotiated agreement. Two new written policies were adopted: one on the use of deadly force and another on arrest and detention procedures. In addition, two new programs were launched, one on police-community relations, the other on minority recruitment.[17]

17. CRS Annual Report, 1975, 18–21.

Addressing the city council on the day of its historic vote, Greenwald noted that Port Arthur's race relations problems were far from settled by that one agreement. He expressed hope that the process demonstrated that future problems could be negotiated. Privately, he also harbored the hope that the deeper understanding that had been developed over the course of the negotiations would prove to be of even greater value for continuing racial progress.

In his description of the case in the *Police Chief,* Dibrell wrote:

> Of the four points on which agreement was reached, the one dealing with firearms and deadly force by the police was most directly related to the original shooting incident. The final agreement provided specific guidelines to be followed in future incidents of this nature. Since for the first time policy was reduced to writing, negotiators felt they had provided a more definitive guide to police officers in the field as well as an aid in assessing the validity of their decisions. The new policy spells out the conditions under which an officer may use deadly force but it also stresses that such force must not be used unnecessarily. And—there should be more understanding on the part of the public as to whether proper guidelines are followed.[18]

Two years later the negotiated changes were still in place. Dibrell was able to tell the *Houston Post* that the police force, which had only six blacks out of a force of ninety-one before the disorders, had ten out of one hundred two years later. While the number of minority officers increased by only four, that amounted to 44 percent of the total growth in the department.

Coming to Terms in Texas

Despite isolated instances of improvements of police performance with respect to minorities, as in Port Arthur, unequal treatment of blacks and Hispanics persisted in Texas as elsewhere. In some places it got worse.

When police-inflicted killings increased throughout the state in 1976–1978, Hispanic anger erupted in a wave of community protests. The Brown Berets and other groups led protest demonstrations of from fifty to a thousand Hispanics in Plainview, Lubbock, Odessa, Houston, Dallas, and Corpus Christi, among other communities, protesting the police killing of sixteen Hispanics in the state in the previous eighteen months.

Mounting acrimony allowed no room for any effort to address the problem. Outraged Hispanics, calling for immediate punitive action against of-

18. Dibrell, "Mediation in Civil Rights Issues," 82.

fending police, had no ear for police explanations; in turn, the police knew only one defense when under attack—to circle the wagons, stand by their own, and admit no wrong.

The CRS conciliation staff working out of the southwest regional office in Dallas was wearing itself ragged going from crisis to crisis trying to deescalate tensions. For every city like Port Arthur that learned to manage its differences with civility, there were countless towns where racial bitterness fed on itself. The futility of trying to restore harmony to fractured communities through city-by-city crisis response became apparent. Something was needed to alter the whole atmosphere of mistrust throughout the state.

CRS knew that the prospects for the success of such an effort would be slim without the cooperation of Hispanic and police leaders. The longstanding adversarial relationship between these two communities grew wider with each incident, and true communication had become virtually impossible.

An opportunity to break the impasse appeared in May 1978, when a coalition of Mexican American organizations from across the country was called together in Dallas by the Mexican American Legal Defense and Education Fund (MALDEF) to review the issue of police brutality. The outrage that police insensitivity had engendered among Americans of Spanish descent created an unprecedented sense of unity among the diverse groups. CRS Regional Director Maurillo (Moe) Ortiz and Bob Greenwald had several discussions with leaders of the coalition, and particularly with Reuben Bonilla Jr., the state director of the League of United Latin American Citizens (LULAC). These conversations led to a decision that CRS would explore the willingness of some of the more prominent Texas police chiefs to meet with Latino leaders on "issues of alleged police abusiveness and ways in which some problems might be moderated."[19]

After receiving informal assurances from leaders in both camps that a constructive, problem-solving discussion, unencumbered by recriminations and review of old wounds, would be welcome, CRS invited six law enforcement executives to meet on September 22, 1978, in the CRS office with an equal number of Hispanic organization leaders. Greenwald later reported that the meeting "produced a sense of achievement beyond anything anticipated. It was evident that both sides were willing to face the issues with a degree of candor and with an inclination to move into uncharted waters."[20]

---

19. CRS staff document: Background Summary for Case Review, March 19, 1979.
20. Greenwald, telephone interview with the author.

Encouraged by the level of communication and rapport experienced at the meeting, the twelve participants formed the Steering Committee on Texas Law Enforcement and Community Relations. Headed by Bonilla and Frank Dyson, the chief of police of Austin, they took the bold step of planning to bring police and Hispanic leaders throughout the state together to look unblinkingly into the face of the critical issues that had long been the source of bitter controversy. They decided to start in south Texas, where two hundred selected leaders, one hundred from each group, were invited to the Symposium on Contemporary Issues in Texas Police-Community Relations.

To underscore their seriousness of purpose, the conveners invited only police chiefs and organization presidents, permitting no alternates. They crafted the invitation carefully so as to make sure that the troublesome nature of the subject would be clearly understood in advance. Five topics were identified: use and control of excessive force; selection and training of law enforcement personnel; complaint process and internal investigation; roles of community organizations; and role and responsibility of the media.

In focusing the program on the issues of critical importance to the minorities, the planners knew that they risked discouraging attendance by the police, whose positions on these issues came under public attack with every allegation of police abusive conduct. But they also knew that any ducking of issues would defeat their purpose. To allay police apprehensions, the conveners took pains to offer the following reassurance: "There is no intention at this conference to discuss details of specific police-citizen incidents. There will be no debate regarding the guilt or innocence of any parties alleged to have committed wrongful acts. We want objective evaluation and honest dialogue on the issue, as presented in the program outline. Those persons in charge of the presentations and workshop sessions will be responsible for assuring that we remain on that course."[21]

The meeting not only drew the desired attendance; it appeared to fulfill the hopes of the sponsors as an unprecedented communications breakthrough between groups who could never before hear one another for the shouting.

CRS insisted that the planners look on the conference as a starting point, not a conclusion. Built into the planning of the San Antonio conference were the nuts and bolts that would assure an outcome wedded to action.

21. Letter of invitation to Symposium II on Texas Law Enforcement and Community Relations, from cochairmen Reuben Bonilla and Glen D. King. Included in "A Symposium on Contemporary Issues Police-Community Relations" (public record of symposium documents), 12.

The steering committee of chiefs and Latino leaders pledged to continue to work together in support of conference recommendations designed to reduce excessive use of force by police. CRS field representatives met with conference delegates back in their hometowns to encourage local programs for better communication and reduction of police-community friction. A notable example occurred in Harris County, which encases Houston. There police and other public agency executives joined with Hispanic leaders to form an association that, for several years, served as a forum for ventilating police-minority concerns and for facilitating the development of collaborative programs.[22]

Within the following year, CRS and the steering committee duplicated the whole process by convening another symposium at Fort Worth, to serve police and minority leaders in west and north-central Texas.

The Impact of Minority Police Officers

The evolving role of the minority police officer was a continual focus of CRS attention. The initial concern was with employment discrimination, which aggravated racial tensions in several ways. The all-white police patrols in Negro neighborhoods reinforced the image of an army of occupation. The token representation of blacks in many departments was seen by the Negro community as a sign that they were considered inferior. Even more troubling was the lack of officers capable of bridging the communications abyss between the different cultures.

In 1967, at the request of the mayor, CRS conducted an assessment of police-community relationships in Akron, Ohio. In this city with a 30 percent minority population, there were 6 black officers on a force of 445, and that had been the number since time out of memory. They were almost all detectives assigned only to cases involving blacks. The occasional patrol assignment was only in black neighborhoods. Special training and assignments and other promotional opportunities were denied them. Regardless of their assignment, for administrative purposes they all reported, in Jim Crow fashion, to the single black sergeant. Negro leaders questioned the good faith of the mayor's appeal for black police recruits. They recounted that the single black candidate who had passed the last written examination had been rejected by the all-white examination board because of personal indebtedness, even though leaders of the black community had offered to make good his debts. They testified that to be young,

22. CRS Annual Report, 1980, 8.

black, and in debt in the ghetto was no character flaw and could certainly be overlooked if the city sincerely wanted able black officers.[23]

As opportunity presented itself, CRS gave support to minority recruitment programs, often helping to work them into conciliation agreements and encouraging minority organizations to undertake training programs to better qualify minority applicants for the civil service examinations. CRS also worked with state and local civil service commissions, encouraging their efforts to eliminate cultural bias that unfairly worked against minorities in civil service testing.

Innovative recruitment approaches were encouraged, such as a 1966 statewide effort in Michigan, in collaboration with the Michigan Association of Chiefs of Police and the Michigan Civil Rights Commission. CRS enlisted the resources of the Advertising Council to create and distribute throughout the state a television commercial designed to attract minority applicants. It featured Robert Culp and Bill Cosby, costars of the popular television show *I Spy* and the only interracial team then appearing on American television. Statewide testing was used to qualify candidates for all of the participating jurisdictions, and individuals failing to meet a special requirement for one department, such as age or height, were referred to other departments where that particular standard was less demanding.

As the number of minority officers grew, CRS worked cooperatively with associations of black officers that were forming as support groups for minority officers who often found themselves in a hostile environment. Resistance took many forms, including open conflict in some departments. Incidents were reported of antiblack graffiti in the station house, of interracial fights and weapons being drawn, and of black officers announcing they would not stand by when they witnessed excessive use of force against blacks. Despite these problems, over time most departments learned to accommodate racial integration.

Racial equity within police departments came more rapidly as minority officers developed their own organizations, and CRS was able to encourage this movement, at times on an after-hours basis. The presence of a CRS conciliator in a city sometimes provided the occasion for a private meeting of unorganized black officers to consider the organizational experience of their peers in other cities. The occasional use of black officers as citizen experts to help CRS in cases outside their own cities also provided opportunities for intercity encouragement for the organization of Negro police associations.

23. Community Relations Service, U.S. Department of Justice, "Report to Mayor John S. Ballard on Police Community Relations, Akron, Ohio," March 1967.

As they grew larger, these minority officer associations sometimes served as a counterweight to the political influence of the predominating association of white police officers. While the mainstream police associations concentrated their efforts on officer benefits and other conditions of work, the minority police organizations often allied themselves with community organizations to support certain social issues, as well as to provide themselves with a political base. Often black police associations would take an active role in minority recruitment, staffing recruitment tables at ball games or conducting training programs to prepare minority applicants for civil service examinations.[24]

In 1975 the Joint Center for Political Studies (JCPS) proposed that a meeting of black command officers (captains or above) be convened to consider ways of dealing with black-on-black crime. The Police Foundation, a nonprofit research organization that had been established by the Ford Foundation in 1970, agreed to support the venture. A major obstacle was the nonexistence of any list of who and where the black command officers were. Robert Lamb and Lee Brown, who had provided CRS assistance to hundreds of police departments around the country, were able to put together the nucleus of an invitation list and became central to the conference planning process. With other planners, they arranged for an informal meeting following the conference, so that the black command officers could consider ways of exercising their influence on a continuing basis. The outcome was a decision to form their own professional association, and thus the National Organization of Black Law Enforcement Executives (NOBLE) was born.

Police Use of Deadly Force

"Death by legal intervention" was the bloodless language used to count every time that a law enforcement officer killed a civilian. According to the National Bureau of Health Statistics, it happened on the average of 342 times a year for the nine-year period following 1968.[25] More than half of the victims were minorities—whose rate of death was nine times greater than that of whites.

Thus, in the decade following passage of the most important legislation in America's war for civil rights, the most symbolic evidence of unequal

24. Robert Lamb Jr., interview with the author.
25. Cynthia C. Sulton and Phillip Cooper, "Summary of Research on the Police Use of Deadly Force," in *A Community Concern: Police Use of Deadly Force* (Washington, D.C.: National Institute of Law Enforcement and Criminal Justice, Law Enforcement Assistance Administration, U.S. Department of Justice, 1979), 69.

justice was highly visible to residents of the nation's racial ghettos. Scientific studies were later to document this experience.

A 1975 study of the decade 1960–1970 showed that 30 percent of civilians killed by police were not involved in criminal activity. Of 1,500 police homicide incidents studied, in only three instances was a police officer convicted of a criminal offense. Black males were killed by police at a rate ten times higher than white males. The study found that between 1960 and 1972, police killed 1,899 black males and 1,914 white males in a population in which about 10 percent were black.[26]

Another study found that in 1978 excessive-use-of-force complaints from Hispanics rose 50 percent. Data from the twenty-four-year period from 1950 to 1973 showed an average of 245 persons killed by police in the years prior to 1967. For the seven years after 1967, the yearly average increased to 359. Of these, 50 percent were black.[27]

Throughout the midseventies, CRS saw police violence dominating its total caseload and exacerbating racial tension nationwide. Nothing was more offensive to a minority community than a wrongful death of one of its own at the hands of police and the subsequent failure of anyone to admit or redress the wrong. The ensuing controversies caused elevated levels of bitterness lasting for years.

By 1978 public protest rose to a crescendo. In Philadelphia, where more than four hundred brutality complaints had been filed against the police the previous year, crowds ranging from fifty to three thousand demonstrated repeatedly through the summer. In November a committee of the Pennsylvania legislature reported that police brutality in Philadelphia had, at times, "reached the level of homicidal violence." In August, in St. Petersburg, Florida, two hundred and fifty black residents took to the streets in a rock-and-bottle-throwing protest of the shooting death of a twenty-year-old black man at the hands of the police. In July, two thousand participated in a protest march in New York City over police violence.[28]

In 1978, Gilbert Pompa, who had been appointed CRS director by President Carter in 1976, acting on the recommendations of a staff study,[29] elevated police use of deadly force to the agency's top priority. Henceforth, instead of engaging only in case-by-case responses to deadly force con-

---

26. Paul Takagi, "Issues in the Study of Police Use of Deadly Force," August 1978.

27. Gilbert G. Pompa, at tenth annual conference of the National Association of Police Community Relations Officials, in LEAA *Newsletter* 8, no. 6 (June–July 1979).

28. Gilbert G. Pompa, "A Major and Most Pressing Concern," *Engage/Social Action,* November–December 1976, 10.

29. CRS staff memorandum to Gilbert G. Pompa from Robert Lamb Jr., "Excessive Force Task Force Memorandum," July 5, 1978.

troversies, CRS would also initiate programs at the national and regional levels to speed the alteration of police practice. Bob Lamb was the moving force bringing CRS to this initiative. It was his memorandum to Pompa setting forth the criticality of this issue that prompted the director to set up the special staff study group, led first by Ozell Sutton and later by Lamb.

Bits and pieces of his experience had led Lamb, over many years, to his understanding of the centrality of this issue to the quality of police-minority relations in America. He recalled the shock when, as an Atlantic City rookie policeman being trained by the New Jersey State Police, he heard the training officer advise the class always to carry a rusty knife or similar weapon, to be dropped at the scene of the crime, whenever it was necessary to shoot an unarmed person. He later learned that the use of the drop-weapon was not an unfamiliar practice in police work throughout the country. It made the justifiable homicide defense that much easier.[30]

In contributing to the movement to change police behavior with respect to the use of deadly force, CRS worked at both the "retail" and "wholesale" levels. The retail effort was the natural consequence of responding to individual outbreaks of racial conflict. This city-by-city negotiation of change in police practice gradually helped to elevate the national norm. At the same time, at the wholesale level, CRS worked with an array of organizations serving the police, religious, minority, and civil rights communities, to change state and local laws as well as police practice through advocacy and education.

A frequently used tool for starting local programs without waiting for a crisis to develop was the regional conference of public officials and minority leaders to address police problems. In Providence, Rhode Island, in October 1978, two hundred law enforcement officials, mayors, judges, and community leaders searched for solutions to problems of police-civilian violence and inadequate procedures for resolving citizen complaints against police. An area conference in St. Petersburg, Florida, drew a hundred and fifty participants to focus on problems of excessive police force and unequal employment opportunities in police departments.

In June 1978, CRS was invited to sponsor a workshop on police use of deadly force at the annual conference of NOBLE. This was followed by passage of a resolution by NOBLE calling for use of deadly force only to preserve the life of the officer or other persons. FBI director William Webster was the guest speaker at the conference. He publicly praised NOBLE's position on deadly force and announced that the protection-of-life-only policy had long been the rule in the FBI. Many advocates of change felt

30. Lamb interview.

that this public announcement of the FBI's restrictive shooting policy was an important contribution to the campaign to reform the practices of local police departments. On the following day, CRS held a meeting for representatives of a dozen national voluntary organizations who had been guests at the NOBLE conference, so that they could share their common concerns about police use of deadly force and seek opportunities for mutual assistance.

Soon other serious efforts were afoot to develop uniform standards on the use of deadly force to guide police jurisdictions throughout the country. NOBLE followed up by drafting and publicizing a model policy on the use of deadly force. The Police Foundation produced a model policy a year later. In 1980 CRS served on a Justice Department task force studying statutes and regulations governing police use of deadly force, preliminary to the development of federal recommendations of uniform standards to be proposed for use throughout the country.

CRS convened the National Consultation on Safety and Force in December 1979, cosponsored by the National Urban League and the League of United Latin American Citizens (LULAC). For three days, police chiefs, city officials, and minority leaders from throughout the country huddled with experts in law, sociology, and research to determine when and under what circumstances the police officer should use a gun. Input was drawn from statisticians, liability insurance specialists, civil rights experts, and police union executives. CRS, the Urban League, and LULAC followed up on the conference by launching joint local programs, in cooperation with the local police, designed to reduce the incidence of police use of deadly force. By the end of the year, nineteen such programs had been initiated. Of the thirty-one recommendations for national, state, and local action produced by the national consultation, the most vigorously favored called for "the Department of Justice to promulgate a model policy requiring that police use deadly force only to defend or protect human life, and that the policy be enforced through civil rights prosecutions."[31]

Using the experts who had appeared at the national consultation and others, CRS staged workshops on the topic at national organization conferences and other meetings around the country.

Municipal Liability Training

While the number of people killed by police did drop significantly, change would have come more slowly if it had depended on advocacy

31. CRS Annual Report, 1980, 11.

alone. In the late seventies there suddenly appeared a powerful incentive for municipalities to curb itchy trigger fingers. A court decision increasing municipal liability for employee misconduct provided an imperative to public officials to pay attention to a matter they had earlier found it convenient to neglect.

The U.S. Supreme Court, in 1978, in the case of *Monell v. Department of Social Services of the City of New York,* held that municipalities were no longer immune from civil suits under the post–Civil War civil rights legislation and could be sued directly for monetary, declaratory, and injunctive relief. In other words, the cities themselves could now be held liable for the misconduct of their employees.

Prior to 1978, civil suits charging police with civil rights abuses were discouraged by a formidable array of circumstances. The city itself could not be held liable, so only the police officer could be sued. Police officers are trained to be effective witnesses and to impress jurors. Jurors tend to respect police as protectors of the public. Since police officers have limited financial resources, any judgment against one was likely to be small and difficult to collect, making such cases unappealing to attorneys who would be dependent on contingency fees. Of the small number of lawsuits that were pursued, the overwhelming majority were decided in favor of the officer.

In the *Monell* case the court reversed an earlier ruling and held that a unit of general local government (such as a city, town, or county) did indeed meet the definition of a "person" under the law and thus was not immune from civil suit under the post–Civil War legislation giving bite to the Fourteenth Amendment. The court ruled that under certain conditions the municipality could be sued along with the public employee if the alleged conduct was consistent with the policy or custom of the agency involved.

That change suddenly gave the plaintiff access to the deep pockets of local government. Once the municipality became the defendant, a change occurred in the jury's perspective. Local government is a less sympathetic and less trusted defendant than the individual officer; besides, the city has plenty of money—or so the juries think.

Another factor also came into play that broke new ground for the admission of incriminating evidence that had formerly been banned. In the past, when the individual officer was sued, actions of other officers were deemed irrelevant and inadmissable as evidence. Following *Monell,* however, the pattern of police practice became highly relevant in order to establish whether or not the alleged act was consistent with custom in that department. The alleged misconduct of fellow officers could now be paraded before the jury.

One other new development contributed to the sudden increase in municipal liability litigation. The costs of suing City Hall were no longer a deterrent to plaintiffs. The number of lawyers available to take police misconduct cases on a contingency basis suddenly mushroomed. The Civil Rights Attorney Fees Awards Act of 1976 had decreed that in all civil rights cases, if the plaintiff prevailed, attorneys' fees could be assessed against the defendant local government. Suddenly the increase in lawsuits, and in the size of jury awards and settlements, became a significant drain on the coffers of hard-pressed local governments.

In 1981, more than thirty-five thousand lawsuits were filed under the *Monell* decision. The majority involved allegations of police brutality and excessive use of force. Many cities were badly bruised.[32]

The city of Detroit, with one $12 million judgment against it, had a total of ten cases with judgments over $1 million each. In another major city, more than one hundred lawsuits were filed in 1980–1981 against the police department and its officers. Twenty-seven involved the use of force or police brutality. Of twelve cases that went to trial in that period, jury verdicts favored the plaintiffs in nine instances. When Washington, D.C., decided it might be cheaper to settle cases rather than go to trial, it set a limit of $10,000 per case. The city soon had to remove the limit as defendants opted for the far more generous jury awards. In 1982 Washington spent a total of $4.1 million in out-of-court settlements—double the previous year. In that same year San Francisco paid out $6.5 million.

The skyrocketing of claims, awards, and settlements hit municipalities in other ways.[33] Legal costs to defend suits escalated as law departments were enlarged and/or outside counsel had to be engaged. The cost of liability insurance went sky-high. Some jurisdictions could not find coverage, or could not afford it. More cities turned to self-insurance. Others experimented with cooperative insurance pools in which several jurisdictions banded together for self-insurance.[34]

To protect their treasuries from this ravaging attack, cities resorted to two strategies. The first was to reduce the number of suits for misconduct

32. Bertram Levine, Draft of Remarks on Municipal Liability, prepared for CRS-sponsored symposium of Cape Cod police executives, January 27, 1983.

33. Police brutality was by no means the only offense bringing the city within the reach of *Monell* type cases. The damage resulting from high-speed chases by police also engendered claims against local government, as did the alleged missteps of municipal departments other than the police. Nevertheless, the cases resulting from police use of deadly force were the most visible and the most costly.

34. "CRS Activity Regarding Consequences of Municipal Civil Liability," staff memorandum to Administration of Justice Team from Howard P. Carrington, national administration of justice specialist, February 17, 1983, 5.

by reducing the instances of officer misconduct. The second was to reduce the losses resulting from the remaining suits by showing documented records of training, policies, and supervision that might convince a jury that inappropriate conduct was not consistent with department policy or custom. Both strategies persuaded many cities to ask CRS to help with training their police. If not for the fiscal consequences of the *Monell* case, CRS assistance would have been far less in demand.

CRS was quick to see the *Monell* decision as the long-sought imperative needed to spur cities to pay attention to problems of excessive use of police force. To mayors, city councils, and police chiefs, CRS presented the pocketbook incentive. In the Dallas regional office John Perez,[35] who had succeeded Moe Ortiz as CRS's southwest regional director, saw an opportunity to spread the gospel of responsible use of police force more rapidly than through crisis assistance to one city at a time. He developed a training format that enabled CRS to carry the message of *Monell* to most police jurisdictions in Texas, and later to other states in the region, including Arkansas, Oklahoma, Louisiana, and New Mexico.

The first step of this approach was to persuade a police chief to accept a CRS-conducted workshop on *Monell* for his top staff and commanders. This would provide the foot in the door for the second and third steps. The second would be a review and, where necessary, a revision of department policies regarding police use of force. The third would be a review and revision of training and supervision practices in order to improve police performance. CRS would then make itself available to assist with follow-up training and policy refinement. Generally, the chief would be encouraged to invite neighboring chiefs to the workshop, thus extending the reach of the CRS message to smaller departments in the area.

The most enthusiastic allies supporting CRS's efforts on municipal liability were district attorneys, who had the hated responsibility of prosecuting police charged with unlawful violence, and city attorneys, who had to defend municipalities against civil suits for officer misconduct. Perez enlisted the city attorneys of six of Texas's largest cities to help make a training video. The six came together as a panel, with CRS general counsel Gail Padgett as moderator, to spend six hours sharing their experiences and concerns about the price cities had to pay because individual officers, and sometimes their supervisors, "screwed up." The videotapes of the seminar,

35. Perez, who had come to CRS after serving San Antonio as a police officer and then as a schoolteacher, was a vigorous advocate of police training. But he was wedded to the CRS doctrine that training was only one leg of a three-legged stool; it was useless without the other legs: written policies that insisted on correct performance, and supervision that assured faithful implementation.

boiled down and edited into five fifteen-minute segments, proved to be persuasive tools inducing police and their commanders to pay more attention to training in an area of police behavior too long ignored.

By 1983 CRS was offering the training to police agencies across the country. In New England, CRS reached out to many departments through areawide meetings convened by local chiefs. In Pennsylvania, the Pennsylvania Association of Chiefs of Police provided the auspices. In Louisiana, the State Police Academy offered the training to the fifty-two local police academy directors who had responsibility for training 90 percent of the state's law enforcement recruits.

Conclusion

The change in police practice with respect to the use of deadly force against minorities was the single most important factor in the revolutionary transition that took place within the broader field of police-minority relations. CRS was only one of many agents and influences generating this transformation, but this is one of the few areas of broad social change on which the footprints of CRS can be so clearly identified.

Other agents for change included the Law Enforcement Assistance Administration (LEAA) of the Justice Department, and particularly its National Minority Advisory Council on Criminal Justice, which helped to impart direction and substance to LEAA's grants addressed to community relations and problems of inner-city policing in general. Another forceful influence leading to change in police practices was the Police Foundation. It was originally headed by Patrick V. Murphy, a former director of LEAA.[36]

By 1980 CRS's director, Gilbert Pompa, was able to tell Congress that over a ten-year period, the annual rate at which minorities had died at the hands of law enforcement personnel had been cut by better than 50 percent. From 1970 to 1979, the annual total of all killings by police had gradually come down from 354 to 170. The total number of Caucasians killed had remained constant; the reduction had been mostly among minorities.[37]

36. One of America's most distinguished law enforcement executives, Murphy, who rose through the ranks of New York City's police department, also served as chief of police in Syracuse, New York, as public safety commissioner in Washington D.C., and as police commissioner in New York City.

37. A definitive study covering this ground for the fifteen-year period 1970–1984, conducted for the Crime Control Institute by Lawrence W. Sherman, Ellen G. Cohn, et al., and published in 1986, reported among its findings: "At least 353 citizens were killed by police in fifty cities in 1971; only 172 were killed in 1984. . . . Citizen killings of police in those cities fell by two-thirds in the same fifteen-year period."

While reluctant to claim credit publicly for its contribution to social change that stemmed from a host of inordinately complex interactions of events and circumstance, CRS believed that with respect to patterns in police use of deadly force, it had to be recognized as a major player. Since the early seventies CRS had been the loudest and most insistent drum beater for the cause of ending excessive use of force by police. At the retail level, in hundreds of communities where police abusiveness had triggered community disruptions, CRS's peace efforts not only helped to encourage improved practice; they also fertilized the soil for change by pounding away at the message that modern police management was capable of producing better policies, conducting better training, and providing better supervision of patrol practices, thus reducing the amount of unnecessary force and producing higher levels of police-minority cooperation. At the same time, CRS's technical assistance to minority organizations and other advocate groups at local and national levels led to the demand for higher levels of police performance all over the country.

By 1989, there were signs that progress in lowering fatalities as a result of police encounters was eroding, a victim of the drug-induced increase of inner-city violence. Nevertheless, by that time the nature of community relations problems in the inner city had changed. Police use of deadly force was no longer seen routinely by residents as evidence of brutal disdain of minority life. Although questionable shootings still occurred, and could still trigger community rage, there was a greater willingness to give police the benefit of the doubt. The impact of the view of the police as a brutal oppressor had been downgraded from a hurricane to a tropical storm—or perhaps gale-force winds.

Decreased alienation between police and minorities resulted from many factors, including increased minority political power, the growing numbers of minority elected officials, including mayors, the growing number of minority police officers, including chiefs, and significant reductions in the amount and intensity of police discourtesy and harassing police practices. Other markers of change included the termination of the use of degrading language by police; the diminution of aggressive patrol practices that gave rise to the ghetto perception of police as "an army of occupation"; the advent of more equal opportunity in police employment and the rise of minorities to positions of command; improved delivery of police services to minority neighborhoods; greater accountability for acts of police brutality; increased consultation and collaboration between the police and the minority community on problems of public safety; and new and more restrictive rules governing police use of deadly force.

Mostly the change resulted because minority communities refused to accept unequal treatment and because their insistent protests and demands for fairness focused public attention on the need for police reform. Improvement has come in every aspect of police-minority interaction, and in every case it resulted from community-by-community protest and issue-by-issue negotiation.

CRS bore close witness to how the struggle of minorities for equal treatment helped to bring greater enlightenment to the police profession. While police work in 1989 still fell short of delivering 100 cents on the dollar of equal justice, monumental progress had been made in the quarter century following passage of the Civil Rights Act and the creation of the Community Relations Service in 1964.

Seven

Education amid Turmoil

On September 12, 1974, thousands of angry whites took to the streets of Boston in an effort to terrify and turn back black students being bused to newly assigned schools. Adults, carrying protest signs of the "nigger-go-home" type, and children, many in Ku Klux Klan outfits, screamed epithets as the yellow buses, some with stone-shattered windows, pulled up to the gates of South Boston High School. Police cordoning off the roadways had difficulty holding back the surging crowds. From the stoops of the row houses lining nearby streets, second-, third-, and fourth-generation home owners, having been assured by their political leaders for a decade that this day would never come, jeered the passing buses.

Object Lesson in Boston

After ten years of successful resistance to the state law requiring school desegregation, Boston had been sued in federal court by the local NAACP, and now, in the ruling of Judge W. Arthur Garrity, it found a judgment it could no longer refuse, evade, or defer.

On the opening day of school, CRS conciliators, assembled at the last minute from other assignments around the country, were paired with school-board employees in radio-equipped cars that sped from one crisis site to another to help defuse the confrontations. Lack of adequate preparation had placed Boston—and CRS—behind the violence curve, requiring a long and costly game of catch-up.

In 1974 CRS was still reeling under the previous year's two-thirds cut in staff. Adjusting to the demands of the budget masters that it cut preventive work and focus on crisis response, the agency had been slow to offer assistance to Boston. Not until the weekend before the buses were to roll did an emergency team of a dozen conciliators arrive to reinforce the small regional staff based in Boston.

So highly charged was the hatred that the emergency team would not be fully disbanded until December; so deeply imbedded were the roots of discord that six years would pass before the return of community stability would permit CRS to close the case. Boston would prove to be America's high-water mark of violent resistance to school busing as a means of desegregation. The nation and the world were scandalized that this cradle of American civilization and culture had fallen victim to the naked hatred and unrestrained passions of the mob. From its efforts to help restore racial harmony in Boston, CRS was able to sharpen the techniques and strategies that, in the succeeding years, it shared with scores of urban school districts throughout the country. For all of them, the watchword would be, "Let's not have another Boston."

Community Conflict and School Desegregation

Local refusal to implement the Supreme Court's 1954 school desegregation requirements had produced firestorms of community controversy throughout the nation for two decades. Throughout the South, under the banner of "massive resistance," state and local governments, private and religious organizations, newspapers and broadcast media linked arms in a die-hard defense of racially separate schooling. The region's leading citizens mobilized for resistance through newly formed White Citizens Councils, while many of the hoi polloi rallied behind the banners of a resurgent Ku Klux Klan, which again lighted the fires of terror and intimidation. In many jurisdictions private academies were formed for the education of white children, and some school districts even closed their schools, leaving black children and some whites with no education whatsoever, while most white families managed some private arrangement. Some states pursued the spurious legal doctrine of interposition in a vain attempt to shield local districts from the reach of federal courts.

Court decisions and federal and state civil rights legislation did not, of themselves, bring Jim Crow schooling to an end. They only established the legal requirements—with which relatively few school jurisdictions voluntarily complied. In most instances change would require some specific act of enforcement. Enforcement mechanisms included the Civil Rights Division of the Justice Department, the U.S. Office of Education, state enforcement bodies, and state and local courts. But many fewer changes would have resulted had it not been for specific demands being made by local African American or other minority groups. These demands—and resistance to them—led not only to additional lawsuits and administrative complaints but also to a plethora of petitions, protests, rancor, rage, confrontations, violence, and negotiations.

From this welter of acrimony arose hundreds of requests for CRS assistance. Seventy-seven desegregation conflicts were presented to CRS in its first year—fifty-two in the South.[1] The number grew steadily. Year after year education cases would make up one-quarter to one-third of the entire workload of the CRS conciliators.

At first the focus was on the rural South, where the major issue was unification of the now illegal dual school systems. Later on, the battlelines moved to northern communities, where the de facto segregation experienced by racial minorities was also being found by the courts to be the result of government support and contrivance and therefore beyond the pale of constitutional requirements. By the time CRS was drawn into the volatile conflicts of desegregation in northern cities in the early seventies, it had the experience of more than a thousand school cases under its belt.

Helping Communities Adjust to Change

It was violence and the fear of violence that summoned CRS into most of its early desegregation cases, rather than education issues per se. The search for peaceful resolutions, however, often extended into other matters because the parties in conflict were the same city officials and the same minority community leaders who were also contesting issues of voting rights, fair employment practices, and equal justice. The CRS-negotiated settlements generally focused on solving those issues that would permit the restoration of community stability. A CRS goal in all cases, though not always achieved, was not only to resolve the issues immediately at hand but also to leave the adversaries better disposed to negotiate the many issues remaining between them.

The intensity and effectiveness of CRS intervention varied from school district to school district, depending on the level of tension, the needs of

1. CRS Annual Report, 1965, 23.

the district, and the opportunities for being useful. Conflict mediation and prevention were only half the job. Serving as a resource for technical proficiency was the other. Experience had shown CRS that conflict feeds on confusion, and a poorly designed desegregation plan or a badly managed school invites disaster. CRS helped local officials find the experts—and the funds to pay them—for designing desegregation plans and training personnel, for helping police improve proficiency in crowd control, for enlisting the support of opinion molders, and for gaining minority input in the planning process. CRS often worked in partnership with the desegregation assistance centers established and funded by the U.S. Office of Education at various universities to provide expertise for local school districts. In this symbiotic relationship, the assistance centers would often give priority to situations identified as critical by CRS and would accept CRS's guidance as to local sources of information that should be consulted to assure that the desegregation planning process did not subordinate minority interests. CRS also helped the centers by identifying qualified minority educators to work as desegregation consultants.

The number of new education cases in the South suddenly accelerated in 1970 when the federal enforcement effort moved into higher gear. The Civil Rights Act of 1964 had empowered two federal agencies to enforce school desegregation. The Justice Department's Civil Rights Division was authorized to accept complaints and sue segregated school systems to compel compliance. The Department of Health, Education, and Welfare (HEW), through its Office of Education, was required to withhold federal funding from segregated school districts. Nevertheless, foot-dragging by resistant school systems had been allowed to slow these enforcement programs to a crawl. According to the Southern Education Reporting Service, the number of Negro children in segregated schools in the South in 1966 was greater than it had been at the time of the *Brown* decision in 1954.[2]

On October 29, 1969, a unanimous Supreme Court decision changed the time frame for desegregation from the "with all deliberate speed" of the 1955 decision to a doctrine requiring school districts to end segregation "at once."[3] The effect of that decision, which had been specifically directed at thirty-three school districts in Mississippi, was to impel the Nixon administration to pursue enforcement with greater urgency. The decree

2. Community Relation Service, U.S. Department of Justice, "Activities Related to the Desegregation of Public Schools," August 15, 1970, February 15, 1971.
3. *Alexander v. Holmes,* 396 U.S. 19 (1969).

was the first major decision handed down by the court under Warren Burger, President Nixon's newly appointed chief justice. The *New York Times* called it a "stinging setback for the administration," whose Justice Department had argued that delays were permissible. The administration immediately pledged to support the decision.[4]

Fearful of the consternation that might result from a highly energized federal push all across the South to terminate segregation "at once," the administration directed CRS to back up the Justice Department and HEW enforcement blitz with a program to reduce the likelihood of violent resistance. CRS was provided with special funding to reinforce its field staff. Aided by the infusion of forty-seven specially trained temporary conciliators, CRS was able to give assistance in 492 communities in nine states between August 1970 and February 1971.

The level of help varied from marginal to critical, depending on an assessment of the need and the chances of making a difference in an individual school district. A record of the program shows that its mediators drew on the full repertoire of CRS approaches and techniques. They worked in the school systems and in the communities. The need to help establish or improve interracial communication was basic. Setting up biracial committees and helping them to communicate and to overcome specific impasses was common. Help was given for the design and operation of rumor control programs and student grievance mechanisms. Schools were helped in improving the fairness of disciplinary systems, student government, and extracurricular programs. Campaigns were launched for the elimination of provocative racial symbols and derogatory language. Help was provided to school systems for the design of in-service training in race relations and conflict management for school personnel and for the drafting of proposals for emergency federal funding for special desegregation-related programs.

In the broader community, efforts were made through special media projects, and in meetings with even the most hostile community groups, to explain the law, the court decisions, and the special programs the federal government was offering to help make desegregation work. Parent associations were given assistance in increasing interracial cooperation. Minority groups received training in how to get their story told more effectively through the media. Police departments were helped with recruiting minorities and establishing police-community relations programs. Civic and business leaders were encouraged to exert their influence so that desegregation would take place without violence. In not a single instance

4. *New York Times,* October 31, 1969.

was this special conflict prevention effort marred by a report of significant disorderly resistance.[5]

Three years later, in 1973, CRS was again enlisted for a similar special conflict prevention effort when U.S. District Court Judge John H. Pratt found a number of southern school districts not in compliance and ordered HEW to step up its compliance efforts even further. Within four years of the decision requiring the end to desegregation "at once," 46 percent of black children in the eleven southern states were attending mostly white schools.

Aided by its experience in helping southern cities to desegregate peacefully, CRS, in the midseventies, exerted a major influence on the efforts of northern cities to forestall disruption of their efforts to implement desegregation plans.

CRS and the U.S. District Court

When the Supreme Court outlawed school desegregation in 1954–1955, no thoughtful observer expected that the necessary alterations would take place without major resistance. The pervasive changes required in school operations and relationships would present difficulties even in the most cooperative school districts. Resistant school systems would be able to find a hundred ways to thwart the court's decision by making sure that desegregation would not work well. Moreover, citizen action also could frustrate a desegregation order if student boycotts, intimidation-induced absences, and rancor inside the schoolhouse destroyed the atmosphere necessary for learning. The Supreme Court expected, therefore, that lower court judges, in ruling on desegregation cases, might have to continue their jurisdiction throughout the implementation process.

Resistance to the courts' decisions could take many forms, including inadequate planning, foot-dragging in implementation, and slipshod supervision, as well as intimidation and street violence. A number of American cities found themselves beset by the intervention of a federal judge not only in the management of their school systems but in the operations of police agencies as well, where disorder in the streets threatened the implementation of court decisions.

Nowhere did the reach of the court appear more assertive or longer lasting than in Boston. According to Martin Walsh, the CRS regional di-

5. CRS Annual Report, 1971, 10, 11.

rector who worked closely with the judge for many years, the reason was that in no other city was the resistance so great and so persistent. Walsh noted that every time the judge had been charged with being overly intrusive, his position had been confirmed by the Court of Appeals, and every effort to gain review by the U.S. Supreme Court had been denied.[6]

A special CRS role in a score of cities where the desegregation fight was most troublesome began in the seventies when U.S. district court judges sought CRS assistance to prevent their orders from being vitiated by community resistance. In many of these cities the CRS role was written into the court order. Judge Garrity, in Boston, was the first to invoke this groundbreaking partnership.

Ed McClure, a CRS conciliator covering Boston, called upon the judge in August 1974 to inform him of the availability of CRS to negotiate in situations of community conflict and to assist in solving racial problems from the street level up. Garrity immediately saw an ally for dealing with what he feared might be one of the toughest parts of his case—how to keep violence from escalating, and how to keep interracial animosity from sabotaging the quality of desegregated education.

CRS's director, Ben Holman, while welcoming the opportunity to work with the court, was concerned about the impact such a relationship might have on CRS's independence and on its reputation as an impartial troubleshooter. He had to make sure that the embrace would not develop into a bear hug. He therefore assigned CRS's general counsel, Hayden Gregory, to head the emergency team to be sent to Boston to contend with any disruptions surrounding the opening day of a desegregated school system. Gregory worked with the judge to establish appropriate guidelines to govern a continuing relationship.

Both Garrity and Gregory recognized that a collaborative relationship between CRS and the court would require that they walk a delicate line. CRS recognized that in some ways its effectiveness would be enhanced by evidence of the respect in which the court held its advice, as well as by its ability to informally interpret the court's thinking to the community. At the same time it was important that CRS, as an independent and objective mediator, should not be seen as subservient to, or a creature of, the court. With city hall as well as the school committee coming under the court order, CRS held a level of clout that had to be used with the utmost circumspection lest it destroy the agency's credibility as an objective negotiator of voluntary agreements.

6. Martin Walsh, interview with the author.

High among Garrity's concerns was a need to encourage the constructive elements among the Boston populace to serve as a counterweight to the wrecking crews. To do this, he would have to understand the views and feelings of key groups and their leaders throughout the city. He hoped that CRS might provide an effective and appropriate channel of communication by which this process could be encouraged. Garrity amended his desegregation order to request CRS's assistance and to require the parties to cooperate with CRS's efforts to harmonize relationships so that desegregation could go forward with a minimum of turmoil.

In the ensuing years U.S. district courts in more than a score of cases were guided by Garrity's lead in reaching out for CRS support. In more than a dozen instances the dictum to cooperate with CRS was written into the court order.

School Desegregation in Boston

By 1974 the opposition to desegregation in Boston had been building for ten years. A generation of political leaders had won their spurs by assaulting the 1965 Racial Imbalance Act of the state legislature, which stated that thenceforth all public schools were prohibited from being more than 50 percent black. But passage of the law did not guarantee its enforcement, and efforts to ignore or repeal the law sparked legal and political battles throughout the state.

In Boston, grassroots opposition organizations had been born and had grown large by using the issue as a litmus test for office seekers for every position on the ballot. Antisegregation sentiment had provided the springboard for every victorious candidate in Boston's local elections, including those for the school committee. It had propelled into prominence City Councilperson Louise Day Hicks and School Committee Chairman John Kerrigan. Hicks, who had led ROAR (Restore Our Alienated Rights), a citywide resistance group rooted in her South Boston power base, had become the archetype of a new breed of local kingmakers. Political pressure had grown so great that even Governor Francis Sargent, a traditional supporter of desegregation, had recently abandoned his support of the state's Racial Imbalance Act.

In March 1973, the Boston NAACP filed suit in federal court seeking an end to segregated schools. In his June 21, 1974, ruling, Judge W. Arthur Garrity Jr. found that the Boston School Committee had deliberately carried out "a systematic program of segregation affecting the city's students, teachers and school facilities, and [had] intentionally brought about and maintain a dual school system." He ordered it to use all legal means, including busing, to secure the rights of the plaintiffs.[7]

Garrity specified that, as the first phase of its remedy, the city must implement an already ordered state plan for the one-third-black ninety-six-thousand-student school system. The state plan called for reduction of the number of all-black schools from sixty-eight to forty-four, with the number of black students in such schools reduced from twenty-six thousand to less than ten thousand. This change would add six thousand to the number of Negro and white students already being bused, bringing the total to thirty thousand. Judge Garrity's order noted that this first phase of the remedy would have to be followed by a second phase, which the school committee would prepare for his approval for the following year.[8]

Evidence of the passion that was to fuel violent resistance to the Boston busing plan was revealed throughout the spring and summer. In March, Boston's mayor, Kevin White, was jeered as he led the St. Patrick's Day parade because his opposition to desegregation had been no more than moderate. In April, thousands of parents and schoolchildren marched on the Massachusetts State House to protest a state court order that Boston comply with the state's racial imbalance law, and the legislature began hearings on a proposal to repeal that law. In May, in a politically motivated nonbinding referendum, Boston citizens voted fifteen-to-one against busing to achieve integration. In September, Senator Edward Kennedy was driven from the platform at an antibusing rally under a storm of catcalls, a shower of eggs and tomatoes, and the shattering of plate-glass windows.

As the day of desegregation approached, those who had been stirring the kettle of passion suddenly became fearful of the possible consequences of their activity. They issued public statements appealing for the safety of the schoolchildren. However, Mayor White was alone among Boston's elected officials in calling for compliance with the court's order. As a defendant in the case, and as the city's executive officer directly subject to Judge Garrity's ruling, he could do no less. But his situation was far more complicated. As a young, vigorous, ambitious mayor of a major city, with liberal credentials, he was seen by many as a rising star on the national political stage. He was among those whose names were being mentioned as vice presidential possibilities for the Democratic Party in 1976. He could not oppose desegregation without damaging his national reputation; he

7. *New York Times,* June 22, 1974.
8. Ibid.

could not support it without risking the loss of his political launching pad in Boston. The tightrope he had walked successfully thus far was becoming increasingly precarious.[9]

The city agencies, under the mayor's leadership, had undertaken frenetic measures to keep the city calm. Communication centers had been established to coordinate between the school system and police and fire agencies, youth workers, and rumor-control centers. Church and civic volunteers had been mobilized to serve as safety monitors on streets, buses, and school grounds. The mayor spoke on television, sympathizing with the distress felt by white parents but emphasizing the paramount responsibility of complying with the law.

Even though the police department was prepared to escort buses and to protect bus routes and school areas, spokesmen for the police union questioned the mayor's authority to require officers to arrest protesters. To remove any and all uncertainty as to the city's will to enforce the law, Judge Garrity found it necessary—on the day before schools were to open— to issue an order directing Boston's police to arrest anyone blocking school doorways or interfering with the implementation of the desegregation plan.

The focus of attention was on South Boston High School, the physical and emotional landmark for generations of Boston's largely working-class Irish community. "Southie," everyone knew, would be the hotbed of resistance. Even though its educational credentials left much to be desired,[10] the high school was the crown jewel of a lily-white neighborhood, whose families had attended it for many generations.

Southie had been paired for desegregation purposes with newly established Roxbury High. The two high schools and their respective feeder schools had been merged into a single district, with racial balance in each school to be achieved by busing some blacks from Roxbury to South Boston and some whites from Southie to Roxbury. Similar cross-racial pairings had been accomplished with other neighborhoods, such as that between white, middle-class Hyde Park and the black Mattapan neighborhood.

On opening day crowds gathered on the streets of South Boston and along bus routes across the city as early as 7:00 a.m., an hour before school began. Buses were greeted with boos and curses. Anti-Negro graffiti had been painted and then only partially obliterated from South Boston High's doors.

9. *New York Times,* April 14, 1974.
10. Because the high school population of the South Boston neighborhood was "skimmed" by Boston's three elite "exam schools" and a highly desired parochial school system, Southie qualified few students for college, only three having made the grade in the previous year.

Several black students and a bus monitor were hurt by flying glass from the windows of three of the many buses that had been stoned, and policemen had been hit by bottles. At the end of the day black students were besieged at Southie, and it took three escorted patrol wagons to remove them safely. Five white youths had been arrested on disorderly conduct charges. Fear of greater violence the next day prompted the mayor to issue orders barring crowds and ordering police to arrest unauthorized gatherings of three or more in the troubled neighborhoods.

The fires of resistance continued to be stoked by political leaders. Having failed to stop the desegregation plan from going into effect, the opponents seemed determined to keep it from working. The school committee appealed the court order; City Councilperson Hicks and State Senator Bulger issued a public statement criticizing police efforts to control the mobs, which they called a "violent police siege." Other foes of busing pursued a course of provocative protest and a school boycott to prove that desegregation would not produce effective education for Boston's children. Hostile crowds at schools and along bus routes prompted some black parents to keep their children home. Those who ran the gauntlet arrived at their classrooms fearful and hostile. While many white parents recognized the futility of a boycott, others remained responsive to the continuing protests of resistance leaders.

Interracial fear and loathing blanketed the city. Disruption and reduced attendance were intertwined. Protest and disorder in the streets led to disorder in the schools; violence in one school led to increased absences throughout the city. It took more than three months before most of Boston's classrooms could claim a stable attendance in an environment in which educational progress could take place.

Those who wanted desegregation to work—the minority community, Judge Garrity, the professional leaders of the school system, as well as CRS—found that their immediate objectives were determined, in part, by the tactics of the opposition. Two priorities became uppermost: to restore attendance to normal as soon as possible, and to douse the fires of disruption that led to fear and hostility in the classroom.

Citywide attendance on opening day was one-third less than usual, reflecting the fears of black parents and calls for a white boycott. At Southie, only 40 of the assigned 940 blacks appeared and only 25 of the 1,600 whites. While attendance rose gradually, it fell off repeatedly as a succession of disruptive acts by desegregation opponents fueled successive cycles of confrontations, violence, and absenteeism.[11]

11. *New York Times Index*, 1974, 660–64.

September 17. A massive police presence brings calm to South Boston where four buses bring 150 black students. Only 60 whites attend. Citywide attendance is 73 percent.

September 18. An interracial fight breaks out at Roslindale High School.

September 19. Four students are injured in an interracial fight at Hyde Park High School. School is closed while parents and students attend meetings to resolve problems.

September 20. Two buses are stoned, there are seven arrests, and attendance is down to 69 percent following a high of 76 percent the day before.

September 21. Police are called to a housing project near South Boston when three hundred gather in the streets. Crowds try to prevent distribution of the Sunday edition of the *Boston Globe.*

September 23. Four hundred walk out of Charlestown High, protesting the desegregation plan, which won't affect them until the next September.

September 30. Pro- and antibusing rallies take place.

October 1. Eighty percent attendance is the highest since school opened.

October 2. Repeated scuffles between white and black students at South Boston High are broken up by police, with nine arrests. Attendance is set back.

October 5. Five thousand protesters march through South Boston, behind the banners of the Home and School Association, including members of the school committee, city council, and state legislature. Order is kept by massed police forces. Four young men are treated at local hospitals after a run-in with a police tactical patrol. Judge Garrity's home is picketed. Two hundred and fifty gather in front of Cardinal Madeiros's house to protest his statement that parochial schools will not be a haven for those fleeing desegregation. A thousand people in a four-hundred-car motorcade demonstrate at police headquarters demanding the removal of the tactical patrol force from South Boston and its replacement with local police.

October 7. A black man is beaten by a crowd in South Boston.

October 8. There is widespread stoning of cars with white riders by youths in Roxbury. The neighborhood previously had been quiet.[12]

---

12. Up to that time the black neighborhoods had been models of physical safety for all—in contrast to the intimidating climate faced by black children in white neighborhoods. The black community had mobilized to assure an atmosphere of welcome

Oct. 9. Judge Garrity refuses Mayor White's request for U.S. marshals to reinforce police in view of the growing violence. The judge cites local and state responsibility. White confers with Governor Sargent, who assigns 425 Metropolitan and State Police to help secure the streets of South Boston.

Violence waxed and waned through November but crescendoed in early December with a series of student fights at South Boston High—mostly between girls. White students had to be sent home early one day after they marched through the halls shouting antiblack epithets. After that, a black girl was struck in the head with a padlock, requiring six stitches. The next day Michael Faith, a white student, was stabbed by a fifteen-year-old black youth.

CRS conciliator Silke Hansen was on her daily tour of Southie when the knifing occurred. She witnessed the outrage of white students mounting to a boil as groups bent on retaliation began to tour the halls. On more than one occasion she found herself trying to reason with a white group, giving their intended prey time to take off. Eventually most of the blacks took refuge in a few classrooms, where teachers locked the doors against marauding white students.

Schools in the South Boston–Roxbury cluster were dismissed early, but 135 black students were besieged in Southie by a crowd of a thousand angry whites. Buses trying to approach the school to evacuate the black students were turned back by the human wall. Mounted and riot-clad police repeatedly moved to force the crowd back, only to have it re-form. Seven residents and three policemen were treated in city hospitals. Two parked police cruisers were demolished and one was overturned. Finally, the mob was distracted by a diversionary massing of buses and police at the main gate while the black students were led out a rear door and down back streets to an alternate set of buses.[13]

Fearful that the knifing incident would reawaken the white boycott of South Boston High, school authorities decided on Friday afternoon to re-

---

for the newly transferred white students and to guarantee secure streets in the Negro neighborhoods. The October 8 incidents were the lone exception.

Boston's black community had for twenty years sponsored—either by itself or on an interracial basis—a variety of projects to improve the education of its children, including school boycotts, experimental "freedom schools," a program known as "operation exodus" in which the black community raised money to pay for buses to take children to white schools under an open enrollment policy, and the Metco program by which black students were voluntarily bused to suburban schools.

13. Silke Hansen, interview with the author.

assure parents by installing airport type walk-through metal detectors, and to have them in place at the opening of school Monday morning. CRS was called upon to make the arrangements. A request to Logan Airport revealed that the airlines, not the airport, were responsible for security at the gates and that the equipment was the property of the airlines. No airline at Logan had equipment to spare. The CRS team enlisted the co-operation of the Federal Aviation Administration, which located two available devices at the headquarters of United Airlines in Seattle. Shipped on the first available plane, they were installed at Southie by United technicians Sunday afternoon.

On December 15 civil rights forces staged a counterdemonstration to protest the antibusing violence, with five thousand participants coming from cities across the country, drawn from civil rights organizations as well as a variety of left-wing activist groups. They clashed briefly with the police tactical patrol, which turned them back with the same impartial rigidity it maintained against the antibusing mobs. The following day six thousand antibusers countered with a march of their own.

On December 19, the U.S. Court of Appeals upheld Judge Garrity's desegregation ruling in a strongly worded decision. School Committee Chair John J. Kerrigan announced that the committee would appeal to the U.S. Supreme Court.

The primary objective of the CRS team during those months of disarray had been to help the city and school system regain stability in the classrooms and on the streets. This required effort at two levels: (1) working with public officials and leaders in the private sector to restore a climate of civility and respect for the law within the city at large; (2) monitoring developments in schools and neighborhoods and consulting with police and school officials on tactics and strategies of conflict management, using direct intervention to conciliate confrontations as they arose.

Day-to-day tasks included advising school and police officials and sometimes mediating between the two; struggling to bring coherence to the scores of civic volunteers representing church groups, youth guidance counselors, social agencies, and civil rights groups who patrolled the streets and schoolyards offering help and counseling restraint to students, parents, and local residents; and emergency intervention in school management problems (such as expediting priority repair of a school intercom system to assist a hapless principal who, strangled in red tape, was struggling to manage a distressed school without basic communications). Conciliators helped to find lost school buses to allay mounting parental panic and suggested revised bus routes and schedules to reduce danger. In one school cafeteria, where a black girl seized a kitchen knife to hold off her tormentors, a CRS conciliator calmed the girl, persuaded her to surrender her weapon, and dispersed the crowd, permitting order to be restored. In another instance a conciliator negotiated a modus vivendi between a warring principal and his faculty senate, to restore the school's capability for sensible management. Teachers who had abandoned responsibility for order in the halls to the newly recruited community monitors had to be drawn back to that duty. Guidelines for when police should enter and leave school premises had to be negotiated between school and police leaders. School officials were helped to define and execute training programs for school personnel ranging from teachers to cafeteria workers to the secretaries who fielded calls from anxious parents.[14]

In the absence of any significant effort by the school system to establish racial harmony and cooperation in the school community, Judge Garrity took matters into his own hands. Following the stabbing of Michael Faith at South Boston High School, the judge decreed that a monitoring program be established to measure tension levels and identify problems at their early stages. CRS was asked to design the program and train and supervise the volunteer monitors. The judge later extended the monitoring system to other schools. In October he ordered the establishment of interracial parent councils in all schools with a mixed student population. He also required the high schools to establish interracial student councils. At the judge's request, CRS undertook the responsibility of coordinating the organization and operation of these councils.

"The councils created a means of communicating among students, parents, teachers and administrators regarding solutions to racial problems. Judge Garrity made it clear that they should not shoulder the major responsibility for racial harmony and school safety. The intent was that by meeting regularly to talk only about problems, parents and students of one race could come to understand the concerns of the other."[15]

By the second semester of the school year a semblance of learning had returned to Boston schools, but the desegregation process had only begun, and racial harmony was still beyond the city's grasp. CRS remained closely involved in part because of its special relationship as a community relations consultant to the court. In addition, racial tensions in the schools increased the intergroup friction in all facets of community life. The case remained active for the next five years.

14. Data drawn partially from the author's participation in the CRS Boston task force, including thirty days on-site, from September to December 1974.
15. CRS Annual Report, 1975, 12.

Detroit: Planning to "Avoid Another Boston"

Chastened by the Boston experience, CRS was determined to never again fall behind the violence curve by delaying the offer of preventive assistance to cities facing desegregation. Indeed, events had reversed any predilection on the part of CRS's overseers in the administration and Congress to limit the agency's role to crisis response only.

More than a year before the January 1976 deadline for Detroit to become the largest school district in the country to be desegregated under court order, CRS offered its services to that city. Even then, school and police officials as well as a number of community institutions had begun to examine their readiness to deal with the problems ahead, and they responded readily to the offer.

A framework of civic coalitions concerned about race relations was already in place, sensitized by the disastrous riot of 1967. Business organizations, religious groups, and minority and social action organizations existed in networks of networks. Most prominent was New Detroit, a well-staffed and financed urban coalition of business, civil rights, and community service groups.

In March 1975, New Detroit convened a meeting of twenty leaders of various groups, from which emerged People and Responsible Organizations for Detroit (PRO Detroit), which took as its first responsibility outreach to other organizations to save the city from tumult. It intended to enlist both the advocates and opponents of school desegregation. CRS and PRO Detroit immediately recognized each other as a source of mutual assistance.[16]

The federal judge presiding over the Detroit desegregation case was Robert E. DeMascio. Like Judge Garrity, he was sensitive to the unique aspects of this case, which were intertwined with community attitudes and developments. In his court order of April 30 he formally requested CRS "to provide assistance to the city of Detroit, to the parties to this litigation, and to the court in achieving harmonious implementation of a remedial plan to be ordered by the court and of future long-range plans to eliminate racial segregation to the extent possible in the public schools in the city of Detroit."

16. William H. O'Brien, cochairperson, People and Responsible Organizations for Detroit (PRO Detroit), presentation at the workshop on the role of business communities, at the Conference on Desegregation without Turmoil, sponsored by the Community Relations Service, U.S. Department of Justice, and the National Center for Quality Integrated Education, May 19, 1976.

CRS's director, Ben Holman, set up a temporary field office in Detroit in May to provide full-time assistance to the city. To head the office the regional director, Richard Salem, chose Ed Cabell, who had extensive experience in the Boston school case. To provide Cabell with an appropriately high-powered assistant with a good knowledge of the territory, Salem persuaded Rita Scott, a Detroit resident, to get a leave of absence from her position as education director of the Michigan Civil Rights Commission.

In order to help the new team get off to a rapid start, a special CRS work group was assembled in Detroit to develop a community relations guidebook and resource library for desegregation without turmoil. Veterans of school desegregation cases in Boston, Louisville, Denver, and elsewhere sat down with Salem, Cabell, and Scott to draft a playbook for helping a city prepare for desegregation without violence. They reviewed their own experiences, institution by institution and play by play—what had gone wrong and what had gone right. Case records in Washington were drawn upon for resource materials—examples of police and school contingency plans, operational orders, and sample lesson plans to prepare teachers, school security aides, and police officers; examples of media campaigns and guidelines for rumor control centers. The examination went beyond the school system to look at the role of city hall, the police, social agencies, the media, and religious, business, and civic groups. The outcome was a summary of the full range of CRS's experience in school desegregation.

As exhaustive as the briefing was, Cabell and Scott knew better than to count on it for any pat solutions for the problems of Detroit. Solutions would have to be worked out by the residents of Detroit, problem by problem. But the CRS team would be well prepared to assist.

In the eight months leading up to the day of desegregation, the CRS team met with the leaders of 125 city agencies and community groups to discuss ways of minimizing disruption. Cabell and Scott—and Gus Gaynett, who replaced Cabell in midproject—took part in more than three hundred community meetings at which the status of the case and various contentious aspects were interpreted and discussed.[17] They called upon community groups to enlist the hundreds of volunteers that would be needed to support desegregation. They helped design the assignment and training programs for volunteers and eased recurrent friction between public officials and the civic associations. In addition, CRS helped community groups to

17. Gustavo Gaynett, "Community Relations Service Involvement in Detroit School Desegregation Case," report to Judge Robert DeMascio, February 2, 1976.

design a rumor control and information center that was adopted by the city. Working with PRO Detroit, CRS arranged for media executives from Boston to meet with news executives in Detroit to discuss what they had done to reduce community antagonism toward the desegregation process.

As the new school term approached, the CRS team worked with school and police officials on plans for preventing disruptions within the schools, on school property, in school neighborhoods, and along the bus routes.

CRS made it a point to meet repeatedly with the neighborhood groups that opposed desegregation. While these meetings were focused on concerns for the safety of children, they were also designed to let these opposition groups know that their feelings were respected, even if their view could not prevail over the court's decision. CRS hoped that inclusion of these groups in the discussion would forestall feelings of isolation that could lead to the extremism that might provoke violence. Nevertheless, in three neighborhoods on the northeast side of the city there were expressions of bitter resistance to the pupil reassignment plan. Three one-day boycotts during the fall semester caused heavy absenteeism in more than a dozen schools. The week before desegregation was to take place, several hundred people picketed the federal building, and several hundred participated in street demonstrations and car caravans.

To assure compliance with his orders, Judge DeMascio counted heavily on a blue-ribbon monitoring commission he had appointed for that purpose, following the experience of his fellow judges in Denver and Boston. He relied on CRS for information about the functioning of the commissions in those other cities,[18] as well as for ongoing assistance to the Detroit commission.

The Detroit situation provided a unique example of CRS cooperation with the court to anticipate and forestall problems that could disrupt orderly compliance with the court's orders. From community groups CRS learned that a bitter bone of contention between the black community and the school system was allegations of discriminatory handling of discipline problems. The discrimination led to disproportionate rates of suspension and expulsion, as well as to interracial antagonism and violence. To introduce a controversial school busing plan in such a climate would have been an invitation to widespread disruption.

At the request of the court, CRS prepared an analysis of the school system's student code of conduct and of its policies on students' rights and

18. Lila N. Carol, "Viewpoints and Guidelines on Court-Appointed Monitoring Commissions in School Desegregation," report of a symposium sponsored by the Community Relations Service, U.S. Department of Justice, and College of Education, Ohio State University, May 31, June 1, 1977.

responsibilities. CRS then recommended ways to assure that disciplinary problems would be handled in a more equitable and consistent manner. When a revised code of conduct was drafted by school officials and approved by the court, CRS helped to train the managers who would be responsible for administering the revised program.

Three days before desegregation was to take place, another CRS team assembled in Detroit to help school and police officials with their final preparations and to troubleshoot problems in the schools and on the streets when the buses rolled. They provided a one-day training session for the 150 police officers composing the special desegregation task force that carried the burden for school safety during the opening week.

Once the buses started to role, CRS mobile teams were in constant radio communication with police and school networks, responding to crisis calls on the streets and in school buildings. Following daily debriefings, CRS's assessments and recommendations were shared with school and police officials in preparation for the next day's problems.

Violent resistance to the student redistribution program turned out to be inconsequential. By the third day, when school attendance, which had been down one-third on opening day, returned to almost the normal 88 percent, Detroit's leaders were ready to acknowledge that their careful preparation had paid off. They had dodged the bullet that had devastated Boston. They had succeeded in desegregating their schools without turmoil.

Dayton

Following four years of bitter political struggle, court-ordered desegregation took place in Dayton, Ohio, without incident on September 3, 1976. Despite the cold-blooded murder of the court-appointed desegregation expert by a demented opponent of desegregation, the change, which involved the busing of twenty thousand children, white and black, was planned and executed without widespread violence and with a minimum of rancor.[19]

The successful effort resulted from a determined and sophisticated mobilization of the full community, which, while opposed to desegregation, was resolved, like Detroit, that its city would not be blemished by the violent resistance that had characterized the Boston experience.

Dayton was a thriving industrial city that prided itself on its grace and civility. Its population of two hundred thousand included seventy-five thousand blacks, reflecting a large migration from the South following World

19. Richard Salem, interview with the author.

War II. Thirty-five thousand newer white immigrants from Appalachia re-inforced a solid core of people opposed to desegregation. Racial issues, heavily focused on segregated schooling, had been in the foreground ever since an outbreak of burning and looting in the North End black neigh-borhood in 1967.

Following the riot, a board of education resolution declared that "every reasonable and constructive measure" would be taken to "eliminate racial imbalance." Under a liberal school board a number of changes were made and the school superintendent created a far-reaching desegregation plan. That proved to be too much for the voters, who took their next opportu-nity to oust the liberals and vote in a conservative school board. When the new board rescinded the plan and fired the superintendent, the NAACP filed suit in U.S. District Court.

In February 1972, Judge Carl B. Rubin found the school board in viola-tion of the U.S. Constitution, and in July he accepted the board of educa-tion's voluntary plan for desegregation. That wasn't good enough for the plaintiffs, and on two appeals Judge Rubin's decision was overruled as too lenient. The appeals court ordered that a satisfactory systemwide plan be prepared for implementation in September 1976.

Despite their effective resistance to desegregation, which had been man-dated by state law since 1926, and by Supreme Court decision since 1954, Dayton's civic leaders now recognized that forty-four months of opposi-tion through litigation had brought them to the end of the line. The city now determined to mobilize its full resources to assure peaceful imple-mentation of the desegregation plan.

The movement for a community coalition to avoid disorderly resistance to desegregation started in Dayton more than a year before the final court order. The initiative was taken by Metropolitan Churches United, which brought together thirty community organizations to explore activities and concerns. The business community, long dominated by corporate execu-tives accustomed to working together on projects for civic improvement, also weighed in to make sure that since desegregation was inevitable, Day-ton would usher it in gracefully. A public relations campaign, staffed and financed by the business community, developed a speakers bureau, media campaigns, a rumor control center, press releases, brochures, bumper stickers, and posters, all designed to educate the community and make it clear that the law would be respected. CRS offered support and guidance to help develop programs, solve problems, and facilitate cooperation.

Judge Rubin complied with the edict of the appeals court by selecting an outside expert to draft the final desegregation plan. Dr. Charles Glatt, the chosen expert, was at work in his office at the U.S. Courthouse on September 18, 1975, when an intruder burst in and shot him to death. At the time of his death, Dr. Glatt was in conference with Tommie Jones, a black woman working her first day on the job as a CRS conciliator.

A former chemistry teacher in the Dayton schools, Jones was well known throughout the city as a civil rights activist who had, on a volunteer basis, presented intergroup workshops during previous periods of racial tension. With the guidance of CRS's Chicago-based regional director, Richard Salem, who had captained CRS's desegregation work in Detroit and several other cities, CRS designed a low-key catalytic role tailored to the particular circumstances in Dayton and the unique reliance placed on CRS by the U.S. District Court.

Judge Rubin was concerned not only that his plan be initiated peacefully but also that its intent of equitable education not be thwarted either by community resistance or by inept implementation by the school administration. Yet Rubin knew that the court itself should not have to provide day-by-day oversight; this should come from community resources. Rubin found an answer to his dilemma when he learned from a conversation with Salem of CRS's collaboration with the U.S. District Courts in Boston and Detroit. He studied both those experiences and adapted them to the case at hand. In January 1976, eight months before the scheduled desegregation, he issued an order asking for CRS assistance in the "establishing and functioning of a Citizens Monitoring Commission," which he was about to create, and directing all parties to the case "to cooperate with the Service and to afford it all reasonable assistance." He also indicated that CRS would have ready access to the court "as to all matters which bear upon the speedy and harmonious implementation of the desegregation plan."

Behind the formal language was the clear expectation that CRS would energize, and where necessary provide guidance to, the development of community support, and that the monitoring commission would ensure the quality of the school system's preparation. Further, the judge looked to CRS to work unobtrusively with the monitoring commission and to keep the court informed of whatever it needed to know in order to assure that the desegregation that resulted would be consistent with his intent.

How CRS acquitted itself of that responsibility as well as its other tasks was reported in detail by Graham S. Finney in a study of the Dayton desegregation experience. As an example, Finney cited the addition to the court order of a requirement for the training of school personnel "when it appeared in the spring that school administrators were moving too slowly to equip their staff with the skills needed to make desegregation work in the classroom." He marveled at the energy and resourcefulness with which

Jones pursued this delicate task, indicating, however, that while much of the work was done behind the scenes, "some bruised relationships were an almost inevitable consequence." He was particularly impressed with the wide diversity of community elements that CRS brought into the desegregation process. He cited the salutary planning work of the city government; the effective police training supervised by Colonel Tyree Broomfield, the police department's chief of staff, who, as a sometime CRS consultant, was familiar with CRS work in other cases; the active support of the church organizations; the enlisting of the national leadership of the AFL-CIO to bolster local labor organization support. Finney reported: "In all these efforts the hand of Jones and the CRS was in evidence, sometimes so subtly that its imprint was barely detectible. Hers was, in fact, the only presence that managed to touch base with all the various parties. This network capacity proved crucial as events unfolded."[20]

In March 1976, Metropolitan Churches United conducted a community conference that, with CRS assistance, featured veterans of Detroit's successful desegregation as speakers. The conference enlisted two hundred and fifty volunteers to build community support in the final months before desegregation. Area committees were formed throughout the city, and dozens of churches issued endorsements. Many churches conducted all-night prayer vigils the day before school opened.

Dayton's Appalachian community of working-class whites expressed its resistance to desegregation and its support for neighborhood schools largely through a community group called Our Common Heritage (OCH), which was foremost among the groups opposed to desegregation. Tommie Jones met often with such groups, discussing their problems in the context of the federal government's concern with peaceful enforcement of the law. After a meeting with Jones in August, OCH declared publicly that it would support compliance with the court order. According to Graham Finney's evaluation, "The OCH endorsement set the tenor of the city's mood in the weeks remaining until the opening day of school."

Desegregation without Turmoil

The turbulence that the fight over school desegregation brought to American cities would have been much worse in many places if civic volunteers had not rolled up their sleeves to make sure that things worked out peacefully. At national and local levels the outpouring of resources and

20. Finney, "Desegregating the Schools in Dayton."

personnel was tremendous. Detroit and Dayton and Dallas did it one way, organizing at the top, with the power structure mobilizing the community. Elsewhere the rallying cry was first sounded closer to the grass roots, as in Prince George's County, Maryland, where in 1971 CRS, on its arrival on the scene, found the League of Women Voters and the Ministerial Association making the case for rational and planned acceptance of inevitable change. In some cities where joint civic action was no more than rudimentary, many groups were hesitant about taking a stand in support of peaceful desegregation because they were uncertain about how to proceed and how prominent a role to play.

The federal conciliators helped the coalition effort in two ways. The first was as a catalyst for community organization. Civic leaders concerned about an impending desegregation crisis could be readily brought together in small groups to talk about the problem informally—and confidentially, if necessary—with someone from the Department of Justice. Such meetings provided encouragement to enter the fray.

CRS pointed out that school desegregation was a new phenomenon, and history had shown that even the most competent of school systems, police departments, and city halls did not have the requisite motivation, experience, or expertise to navigate the minefield of community turmoil. Moreover, since the forces of discord fed on resistance to unpopular change, the thoughtful sectors of the community needed to assert leadership to assure a peaceful transition.

CRS helped community groups to learn from the successes and failures in other cities. This was done by sharing sample materials from other cases, by arranging direct contact via mail and phone, and by intercity visits. In May 1975, 570 coalition leaders from more than seventy cities came together to share experiences at the Conference on Desegregation without Turmoil. Their how-to-do-it exchanges ranged from ideas for working with the schools, police, and city hall to assure adequate advanced planning to suggestions for enlisting the media to build public support. The local coalition leaders learned how to prepare themselves to consult productively with—and sometimes to challenge—school and public safety officials on the adequacy of preparations to avoid and control violence.

Groups shared tips on how they had successfully dealt with common problems—like the charge that the local desegregation decision was the unconstitutional work of a misguided judge. The suggested solution had three stages. The first was to get the local bar association to issue its analysis of the court's decision. Such a report would generally make it clear that the ruling was not only constitutional but also fully consistent with the findings of the appeals courts. The second was to form a media committee to win support for the bar association's position from newspapers and broadcast outlets. The third was to form a speakers committee to stimulate discussion of the bar association position before community groups.

In the campaign to build and strengthen local coalitions to support peaceful desegregation, CRS found powerful allies among national associations. Religious organizations were interested in furthering social justice; business organizations knew that community violence was bad for business. The International Association of City Managers, the U.S. Conference of Mayors, the National Association of School Superintendents, and the National Association of Secondary School Principals were all concerned with providing their constituents with information and resources to deal with critical problems. Several national organizations were helpful in identifying local constituents who might be interested in leading local efforts. Among them were the American Jewish Committee, the AFL-CIO, and the various social action arms of the national religious denominations.

The Conference on Desegregation without Turmoil was cosponsored by CRS and the National Center for Quality Integrated Education, a project of the National Conference of Christians and Jews. Assistance was provided by the National Education Association. The U.S. Chamber of Commerce published and circulated to its membership the conference reports on how business associations in Detroit, Dayton, and Dallas took the lead in building coalitions to assure peaceful implementation of school desegregation decisions. The AFL-CIO contributed $10,000 to help fund the conference.

The AFL-CIO played a unique behind-the-scenes role in working for peaceful school desegregation. Even though the national organization was a strong supporter of civil rights, many members of local unions were deeply opposed to school desegregation. George Meany, president of the AFL-CIO, was an uncompromising foe of segregation.[21] He instructed William Pollard, director of the organization's Civil Rights Department, to give top priority to the task of winning local support for peaceful desegregation and for stifling opposition efforts by local labor groups. When alerted through CRS, or his own channels, of the intent of a local central trades and labor council, anywhere in the country, to take a public position against desegregation, Pollard would meet with the leaders of the local council. He would advise them, in no uncertain terms, of how deeply unhappy Meany would be at such a turn of events.

21. Meany came out in favor of the Supreme Court's school desegregation decision immediately after it was announced in 1954. He called it an act of "simple justice" and lobbied within the labor movement for its support.

Historical Perspective

Martin Walsh became CRS's regional director for New England in November 1974, shortly after the agency entered the Boston school desegregation case, and he managed that case until its closure six years later. For three decades he presided over CRS efforts to resolve racial conflict throughout the six-state area. In recognition of that work Attorney General John Ashcroft presented him, in 2001, with the Attorney General's Distinguished Service Award. It was the second time Walsh had been so honored.

For almost thirty years, he and the men and women working under him had grappled with literally thousands of racial conflicts, working in settings that ranged from disorder in the streets to negotiation around the conference table. They had worked with governors, mayors, police chiefs, school superintendents, business leaders, and the heads of religious and civic communities, as well as civil rights activists and those who carried forward the banner of every embattled minority group. They had learned to assess the tension level in every community in which they worked. They had studied the dynamics of conflict in the most volatile cities, so that they could counsel local leaders on the best approaches for avoiding outbreaks of racial violence.

Walsh made a specialty of helping communities develop preventive strategies. He worked with the bellwethers among public officials—outstanding mayors, educators, police chiefs, and district attorneys—to convene regional or statewide conferences of their counterparts in other communities. These conferences brought together civil rights leaders and experts within each profession to identify emerging racial problems and consider, in advance of a crisis, methods and resources for dealing with them.

Interviewed in June 2001, Walsh identified Boston's school desegregation ordeal as an exorcism, following which the resolution of other stubborn civil rights problems became possible. He thought the school conflict exposed the city's "racial malaise" and bared problems in the underpinnings of other institutions in Boston. He saw it as a turning point for the people of Boston, "stirring them to redeem themselves from being, what Mayor Kevin White himself was to acknowledge as, 'the most racist city in America.'" He felt that "Judge Garrity's steadfastness, over a period of six years, in requiring the city and the school system to do what was necessary to make desegregation work made it clear that the opposition was not going to win." It set in motion changes in the political system that could accommodate subsequent court-ordered reforms such as those affecting the police, the firefighters, and public housing.

Walsh recalled: "Those who were to lead the reform in the 1980s included some of the leaders of the resistance in the seventies. Kevin White, before leaving office as mayor in 1980, created the Boston Committee, to work for improved human relations. Ray Flynn, who had been among the South Boston politicians opposed to Judge Garrity's order, ran for mayor in 1983, promising to try to bring the city together. When elected, he followed through on his pledge. Since that time, race has never been a negative issue in Boston mayoral elections."

Walsh also stated his belief that the Boston experience with school desegregation had a profound influence beyond Boston. The image of intractable hatred and mob violence in one of America's greatest cities, which Boston had communicated to the entire nation, demonstrated the consequences of failed leadership in a time of crisis. It stirred those responsible for the fate of other cities to make the preparations that would enable them to "avoid another Boston."

In 1979 CRS, in cooperation with the National Urban League and the Anti-Defamation League of B'nai B'rith, created the Greater Boston Civil Rights Coalition, an association working for racial harmony. Walsh pointed out that both that coalition and Kevin White's Boston Committee still exist. "By 2001," he said, "the overtness of discrimination and the negative voices of the demagogues have been shunted aside as aberrations. Improving relationships—that's where the dynamic of race is being played out now."[22]

22. Walsh interview.

Eight

Mediation

The Road Less Traveled

In 1972 the commissioner of corrections for the State of Louisiana made sweeping changes in the living conditions of prisoners throughout the state's penal system. Her objective was to reduce racial discrimination and conflict and to raise the standards of respect for the rights of all prisoners. At the root of the change was a written agreement negotiated by CRS the year before, settling civil rights complaints filed by prisoners in the state's maximum security facility at Angola. This agreement was embodied in a consent decree issued by Judge E. Gordon West, who had asked CRS to mediate civil rights issues between the prison authorities and the complaining prisoners.[1] The form of the court's judgment made it easier for the reform-minded corrections commissioner to extend its benefits throughout the state's entire correctional system.

In the eyes of some judges, Judge West's experience suggested a more satisfactory way of resolving many of the issues involving the civil rights of prisoners that were contributing to the overcrowding of federal court dockets. The case proved to be an eye-opener for CRS as well, as its staff perceived the far-reaching social change that might result when a CRS agreement, reduced to writing, was embodied in a court order.

Mediation or Conciliation—Which Way to Go?

In its early years CRS used only one word to describe its peacemaking process—conciliation. Broadly speaking, the term meant "whatever it takes to resolve the conflict." Conciliation encompassed a broad range of meth-

1. Robert Greenwald, interview with the author.

ods, techniques, strategies, and resources to be drawn on in whatever combination would get the job done—including, at times, the use of a written agreement. Sometimes that written agreement required formal mediation, a process with which CRS's conciliators had little experience.

In contrast to the wide-ranging, flexible forms of intervention permitted by conciliation, the activities called for in mediation were prescribed, disciplined, and tightly choreographed. Mediation consisted of formal cross-table negotiations between the conflicting parties, presided over by a trained mediator, following specific rules of procedure and with the intention of producing a binding written agreement for the solution of specific predetermined issues.

In the early seventies, CRS's director, Ben Holman, reviewed the agency's limited but growing experience with mediation cases. In the Southwest region, Robert Greenwald had used mediation in Louisiana prison cases. In the Midwest region, Jesse Taylor had produced impressive agreements in school cases and in conflicts between minority groups and industrial corporations. There had been a few other uses of mediation as well. Holman commissioned a staff study that concluded that, while mediation was not suitable in most of the conflicts CRS dealt with, there were instances where it might achieve lasting solutions not otherwise possible. But there were problems. Often, it was not the immediate conflict but the underlying problems that might be amenable to mediation. Additional casework time would be necessary to determine whether a mediated outcome would be more desirable than the settlement worked out through conciliation alone. Also, the antagonists might have to be persuaded to revise the way they looked at the problem before they would buy into the mediation process.

Holman decided that there was a distinct place for mediation in the CRS program, but its use should not depend on happenstance or upon the propensity of the individual fieldworker. Intensive mediation training was begun, and special rules of engagement were set forth as well as guidelines for "marketing" the use of this new and potent tool. Eventually, the agency developed an impressive track record for mediation of cases involving prisons, schools, police agencies, and industrial conflicts.

Mediation cases presented CRS's management with a cost/benefit dilemma. On the plus side, these cases often involved conflicts that were bitter, stubborn, and important. Such cases were mostly successful, producing binding written agreements that often provided long-range as well as short-range solutions. On the minus side was the cost. Conflicts that might profitably be dealt with by mediation were not always readily apparent. The preliminary process of recasting the conflict into negotiable issues and persuading the parties that a mediated written agreement could be in their best interest often took as much or more time than the mediation itself. On the average, five conciliated settlements could be worked out in the time it took to conclude one mediation agreement. That meant that for every mediation case resolved, five other cases had to be either rejected or added to the backlog of cases waiting to be resolved.

The Dividends of Mediation

Prisoner Civil Rights Cases in Louisiana

It had all started the year before when Judge West, in an effort to relieve the swollen calendar of cases before him, noted that thirty of them stemmed from civil rights complaints filed by prisoners (most of whom were black) in Angola. He asked the prison authorities and the lawyers for the prisoners to try to work out some sort of comprehensive settlement using Robert Greenwald of CRS as a mediator.[2]

Greenwald began an intensive period of preparation, helping in the selection of negotiating teams for the prisoners and the prison, establishing an agreement on procedures and guidelines, and getting consensus among the prisoners on the substance and wording of the specific complaints to be mediated. In three marathon mediation sessions, the negotiating teams were able to reach agreement on twenty-eight of the thirty-some-odd issues that had been raised. The outcome, as reported in the CRS Annual Report for 1972, included:

> closing some notorious isolation cells, ending lockdown abuses, eliminating certain restrictions on correspondence and hairstyles, establishment of a grievance process, creation of a joint committee to prepare revisions to the existing rules and regulations, improvement in medical attention to inmates, and increased access to showers. . . . As a result of CRS mediation, many of the complaints filed in court were declared moot. Moreover, subsequent reports from prison officials and inmates indicated that inmate-staff relations improved, and that disciplinary infractions decreased.[3]

2. For a description of this case and the one discussed following, as well as a comprehensive delineation of the CRS approach to mediation, see Robert F. Greenwald, "CRS: Dispute Resolution through Mediation."

3. CRS Annual Report, 1972, 26–27.

On the heels of the Angola case, a second federal judge, Jack M. Gordon, asked CRS to mediate a similar case at the Jefferson Parish Jail in Louisiana. Judge Gordon, enthused about what he saw as an innovative approach to a sticky problem, included in his opinion a detailed description of the process. As he explained in a letter to Greenwald: "I devoted a substantial portion of the opinion to outlining the mediation efforts and the manner in which they were carried out, as well as commenting upon my views as to their efficacy in such situations. I felt that issuing the opinion in this form would be as good a way as any of acquainting others with the success we met in this case."[4]

The opinion to which the judge referred had also noted: "In addition to the formal agreements, the Court also appreciates certain fringe benefits that resulted from this series of negotiations; among the valuable extras are a higher level of rapport between the authorities and the inmates, and, of no small import, the introduction of mediation to both sides as a potentially viable and permanent alternative to the courts in resolving the complaints of inmates."[5]

Integration of the Cook County Jail

Because the five thousand inmates of the Cook County Jail near Chicago were segregated by race, the Civil Rights Division of the Justice Department sued the county early in 1979. Trial was scheduled for 1980. Seeking to avoid a long trial, Judge Hubert L. Will of the U.S. District Court encouraged the parties to work out a settlement. When, in May 1979, they reported to him their inability to make any progress, he directed them to utilize the mediating services of CRS. Six months later the judge was able to issue a consent decree based on the CRS-produced agreement. As a result of that mediation, the county pledged to desegregate the jail, utilizing a plan that would be worked out by the Justice Department's National Institute of Corrections.

In congratulating mediator Jesse Taylor for achieving a settlement without trial, which others had thought impossible, the judge remarked in court that he had never even heard of CRS until the day before he made his referral. At a workshop of the judges of the Fifth Circuit, he had heard Director Gil Pompa describe the work of the agency. Judge Will later wrote to Attorney General Benjamin R. Civiletti, "The agency's demonstrated ability to mediate complex civil rights cases could result in substantial sav-

4. Judge Jack M. Gorden to Robert F. Greenwald, August 29, 1974.
5. *Frazier v. Donelson,* U.S. District Court, E.D. Louisiana, August 23, 1974.

ings of time and money to both the court and the parties and result in earlier settlements which both the parties and the court view as equitable."[6]

Over the years CRS successfully mediated a number of prison cases that often seemed intractable. Some were court-referred; others were instigated by prison authorities. These cases divided broadly into two categories—discriminatory conditions of confinement, and racial tension and violence. While CRS was often successful in working out far-reaching settlements, the overall number of such cases was few. For one reason, prison officials tended to be reluctant to bring in outsiders to help solve the problems of their closed institutions. Second, CRS found that, compared to other issues, there was little community concern about prison conditions and no significant constituency to invite the agency's attention. Third, settlements were inclined to erode with time because of the turnover of inmates as well as of corrections personnel. Fourth, the CRS regional directors, often hard put to choose among the cases competing for the attention of an already overburdened staff, were reluctant to make commitments to prison cases, which were very time-consuming.

Voting Rights in Cairo, Illinois

The racial history of Cairo, Illinois, had been conditioned in part by its pre–Civil War role as a collection point for captured runaway slaves being shipped back to their owners along the Mississippi River. Despite its population of only six thousand, it had been one of the worst hotbeds of racial violence and civil rights protest in the late 1960s and throughout the 1970s. Recurrent periods of tension were marked by protest demonstrations, boycotts of white merchants, vigilante assaults on a black housing project, armed confrontations, and shootings. The black population, amounting to about one-third of the city's residents, was large enough to resist white domination but not large enough to exercise political influence. At-large elections for the city's mayor and council had effectively barred blacks from elected representation since before 1900.

A class-action suit filed in behalf of fourteen hundred eligible black voters had been in the U.S. District Court for six years when Judge James Foreman, in October 1979, asked CRS to mediate. A far-reaching settlement was worked out in three months and embodied by the judge in a consent decree ending the protracted litigation.[7] The agreement replaced

6. Judge Hubert I. Will to Attorney General Benjamin R. Civiletti, January 14, 1980, copy in author's collection.
7. *Chicago Defender,* March 15, 1980.

the five-person mayor and council, which had been elected at large, with a seven-person council, five of whose members would be elected from newly designated wards. The new arrangement guaranteed the election of at least two blacks.

The judge and attorneys were exuberant to have the matter behind them. They had anticipated a three-week trial followed by a lengthy appellate process replete with costly discovery, possibly lasting three more years. They calculated a possible savings in future legal costs and court expenses of $300,000. Further savings accrued to the U.S. Justice Department, which had been poised to enter the case as amicus had it gone to trial.

To CRS and the people in both the white and the black communities, the greater value of the settlement was to be seen not in monetary costs but in social benefits. The termination of political disenfranchisement of Negroes was expected to usher in other gains that would result in more equitable sharing in the decision-making process. Several bitter bones of contention that had contributed to past conflicts could now be eliminated. The blacks, possessing for the first time a share of political power and influence, would undoubtedly find ways to redress other long-standing inequities that had fueled a century of bad feeling.

In this case, as in many other instances where mediation was utilized as an alternative to litigation, a trial would have been rooted in the adjudication of past wrongs. Mediation, on the other hand, could more readily concentrate on future arrangements that the parties felt would work. From the CRS point of view, mediation was clearly preferable to a trial in those community situations where the antagonists would have to continue to relate to each other. A trial, based on the adjudication of who was wrong or right, would produce a winner and a loser and perpetuate bitterness. On the other hand, a negotiated settlement based on give-and-take often left the adversaries on a first-name basis and better prepared for face-to-face resolution of future differences.

Police Rivalry and the Weakening of Law Enforcement in Atlanta

Atlanta's crime statistics were on the rise through most of the seventies. The erosion of effective law enforcement was attributed by many to bitter rivalry between black and white police officers. It was presumed to date back to 1973 when the Afro-American Patrolmen's League and the Civil Rights Division of the Justice Department brought suit against the mostly white city administration, charging discrimination in hiring and promotion. In 1976, with the by then mostly black city government on the verge of reaching a settlement with the plaintiffs, the Fraternal Order of Police became a party to the suit, charging discrimination against white officers.

Pending settlement of the case, Judge Charles A. Moye took control over personnel matters and froze all new hiring and all promotions. As the number of officers decreased, and black-white antagonism was acted out on the job, crime statistics continued to climb.

Over the years a number of respected third-party institutions were called on to help the antagonists work out an agreement. Fearful of the controversy's negative impact on business, the Atlanta Chamber of Commerce tried to bring the parties together—to no avail. The Atlanta Human Relations Commission was the next to try. Then the city council sought to intervene. Finally, the mayor appointed a blue-ribbon panel to try to end the impasse. Each of these efforts failed.

In September 1979, with the case about to come to trial in what most observers expected to be a long and bitter proceeding that would further fray race relations, the parties were induced to try to mediate their differences with the help of CRS. In view of the high stakes involved, Regional Director Ozell Sutton selected an interracial mediation team that he personally headed. He also arranged to borrow from CRS's San Francisco office mediator Ed Howden, widely acknowledged to be among America's pioneers in racial conflict negotiation.

Two months of mediation activity, climaxing in weekend sessions that lasted well into the night before the trial was to begin, finally yielded an out-of-court settlement.[8]

Presented with agreed-upon detailed plans for recruitment and promotion of both black and white officers, and formulas for back pay for various categories of complainants, Judge Moye accepted the agreement and lifted the hiring freeze—finally bringing an end to the longtime depletion of the Atlanta police force. The judge agreed to retain oversight of the case for three years to assure its full implementation.

The rapprochement between black and white police officers could not have come at a more critical time. Early in 1980, just a few months after the mediated agreement, the city began to face its most severe racial crisis since the height of the civil rights movement, when it experienced what became known as the case of the missing and murdered black children.

Over a period of months, almost thirty black children were either murdered or missing. A white predator was suspected, and the Negro community became increasingly fearful and bitter at what it felt was police

8. *Atlanta Constitution*, November 6, 1979.

inadequacy and white indifference. CRS spent months working with the city's leaders, both black and white, to help bring federal law enforcement assistance to the city and to demonstrate that the community was united in its concern. Ultimately, a deranged black man was found to be the killer. Most qualified observers agreed that if the racial conflicts and personnel shortages within the Bureau of Police Services had not been resolved before the episode of the murdered and missing children occurred, the level of interracial bitterness would have been far more severe.

Atlanta was only one of many cities where class-action suits charging racial discrimination in police employment led to protracted conflicts between black and white officers and consequent deterioration of the quality of police services. Louisville, Kentucky, lived through a similar scenario that, after many years, was also resolved within a few months via CRS mediation. Within a year of the Atlanta case, neighboring De Kalb County used the same course to settle suits within both its police force and its sheriff's department.

A Win/Win Ending to the Long Antagonism between Hispanics and Coors

From the mid-1970s to the mid-1980s, the Adolph Coors Company, then a growing industrial giant that dominated the brewing industry in the mountain states, was the target of widespread protest by the increasingly vocal Hispanic population because of alleged economic and employment discrimination. Public demonstrations against Coors contributed to an atmosphere of racial/ethnic unrest in many communities throughout the region. A Hispanic boycott of Coors products appeared to have little impact in bringing about change. Early efforts by CRS to mediate between local Hispanic groups and Coors management fell apart when labor problems at one of the breweries gave rise to a Coors boycott by organized labor. Subsequently, black organizations also charged Coors with discriminatory practices.

Bolstered by four generations of pride and profit, the fiercely independent Coors family appeared to stiffen its resistance in the face of outside interference. Behind the scenes, however, a shift was under way. The younger members of the Coors family, then moving into positions of control in the company, were deeply concerned about radical changes in the economics of the industry. A wave of mergers and acquisitions was threatening to reduce the number of major breweries to no more than half a dozen or so supergiants. In order to end up among the major players, Coors would have to intensify its drive for growth. The company knew that if it was going to sell its product on a national scale, it could no longer be indifferent to minority markets.

The situation came to a head in 1984 when the chairman of the Coors board of directors, while addressing a meeting of minority business owners, uttered remarks that many in his audience found to be insulting to blacks.[9] The resulting outpouring of anger from many minority groups so embarrassed the company that its leaders became more amenable to the idea of negotiating minority grievances so that they might put the problem behind them.

While Coors expressed willingness to resume negotiations with Hispanic groups, it now wanted discussions to be national in scope. CRS helped to play a role in the formation of a coalition of national Hispanic organizations to negotiate on behalf of the Hispanic community. Parallel negotiations were also initiated between Coors and black organizations. Both Coors and the Hispanics favored using CRS as a mediator. Black leaders, having previous experience in negotiating "fair share" agreements with business organizations, saw no need for third-party assistance.

Leo Cardenas, director of CRS's Rocky Mountain regional office in Denver, was cautious on personal grounds as he sought to assist the Coors/ Hispanic arrangements. A former newspaperman and author, he had been active in civil rights circles ever since, as a college student, he had helped to organize the first campus chapter of LULAC (League of United Latin American Citizens) at the University of Texas at Austin. He was a former national vice president of LULAC, and though that organization had opted to stand apart from the Coors negotiations, he was nevertheless well known to the Hispanic leaders who would be meeting with Coors. Cardenas asked himself whether his role as a third-party neutral would be compromised. CRS later learned that, although some among the Coors leadership questioned Cardenas's familiarity with the Hispanics, he was also well known and respected by Coors's own Hispanic advisers. Moreover, CRS's credibility had already been established among the Coors people as a result of the aborted local negotiations a few years earlier. While the parties raised no question about his neutrality, Cardenas nevertheless assigned Silke Hansen, his senior staff mediator, to preside over the negotiations.[10]

The progress of the mediation was impeded by the complexities of some of the issues, and because Coors felt a need for the agreement with the Hispanics to be in the same ballpark as its settlement with the Negro

9. *New York Times,* November 16, 1984.
10. Leo Cardenas, interview with the author.

negotiators. On the other hand, negotiations were aided by a strong desire on the part of both sides to arrive at an agreement. In addition, the major players on both sides—those who would have to sign off on any settlement—personally participated in the give-and-take of almost all sessions. Peter Coors headed the company team. The leading figure among the Hispanics was Raul Yzaguirre, head of the National Council of La Raza, a major Hispanic umbrella group.[11]

The critical issues centered on equal employment opportunities at Coors and equal opportunities for economic participation, as well as the company's level of community support. The stakes were high for both sides. Coors knew that the bottom line of a settlement would involve the redirection of hundreds of millions of dollars of their community and economic investment. But it would also lead to expanded access to major markets. The Hispanics knew that they were entrusted with two trump cards. One was their likely ability to bring an end to the still-lingering Hispanic boycott of Coors; the other was the influence they could exert on the buying habits of America's Hispanic population. They did not want to bargain away these cards for a pittance. Awareness of the magnitude of the stakes brought the negotiations to an impasse on several occasions. But it also made it easier for CRS to help the parties draw back from the brink.

The signed agreement was a hard-nosed, quid-pro-quo business arrangement, based on the principles of fairness and self-interest—as made clear by the first paragraph: "This partnership is based on achieving equity and parity for the Hispanic community within Adolph Coors Company. Equity and parity are defined operationally as returning a share of company resources back to the Hispanic community in direct proportion to the percentage of business that Coors enjoys from that community."[12]

The final settlement called for, among other provisions, the hiring of Hispanics in all job categories, at a rate of no less than 12 percent for the next five years. An affirmative action plan would require fair promotions, including opening of the executive ranks. The company also agreed to make outright contributions of no less than $500,000 per year to the Hispanic community, of which at least one-third would be earmarked for education. The greater amount of the settlement was to be spent in rechanneling Coors's resources to create new distributorships among Hispanic entrepreneurs. Significant funds would also be directed to Hispanic banks to assist in community revitalization projects. Similarly, a fair share of Coors

11. Hansen interview.
12. "National Agreement between Adolph Coors Company and a Coalition of Hispanic Organizations," signed October 29, 1984.

business would be channeled to Hispanic lawyers, as well as to media, insurance, and advertising services. To make sure that the agreement would be lived up to, an annual audit would be made by an independent Hispanic auditor, engaged by the company with the approval of the coalition.[13]

From an economic point of view, it appeared to be a win/win agreement. Since the size of the total settlement was to be based on the proportion of sales in Hispanic neighborhoods, the Hispanics saw it as an overdue equitable return to the community. For Coors, it promised increased sales, achieved largely through redistribution of the cost of doing business.

The CRS mediators maintained informal contact with members of the committee that audited the contract. At the end of the first five years, both sides indicated satisfaction. While the increase in the number of Hispanic distributorships had not been as rapid as hoped, Coors nevertheless appeared to be leading the industry in that regard.

Successive five-year agreements have been renewed until the time of this writing. The coalition of national Hispanic organizations that CRS helped bring together to negotiate with Coors converted itself to a permanent national organization known as the Hispanic Association on Corporate Responsibility. It seeks to stimulate economic development opportunities for Hispanics and continues to work out partnership agreements, similar to that with Coors, with other major national employers.

Measuring the Costs Versus the Benefits of Court-Referred Mediation

The apparent success of CRS mediation—and especially of those cases referred by the courts—raised serious questions for CRS's management in terms of deployment of resources. Almost all referrals were mediated to the satisfaction of the parties and the court, and with significant cost savings compared to litigation. Moreover, the social benefit of the settlements, in terms of reduced racial friction, often exceeded the scope of the original issues. However, the number of court requests was very few. Most judges had never heard of CRS.

To test whether or not CRS should "market" its services to judges, an experimental program was launched in 1979. With the cooperation of the senior judge of the Seventh Judicial Circuit, arrangement was made to acquaint the judges of the circuit with the service available through CRS's Midwest regional office.

13. CRS Annual Report, 1984, 15.

Within a year, twelve judges had referred nineteen cases.[14] An evaluation of the pilot project answered critical questions: if judges knew about
the service, they would use it; cases referred by the court were consistent
with CRS's congressional mandate; most cases could be mediated successfully; CRS would be able to refuse a referral without fear of offending the
judge. The program also got high marks for consistently achieving settlement at a much lower cost and often with a much better result than would
have been possible through litigation. The pilot program also showed CRS
that cases not only were consistent with the agency's own criteria for case
acceptance but also often addressed critical problems that would otherwise have been beyond its reach.[15]

The downside of the program was the increased cost to CRS and the
greater number of staff hours required. CRS's repeated requests for more
mediators met with little success. Nevertheless, CRS extended the program of outreach to the federal judiciary to all regions, leaving to regional
directors the hard choices of case selection. At the time of this writing,
several years of tight budgets had reduced the number of court-referred
mediation cases to no more than a handful a year.[16]

14. CRS Annual Report, 1980, 8.
15. U.S. Department of Justice, Community Relations Service, "Evaluation of the
Pilot Project on Court-Referred Mediation."
16. Jonathan Chace, interview with the author.

Nine

Not All Black and White

Varieties of Civil Rights Conflict

The rivers of Idaho, which rise at the Continental Divide, were first seen by white people in 1805, when the men of the Lewis and Clark expedition were welcomed to share the bounty of the mighty Nez Percé tribe, whose ancestors had fished those waters since time out of memory. The Nez Percé befriended and guided President Jefferson's Corps of Discovery through one of the most perilous parts of its journey. Seventy years later, the United States cavalry drove the tribe from its homeland and, after a relentless and bloody pursuit, finally defeated the celebrated Chief Joseph and confined the remnant of the tribe on a reservation along the Rapid River.

It was on the banks of the Rapid River, in 1979, during the first week of the salmon run, that CRS mediator Robert Hughes stepped between opposing groups of men and weapons and called out, "You don't want to do this. There's gotta be another way." The law enforcement officials on one side and the Nez Percé on the other took a deep breath, eased back on the revved-up rage and fear, and let the adrenaline rush subside. Things had gotten out of hand. Both sides wanted a way out.[1]

Different Drummers

In 1964 the civil rights revolution was defined by the massive efforts being made to overcome the legacy of slavery. When Congress created CRS to help reduce the social anguish and violence that were likely to accompany the changeover, the only minority group it had in mind was Negroes.

1. Robert Hughes, interview with the author.

But the actual law that set CRS in motion made no distinction among races or ethnic minorities; it described the target as community conflict affecting the rights of all racial and ethnic groups.

Given the way CRS handled many types of cases, it did not make much difference which minority group was involved. The issues were similar, as were the techniques for helping a community find constructive outcomes. But some issues were unique to Asians, or Hispanics, or Native Americans. While each group suffered and fought against unfair denial of equal justice, education, and economic opportunity, the circumstances often varied— especially with respect to Native Americans. The confrontation on the Rapid River that engaged the efforts of Bob Hughes opens a window on this type of case.

Indian Treaty Rights: The Meaning of the Nez Percé

The confrontation in Idaho between the Nez Percé and state fish and game agents had roots in long-running antagonisms about who could fish where and when. The Idaho Fish and Game Commission was authorized by state law to control all fishing. But for the past decade, a number of decisions in federal courts throughout the Northwest had supported the Indians' claims that their treaty rights gave them authority to control fishing on their reservations. The Supreme Court affirmed this, with the qualification that conservation needs had priority over treaty rights. Competition between white sports fishermen and Indians, fueled at times by a limited supply of salmon, was a source of continuing resentment. Game wardens struggled to keep both groups within the bounds of state law.

Early in May, at the start of the salmon run, the state Fish and Game Commission had ordered a conservation closure on salmon fishing in the river. The Indians, who used the fish not only for subsistence but also for religious ceremonies, were not happy with the ban. The Nez Percé Fisherman's Club, composed of many younger members of the tribe, decided to vindicate tradition and treaty rights by conducting a "fish-in" in defiance of the state's edict. Their target would be the state fish hatchery seventy miles south of the reservation. This was where the salmon run was interrupted until the hatchery had obtained its minimum count. Then, to the extent that the run exceeded conservation needs, fish were released in stages to the upper waters, where the Indians satisfied their ceremonial requirements before permitting subsistence fishing. The Indians did not trust the hatchery count, which provided the basis for the amount of fish released into their waters.

On learning that trouble was brewing, Hughes had flown from CRS's regional headquarters in Seattle to Lewiston, Idaho, and had driven to the Nez Percé reservation some hundred miles away. There the tribal chairman had informed him that a convoy of about thirty young men had left a half-hour earlier to drive to the hatchery some seventy miles south. Hughes followed.

For the first day or two it was cat-and-mouse: Indians surveying the river and testing the water; fish and game agents with binoculars on the cliffs above the banks, keeping the scene under surveillance; and other Indians higher on the cliffside, surveying the agents. When the law enforcement contingent was reinforced by the state police, more Indians came down from the reservation to bolster the Nez Percé.

The Indians had set up a camp of eight large tepees along the riverbottom. The agents were bivouacked in trailers in another area along the bank. The situation became more delicate when the Department of Fisheries agents began to conduct sweeps through the Nez Percé campsite searching for fish. The incensed Indians ambushed one of the sweeps, descending on the agents with whoops and invectives and brandishing their ever-present ceremonial war clubs. The agents closed ranks and withdrew up the cliffside path as fast as their dignity would permit, to the area where the vehicles of both sides were parked and where the state police were waiting. Indians and agents raced to their respective vehicles to get their weapons. That was when Bob Hughes made his offer of a better way.

In the tense silence that followed, Hughes arranged for each side to designate three representatives who would meet with him to work out some arrangement to avoid bloodshed. He spent the rest of the day shuttling back and forth between the camps, trying to hold the temporary accord together until he got the rival delegations to agree to meet in his motel room in the town of Riggins, about six miles away. It took until nearly midnight to work out an informal understanding that, while permitting the confrontation to go forward, established safeguards to avoid violence. The Nez Percé agreed to allow the agents to come through the camp, but only with advance notice that would be delivered through Hughes. The agents would be accompanied by Indians, and they would not enter any of the tents. As a step toward a long-range solution, when the salmon were transferred from the trap to the hatchery for counting, the Indians would be allowed to count the salmon jointly with the hatchery personnel, so as to establish the credibility of the count.

The peaceful end of the 1979 standoff on the Rapid River marked the start of a new case for Hughes. To reduce the large number of annual conflicts involving hunting and fishing rights, it would be necessary for all concerned parties throughout the state to work together to plan and enforce preventive strategies.

Working with the governor's office, Hughes set up a meeting between the Nez Percé tribal chairman and the director of the State Fish and Game Commission. This led to the development of an improved formula for tribal harvesting of salmon. CRS also worked with local law enforcement authorities to encourage Indian and white fishermen throughout the state to respect each other's rights. Still, when the next salmon season opened, the situation was touch-and-go and required careful monitoring. Hughes returned for the next two years to survey the scene and conciliate problems.

The Rapid River was typical of hunting and fishing locales throughout the Northwest, as well as in other parts of the country, where the interests and practices of Indians collided with those of white sportsmen and commercial fishers. In other walks of life as well, questions of law and jurisdiction governing white and Indian relationships, often strained, had grown murkier as a result of court decisions. The CRS Northwest regional office, in responding to many such cases over a four-state area, had learned that lack of clarity about the law compounded the conflict.

In 1980 CRS, under Regional Director Robert Lamb, took the lead in recommending, and then cosponsoring, a three-state Institute on Indian Law and Jurisdiction for lawyers and law enforcement personnel from Washington, Oregon, and Idaho.[2] Supported by the three governors, the institute focused on issues of hunting and fishing rights on and off the reservation. It also delved into other problems where the confusion of law was adding fuel to the racial fires CRS was trying to put out. These included criminal justice jurisdiction over Indians and whites and cross-deputization of law enforcement officials on and off Indian reservations, the authority and functioning of tribal courts, and methods of conflict resolution.

The hunting and fishing cases showed CRS that its mandate to help resolve racial conflict could not be limited to civil rights issues alone. If the legacy of slavery had written the CRS agenda with respect to conflicts involving African Americans, the legacy of Indian treaties defined much of the CRS challenge with respect to conflicts involving Native Americans.

Where blacks struggled for integration and the right to be included in the mainstream of American society, many—but not all—Indians were more concerned with distinctiveness. They saw the well-being of their people as being tied up with land and rights that they felt had been illegally taken away by the government, and for which they wanted restitution. For more than a century they had been fighting a rearguard action to preserve or

2. CRS Annual Report, 1980, 14.

reclaim their land, their culture, and their source of livelihood from an expansive American society in pursuit of its manifest destiny. Only Indians had their rights to property and their status under law determined by treaties and special acts of Congress. Only Indians had a special trust relationship with the United States, under which a federal agency had authority and responsibility over the governance of their land and resources, and presumably for their well-being. But Indian well-being had been elusive. Poverty and the social disorder it breeds had been the consequence for both those who had remained on the reservations and the many who had been driven from the reservations to the squalor of the cities. Many of the Indians' quarrels with their white neighbors and with local, state, and federal governments had to do with preserving and reclaiming rights and property and a way of life that many believed had been guaranteed by the U.S. government.

They had battled for more than a hundred and fifty years in the courts, often losing, sometimes winning, and when winning seeing victories eviscerated over time by Congress and by unfair manipulation in the administration of the law. Indian historians record duplicities of the U.S. government with respect to law and policy affecting Indians dating back at least to 1832. In the case of *Worcester v. Georgia* the Supreme Court, in a ruling handed down by Chief Justice John Marshall, determined that the laws of Georgia were null and void on Cherokee lands because of the Indians' treaty with the United States. President Andrew Jackson, refusing to act on that decision, said, "John Marshall has made his decision, let him enforce it." He then forced the Cherokees and other tribes to accept new treaties, sending them to Oklahoma. Since then Indians had been forced to accept almost four hundred treaties or agreements by which they surrendered ancestral homelands in exchange for other lands and the guarantee of rights to safeguard their way of life. For a period of a hundred and fifty years Indians saw their land holdings and treaty rights winnowed away by an unrelenting series of acts of Congress, court battles, and federal administrative decisions. That pattern of giving with one hand and taking with the other, of expropriating by force and false pledges, of negotiating with mental reservations, of consuming the loaf a slice at a time, of the government flouting its own laws, continued in various forms down to modern times.

Many Indian leaders and organizations struggled to improve the lot of Native Americans by playing the hand they had been dealt. Advocacy groups struggled in the courts and legislatures to reverse old wrongs or to gain compensation. But to many Indians nothing seemed to halt the long descent by which the once proud possessors of the continent had evolved to be among the poorest of its poor. And so, one hundred and fifty years after *Worcester,* thousands upon thousands of American Indians, poorly educated but well-schooled about these events by oral history, were ready to be revitalized by the idea that treaty rights might yet be regained.

Reflecting on the emotional underpinnings of Indian activism in the last half of the twentieth century, Indian historian Vine Deloria Jr. wrote: "The Modern Indian movement for national recognition thus had its roots in the tireless resistance of countless Indians who have refused to melt into the homogeneity of American life and accept American citizenship. The idea that Indian problems are some exotic form of domestic disturbance will simply not hold water in view of the persistent attitude of Indians that they have superior rights to national existence which the United States must respect."[3]

Indian Activism and the Trail of Broken Treaties

In 1964 a group of Sioux living in the San Francisco Bay area, citing provisions of the 1868 Fort Laramie treaty between the United States and the Sioux tribes, took over Alcatraz Island, the site of an abandoned federal prison. Ousted by U.S. marshals the next day, the Indians brought suit in federal court, laying claim to the property. The suit was dismissed, but the takeover drew nationwide attention to the concept of illegally compromised Indian treaty rights. Edward Lazarus indicates that the display of bravado at Alcatraz sent an inspiring signal to Native Americans everywhere that militant assertion of historic rights might restore to the Indian people the vaunted pride and dignity that had been eroded by decades of second-class social and economic status. A spate of Indian takeovers of all kinds of institutions followed for the next decade.[4]

Native American society was in flux. Under the Indian Reorganization Act of 1934, ostensibly designed to bring greater self-government to the reservations, the governance of the tribes was conferred on democratically elected tribal councils, each headed by an elected tribal chairman. The Bureau of Indian Affairs (BIA) would initially guide the Indians in the details of self-government, and then gradually reduce its role on each reservation to that of a supplier of resources. The speed, effectiveness, and integrity of the changeover had varied from reservation to reservation. At

3. Deloria, *Behind the Trail of Broken Treaties: An Indian Declaration of Independence,* 20.

4. Lazarus, *Black Hills, White Justice: The Sioux Nation versus the United States, 1975 to the Present,* 290.

the same time, large numbers of reservation Indians still followed old cultural and spiritual practices, scorning the BIA overlordship. Many traditionalists, railing against inefficiency, corruption, patronage, and injustice, questioned the legitimacy of tribal government and its BIA oversight.

Among younger Indians, advocacy groups were on the increase. Some were focused on legal and legislative remedies. Others, inspired by the physical heroism of black civil rights activists, chose civil disobedience as the means to call attention to Indian grievances. At the same time, among young, impoverished urban Indians there arose a movement to reclaim their cultural identity by returning to their reservations, where they sought the tutelage of, and made common cause with, the traditional chiefs.

Of the several militant protest organizations that arose from this ferment, the American Indian Movement (AIM) was the most successful, because of the imagination, daring, and success of its symbolic and dramatic protests. AIM first came together in 1968 in Minneapolis, a group that had been toughened by urban poverty, racism, and, for many, prison experience. Its first and primary focus was on the abuses of the criminal justice system, and it established a reputation for programs that monitored police behavior in Indian neighborhoods. As its activities gained a reputation for reducing arrests and police abusiveness, the group was invited to introduce its approach in other cities.

AIM doctrine coupled resistance to current abuse with demands for strict compliance with treaties of the past century. It took as its gospel the Fort Laramie treaty of 1868, which had ended armed combat between U.S. troops and the Sioux tribes by acknowledging the Indians' right to vast areas of the northern plains. Only after the army permitted and protected white encroachment on the land did the Indians learn that the treaty Congress had ratified was not quite the treaty they thought they had negotiated.

One of AIM's first targets for a "takeover" was Mount Rushmore, the national shrine to four great American presidents located in the heart of the Black Hills of South Dakota. Now administered by the National Park Service, the area had been at the core of the land guaranteed to Indians under the Fort Laramie treaty. AIM sent a caravan of twenty protesters to occupy Mount Rushmore, camping just above the massive heads of the presidents sculpted into the mountainside, in full view of the many tourists below. Park rangers ousted the group after twelve hours, but not before the bold venture had drawn nationwide attention to the grievances the Indians had intended to air. A leading actor in the Mount Rushmore takeover was Russell Means, an Oglala from the Pine Ridge Reservation who had been raised on the West Coast and had first been drawn to the fight for Indian rights as a young man recruited for the Alcatraz takeover of 1964.[5]

The conflict between AIM and the United States government in the early 1970s captured and held the nation's attention and imagination for a year and a half. It was highlighted by the cross-country Indian cavalcade to Washington known as the Trail of Broken Treaties and by the takeover and siege at Wounded Knee. The Community Relations Service, serving behind the scenes in this drama, but directly involved from beginning to end, worked with both sides to help avoid any uncalculated blunder that might have brought on a disastrous outcome neither side wanted.

The starting point for the conflict may have been the violent death of Raymond Yellow Thunder, a Pine Ridge Indian who had been tortured, shamed, and murdered by five whites in Gordon, Nebraska, in early 1972. The developing trial of his assailants took on the appearance of a cover-up, and the accused were charged with no more than second-degree man-slaughter and freed on bond. To Indians in the area it appeared to be a familiar scenario, trivializing the killing of Indians by whites. The family asked for AIM's help in getting justice. AIM brought a caravan of a hundred cars with five hundred people to parade through the streets of Gordon. Demonstrations continued for two days and nights while AIM leaders negotiated with the city's representatives. The Indian negotiators extracted pledges for a second autopsy and a vigorous murder prosecution, as well as the resolution of other grievances of local Indian residents. The apparent victory brought a heroes' welcome to AIM on its return to Pine Ridge and national acclaim among Native Americans.[6] AIM responded to other killings of Indians with similar demonstrations. Some resulted in violent confrontations.

AIM helped to stage the Trail of Broken Treaties in collaboration with Indian protest groups from the Northwest and the West Coast. A leading participant in the venture was Hank Adams, an Indian attorney who had led fishing rights demonstrations in the Northwest in the early sixties and who had filed some successful lawsuits regarding Indian treaty rights. The purpose of this cross-country motor caravan was to petition the government for a comprehensive reconsideration of Indian treaties and how they were being administered. A twenty-point document of grievances was to be presented to Congress and to the Nixon White House.[7]

5. Ibid., 294.
6. Russell Means and Marvin J. Wolf, *Where White Men Fear to Tread: The Autobiography of Russell Means.*
7. Deloria, *Behind the Trail of Broken Treaties,* xi.

Winding its way through Indian country, recruiting adherents on reservations and in urban centers along its route, the caravan delivered a thousand protesters to the nation's capital, arriving a few days before the 1972 presidential elections. CRS's John Terronez accompanied the caravan to Washington, filling the same role that CRS had taken when escorting the Poor People's Campaign to Resurrection City on the Washington Mall a few years earlier. He visited police chiefs and civic leaders a day in advance of the caravan to advise them of the peaceful intentions of the Indians and the wisdom of assuring their uneventful passage.

Faulty planning and poor coordination with BIA resulted in inadequate housing arrangements in Washington and a consequent unplanned takeover of BIA's headquarters by the demonstrators. During the course of the six-day occupation, discipline broke down, leading to appreciable damage to the building and its contents, as well as the removal of some BIA files. CRS conciliators at the scene provided liaison with the authorities and counseled restraint on the part of the outraged BIA police and District of Columbia police ringing the building.

It was the White House itself that resolved the problem. Seeking a rapid and nonviolent termination of the incident, White House negotiators offered three concessions to the Indians. They agreed to consider the twenty-point document on treaty revision;[8] they permitted the occupants to vacate the building without prosecution; and they provided $64,000 to expedite the Indians' return to their homes. A key figure in working out the nonviolent outcome was Leonard Garment, counsel to President Nixon, who was the point man of the administration's efforts to conduct an enlightened approach to Indian affairs.

In January, AIM was called on to protest another Indian murder, this one in Custer, South Dakota. A protest caravan was mounted to insist on justice in the trial of the killers of Wesley Bad Heart Bull. Violence between the caravan Indians and reinforced police forces mounted to riot proportions, ending with widespread damage and twenty-seven protesters jailed.

Other confrontations with authorities occurred in Scottsbluff, Nebraska, and Rapid City, South Dakota. In the wake of the takeover of the BIA building in Washington and AIM's several subsequent standoffs with police, Dick Wilson, the tribal chairman at Pine Ridge, indicated that AIM was not welcome on the reservation and that Russell Means would be

8. In January, the White House publicly announced its rejection in toto of the twenty-point petition of the Trail of Broken Treaties Organization.

barred from all public meetings. The tribal court also issued a warrant for the arrest of AIM leader Dennis Banks. Fear that AIM might attempt to take over the BIA building at Pine Ridge led to reinforcement of the reservation's BIA police unit with a detachment of eighty U.S. marshals.

In mid-February, as tensions rose, CRS dispatched three conciliators to Pine Ridge, where their first job was to try to sort out the issues and the players. They immediately found themselves in a cauldron of fear and anger. Established rivalries among the Indian residents had grown more bitter since the election of Dick Wilson as tribal chairman within the previous year. Supporting him were those whose lives were centered around the administration of the reservation, those on the tribal payroll, and those most strongly linked to the new federal benefit programs resulting from the War on Poverty. This number also included those employed by the Bureau of Indian Affairs, whose support services buttressed the tribal operations.

The opposition group included most of the full-blooded Indians, who were influenced by the traditional headmen and spiritual leaders who envisioned a reassertion of treaty rights to foster the restoration of a more Indian way of life. They accused Wilson of corruption, nepotism, a patronage-laden political tyranny, misuse of the tribal police, and creation of "goon squads" to intimidate his opponents. The opposition, including some members of the tribal council, had organized the Oglala Sioux Civil Rights Organization (OSCRO) in an effort to oust the Wilson forces. An attempt to impeach Wilson had failed, and a second effort was being mounted.

The marshals and the BIA police saw AIM as an outlaw band that had occupied and trashed the BIA headquarters and had a record of engaging in hand-to-hand battle with local and state law enforcement agencies. They were fully expecting and prepared for the possibility of violent confrontation. The BIA building had been reinforced with bunkers, and machine guns were emplaced on the roof. When CRS conciliator Efrain Martinez consulted with an official of the marshals as to how they saw their role, he said they were there to protect federal property, including the BIA building. When Martinez asked if they planned to intervene if AIM leaders resisted the rumored intention of tribal police to arrest some of them on the basis of an expired court order, the officer replied, "If war is to start, let it start here."[9]

With the failure of a second impeachment effort on February 23, OSCRO and the tribal elders began a series of public meetings to enlist

9. Efrain Martinez, interview with the author.

community support. They asked AIM to join with them. The meetings, held in the nearby settlement of Calico, were sometimes fired upon by parties unknown. OSCRO invited CRS to attend the meetings, in the hope that the presence of Department of Justice officials might offer some protection.

In search of a way to moderate or avert the gathering storm, CRS made arrangements for a meeting at which AIM and OSCRO leaders could discuss their problems with the leaders of the marshals. The meeting was to take place on the evening of February 26. The Indians attended, but the marshals did not appear.

At a community meeting on the evening of February 27, the leaders declared that the meeting hall was too small for the crowd and transferred the location to a larger hall in the village of Porcupine, about twenty miles away. En route to Porcupine, a caravan with about fifty cars and two hundred and fifty AIM and OSCRO participants stopped instead at Wounded Knee. They took possession of the hamlet, occupying the trading post and Catholic church and preparing to defend the village. The Catholic priest and the Gildersleeve family, who owned the trading post, were taken hostage but later told that they could leave. They opted to stay in the village.[10]

The traditional tribal leaders, who had asked AIM to support their efforts by some dramatic gesture, had also suggested Wounded Knee as the target. "In directing AIM to Wounded Knee ... OSCRO and the traditionals had selected the most symbolically rich location in Indian America. There, in 1890, Custer's onetime outfit, the 7th Cavalry, had closed the Indian Wars in a burst of runaway savagery. There, 300 Sioux men, women and children lie buried in a mass grave, marking the spot—indelible in Sioux memory."[11]

CRS conciliators John Terronez and Efrain Martinez, who did not arrive at Wounded Knee until after midnight, found most of its new occupants in the Catholic church. AIM leaders Russell Means and Dennis Banks were preparing a statement of demands, which they asked CRS to deliver to the government. The document, drawn largely from AIM's agenda for the aborted meeting with the marshals the night before, focused equally on the need for changes in tribal government at Pine Ridge and on reconsideration of the processes by which the federal government made treaties with the Indians.

As the CRS team members were leaving, they were warned that AIM warriors were posted in the surrounding hills with orders to shoot at anything that moved. They were given headlight signals to use to guarantee

10. Means and Wolf, *Where White Men Fear to Tread,* 267.
11. Lazarus, *Black Hills, White Justice,* 306.

them safe passage. (They later would receive other headlight signals from the U.S. marshals to use for nighttime approaches to the government's positions.)

At the BIA building in Pine Ridge, Terronez and Martinez passed the AIM document to Joseph Trimbach, the FBI's special agent in charge. He told them to wait in the office and then posted an armed guard at the door. Finding themselves under virtual arrest despite the Department of Justice credentials in their pockets, the CRS men phoned Martin Walsh, the headquarters coordinator of CRS's conflict resolution activities, reaching him at his home in Washington, D.C., at 4:00 a.m. Walsh spent the next few hours trying to reach the U.S. attorney whose jurisdiction covered Wounded Knee, to explain the CRS mission and the assignment of its conciliators to the heart of the conflict.[12] When Trimbach appeared in the morning to release Terronez and Martinez, he instructed them not to return to Wounded Knee. They indicated that they worked for the same Justice Department he did, and short of a change in orders from Washington, their duties required them to return without delay. CRS indeed did return to Wounded Knee that day, and for the seventy days thereafter.

Within a day the reservation became an armed camp. Reinforcements were rushed to the three federal law enforcement agencies—the U.S. marshals, the FBI, and the BIA police. Weapons and supplies poured in from army sources. Armored personnel carriers were used to barricade the three roads leading to Wounded Knee. Wayne Colburn, the chief of the U.S. Marshals Service, flew in from Washington to personally take command of tactical operations. Ralph Erickson, a special assistant to the attorney general, had flown in to be responsible for negotiations.

The AIM forces had sacked the trading post at Wounded Knee for shotguns and hunting rifles to enlarge their arsenal. They used a burned-out pickup truck to set up their roadblock and refused access to all federal agencies except CRS. The visitors whom they approved had to be escorted in and out by CRS. All roadblocks were reinforced with bunkers. Nighttime was punctuated by undefined firefights, and random gunshots were heard during the day. A parked FBI car was struck.

In the first two days the CRS team, now grown to seven, set up several meetings between government and AIM representatives that made no progress toward settlement, although they did achieve tentative agreement as to the rules of engagement. The Indians held generally to their previously stated positions demanding changes in tribal government and consideration of treaty reform at the highest levels. The government representatives

12. Walsh interview.

refused to negotiate any matters of substance until weapons were surrendered and the town evacuated. They did, however, agree to help AIM make contact with its lawyers. In exchange for the government's agreement not to move its forces any closer to Wounded Knee than five miles, the Indians would not fire any more shots. Ralph Erickson told a press conference, "We are not optimistic at the progress today."

What followed was two months of a war that was not a war and negotiation about the procedures for negotiation. The government announced that its forces were instructed not to fire except to defend themselves and the property they were protecting. Indians repeatedly declared that they only fired when fired upon. Nevertheless, both sides expended tens of thousands of rounds of ammunition before the close of hostilities. Two Indians were killed, a U.S. marshal was paralyzed, and a dozen other men were wounded. Fear and anger and mistrust were everywhere. CRS emissaries, shuttling back and forth between the two armed camps, often found themselves looking into the muzzles of loaded rifles.

It was apparent that the government never intended for its siege to be airtight. Its armed checkpoints across the roads into Wounded Knee were mostly for purposes of controlling access rather than for barring all entry. Contraband such as arms and ammunition would of course be confiscated. The noose would be tightened or loosened according to circumstances. While importation of food and other necessities was limited, government negotiators never threatened to starve the occupants out—although in times of greatest trouble they allowed the media to infer such a possibility. Food and medical supplies brought in by the National Council of Churches were first inspected by the marshals, then escorted in by CRS. Members of the press could come and go, except when they were banned by federal agents. CRS was allowed to bring in certain supplies from the BIA hospital, such as lye for the latrines.[13] The perimeter of the occupied area was quite porous. Overland routes through hills, woods, and prairie, though difficult, were available to Indians who backpacked food and supplies, to venturesome media folk, and to occupants under indictment who chose to come and go that way rather than risk arrest at the roadblocks.

The federal conciliators had to take on a new role, helping both sides to guard against an unplanned escalation of hostilities. Martin Walsh felt that for more than two months at Wounded Knee the possibility of a bloodbath was never far away. As one of the rotating operations chiefs of the CRS detachment at Wounded Knee in the early phase of the occupation, he had been there when a federal law enforcement officer was

13. Manuel Salinas, interview with the author.

wounded in an all-night firefight in which thousands of rounds had been fired. At the briefing of federal forces the next morning, the prevailing sentiment among law enforcement personnel was that the standoff had been permitted to go far enough. It was time for an all-out assault. Walsh argued for delay so that a new ceasefire might be negotiated. He was given the go-ahead to try.

Flying a white flag on his rental car, Walsh with conciliators Hector Berioz and Pasqual Marquez drove into Wounded Knee while it was still taking intermittent fire. Getting out of the car, Walsh stood to his full six-foot-six to survey the scene. He was promptly dragged down behind the car by his teammates just seconds before a shot struck the wall behind him. The angle of fire made it clear that the shot had not come from government lines. Nor had it come from within Wounded Knee. Further evidence uncovered during the day by both sides raised strong suspicions that the firefight had been triggered by unidentified troublemakers in the hills. Both AIM and the feds came to believe that at least some of the nighttime firefights had been deliberately provoked by shots from vigilante sources.[14]

The dangerous game between AIM and the federal forces was made more volatile by the presence of some provocative wildcards. Tribal Chairman Dick Wilson was suspected by some of seeking total warfare. At one time Wilson threatened that he had a force of nine hundred available to assault the AIM position if the government did not do it. He was supported by white ranchers and other residents who made their living on the reservation. The ranchers had their own grievances with AIM, which, in the past, had advocated resistance to outside exploitation of reservation resources.

A cease-fire was ultimately worked out. The feds withdrew their roadblocks to a distance five miles from Wounded Knee, and the Indians agreed not to fire unless fired upon. Walsh and Dick Salem, who had come in to relieve him as operations chief, decided it was important to maintain a CRS peacekeeping presence in the hamlet twenty-four hours a day to try to investigate outbreaks as soon as they occurred. Salem and Burt Greenspan, standing the first overnight watch in the compound, found themselves warmly welcomed by AIM leaders, who felt that a government assault was less to be feared with two federal representatives in their midst.[15] From then until the end of the siege, CRS provided round-the-clock coverage with twelve-hour shifts by one or more conciliators.

14. Walsh interview.
15. Salem interview.

But cease-fires were never for keeps, and peacemaking was an ongoing process. It was not surprising that, as the siege wore on, angry men manning lonely, often freezing outposts, sometimes tired, sometimes fearful, would be quick to fire and slow to ask questions. Nightly firing, at times heavy, sometimes continued for weeks on end. CRS would broker a cease-fire between the parties and then try to monitor the truce. It was sometimes dicey moving back and forth between the rival outposts during a nighttime firefight in order to convey dialogue that, essentially, went like this:

"My guys didn't start it—"

"Well neither did mine—"

"Yes, we'll stop firing if they pull back—"

"Well, okay—"

"Well. Okay."

On one occasion Efrain Martinez was at a government roadblock where marshals were deployed to fire on a large group of armed Indians coming toward them from Wounded Knee. He asked the marshals to hold their fire until he could check it out. He then drove down to the approaching party to learn that it was an AIM honor guard escorting a group of elders of the Iroquois and related tribes for the benefit of television cameras. The New York State Indians had just completed a ceremonial visit to Wounded Knee. Martinez advised them of what lay ahead and suggested that the honor guard bid farewell to the guests before coming into rifle range. He then returned to prepare the marshals to allow the distinguished visitors and their media escort to pass through the roadblock.[16]

As the standoff went on, CRS conciliators adapted to the routine of being stopped at gunpoint at each of the three roadblocks on every trip in or out of the hamlet. About six miles away from Wounded Knee was the checkpoint of the tribal police, an outpost manned by followers of Tribal Chairman Dick Wilson, whom many of his political foes preferred to call Dick Wilson's goons. Five miles out was the federal government checkpoint staffed by men of the U.S. Marshals Service and the FBI, who made no bones about seeing the CRS assignment as being tantamount to consorting with the enemy. Closest to Wounded Knee was the AIM outpost, where the CRS identification credentials always had to be shown. But it was only at the last barrier that the peacemakers felt their presence was welcome.

While the leaders of the government team accepted the CRS conciliators as necessary neutral go-betweens, some of the law enforcement agents

16. Martinez interview.

on the firing line had mixed feelings. On occasion CRS cars would be stopped at the government roadblock and searched for contraband. Martinez was stopped one day and told by a marshal that he could no longer go into Wounded Knee because the Indians were siphoning gas from cars to make Molotov cocktails. Martinez asked, "How can we settle this? You're out here on this freezing prairie, where you didn't ask to be sent, because the Justice Department told you to be here. The same Justice Department told me to be inside Wounded Knee, so I gotta go. Why don't you send a deputy in with me to guard the car?" The marshal thought for a moment, then replied, "Okay, you can go ahead, but be careful."

CRS had known that AIM was siphoning gas to use in its own cars but thought it to be a useful practice since it helped to make sure that AIM's discipline over its outposted warriors did not suffer from lack of communication and control. For the same reason, CRS also provided batteries for AIM's radios. But the question was soon rendered moot when the tribal police checkpoint refused to pass any CRS vehicle whose gas gauge showed more than one or two gallons. On more than one occasion conciliators had to turn back to drive an extra ten or twenty miles in order to bring the gas gauge down low enough to satisfy Wilson's men.

At one point Wilson ordered CRS off the reservation, until it was made clear to him that the attorney general, not the tribal chairman, determined Department of Justice assignments. His men then denied CRS passage through their roadblock. The CRS absence was immediately taken by AIM's leadership to mean that the government was preparing for an all-out assault, thus destabilizing the cease-fire. CRS then arranged for an armed escort by the U.S. marshals whenever Wilson's people barred its way. On one occasion, Jonathan Chace was at the tribal checkpoint waiting for his escorting marshal, when a car of wannabe AIM supporters blundered onto the scene. They were college students on their way to offer supplies and their services to AIM; they hadn't calculated on roadblocks and armed guards. The guard roughed them up and fired a shotgun into their engine. Chace's escort, who arrived during these proceedings, took stock of the situation. He said to Chace, "This is no place for me to be," and made a rapid departure. Minus his escort, Chace never did get into Wounded Knee that day.[17]

In late April, when it was unclear if a settlement could be reached in the two-month-old conflict, Wilson again demanded that CRS leave the reservation and barred the escorting marshals at gunpoint. The standoff between Wilson's Indians and federal officers did not end until Wayne Col-

17. Chace interview.

burn, chief of the U.S. Marshals Service, personally led a detachment of deputies armed with M-16 rifles to force the termination of the roadblock.

Fully aware of the deadly circumstances of the siege, AIM nevertheless extracted from it the fullest measure of publicity for its cause. Its leaders also knew that the glare of the limelight was their best defense against an assault. The major news media set up full-scale operations on the scene. Supporters, new and old, rushed to AIM's aid. The National Council of Churches took up collections and provided food and medical supplies. Theatrical celebrities and nationally known civil rights leaders visited the encampment, as did Indians representing more than fifty tribes from around the country. Messages of support came from around the world. Prominent entertainers helped to raise funds. Small planes flew in journalists and supplies.

AIM used pageantry and street theater to underscore the seriousness of its intent. It established a symbolic independent Indian nation to negotiate with the United States as a sovereign entity. It asked the United Nations for membership and support of its human rights claims. When it feared a government assault following a major breakdown in negotiations, it invited the media to a traditional ceremony where warriors donned warpaint as a pledge of death before surrender. It frequently invoked Sioux Chief Crazy Horse's famous war cry of a hundred years before, "Today is a good day to die." AIM's leaders understood that their negotiating position as well as their likelihood of survival lay in the credibility of their readiness to die fighting if necessary, and they reinforced that threat in speech and gesture at all times.

Negotiations about negotiations waxed and waned throughout the standoff. The basic position of the government, from which it never wavered, was that it would not negotiate under threat. But safety required that deals be made about day-to-day relations. CRS was sometimes helpful in brokering the arrangements that permitted discussion to proceed. Early on, the government was uncomfortable about negotiating with AIM. Ed Howden, who had flown in from the CRS San Francisco office right after the takeover, proposed that the traditional chiefs, who were aligned with AIM, take a more prominent role in these conversations. Leonard Crow Dog, who had been designated spiritual leader of the forces occupying Wounded Knee, became a key player at that time.

Two weeks after the takeover, Assistant Attorney General Harlington Wood arrived on the scene, to try to break the negotiations stalemate.[18] AIM leaders insisted that the meeting take place within the village, fearing

18. Wood later served as a U.S. District Court judge.

arrest if they met outside their own lines. Wood, against the advice of law enforcement officials worried about his safety, agreed to meet them inside the hamlet. He was escorted into the compound by CRS's Robert Lamb and the Reverend John P. Adams, who headed the National Council of Churches' food and medical distribution program at Wounded Knee, and who also tried to use his good offices as a mediating influence.[19]

Wood and the Indian representatives appeared to develop a good-faith relationship. After hearing their complaints in full, he indicated that he would try to develop some negotiable issues. A few days later he returned to Washington for consultation. He came back with a new proposal, which he presented to the Indians, again meeting inside Wounded Knee. They rejected it. The stalemate went on as the essential impasse remained the same. The government would not negotiate on substance until the Indians surrendered. The Indians would not give up their occupation of the village, which was their trump card, without an assurance of meaningful negotiations.

Assistant Attorney General Kent Frizzell replaced Wood as the government's chief negotiator.[20] Finding a neutral location for the peace talks became a stumbling block. It was finally agreed that the Indians would erect a large white ceremonial tepee in what became known as the demilitarized zone (DMZ). The tepee was located on the top of a rise that was visible to each side's roadblock. On the day of the first meeting, random firing from the hills delayed erection of the tepee until CRS was able to resolve the incident. Dick Salem, who was then the CRS chief of operations, sent Frizzell a message to advise him of the delay and asking him to await Salem's call on walkie-talkie before bringing in the government's delegation. About an hour before arrangements were completed, Frizzell and his party arrived by helicopter, landing about a hundred yards from the site. Salem ran over to explain the situation again and to warn that early arrival might well be interpreted as lack of appropriate ceremonial respect, which could start the discussions on a bad note. The feds took off, to return following Salem's call.

19. Adams, *At the Heart of the Whirlwind*, chap. 11. The Reverend Adams served for many years on the staff of the Board of Christian Social Concerns of the United Methodist Church and spearheaded the church's work on conflict resolution. He often played an influential role in the leadership of multidenominational efforts addressed to civil rights. His appearance at the site of many of America's major civil rights conflicts had made him a familiar and trusted figure to CRS conciliators.

20. Frizzell later became solicitor of the Department of the Interior, continuing, in that role, as a principal negotiator at Wounded Knee.

To get around the sticking point that the government could not negotiate under duress, CRS came up with the formulation of negotiating on two separate tracks, one on security and the other on substance. That way, at least conversations aimed at developing a framework for settlement could go forward, with the timing of its implementation to be worked out later. Under that arrangement a tentative understanding evolved that when the time came for the Indians to surrender they would lay down their arms to CRS, which would then monitor whatever other arrangements were agreed upon to assure their safety.

Within a few days the negotiators worked out what appeared to be a formula for settlement of the siege—the Indians would lay down their arms simultaneously with a meeting at the White House to discuss AIM's proposals. They achieved agreement on the issues that would be discussed and also worked out the conditions for ending the occupation. In order for Russell Means to be a member of the four-man Indian delegation, he would agree to be arrested on charges against him, to be arraigned in federal court in Rapid City, and then to be released on bail. Dennis Banks, remaining in charge at Wounded Knee, would order the end of the occupation when he received a call from Russell Means at the White House.

The Indians arrived in Washington for the April 7 meeting scheduled to take place in the office of Leonard Garment, counsel to the president. The entire arrangement then broke apart over a disagreement as to whether Means would call Banks at the start of the meeting (the government's position) or at the conclusion of the meeting (Means's position).

The difference could not be reconciled. The meeting never took place. At Wounded Knee, it was back to square one—except that the tension had escalated. Two thousand rounds of ammunition were exchanged on a single night.

On April 24, the occupants of Wounded Knee sent a message through CRS that they were prepared to enter into new talks designed to end the takeover. In the negotiations that followed, tribal elders who were supportive of AIM, rather than AIM's acknowledged leaders, acted as spokesmen for the insurgents in working out a new draft agreement. Frank Fool's Crow and Matthew King were the recognized leaders among the elders.

A tentative agreement, which Frizzell worked out with the elders, provided that within two weeks of an evacuation of Wounded Knee, a delegation from the White House would come to the reservation to consult with the elders regarding the grievances that had been presented. Other terms of the agreement provided that the government would undertake "an extensive investigation of the operation and finances of the reservation and would protect all legal rights of individual Indians against unlawful abuses by tribal governing authorities."[21]

The Indians agreed, subject to written confirmation from the White House. A letter to the elders from Leonard Garment, confirming the pledge of a White House delegation, was received by the elders at the home of Frank Fool's Crow on May 6. The letter was immediately taken to Wounded Knee, forty miles away, for final review of the tentative agreement by AIM's leadership. The leaders raised some concerns about the details as to how the surrender would take place and demanded clarification. Leo Cardenas, head of the CRS contingent, immediately phoned the government's chief negotiators, Frizzell and Richard R. Hellstern, deputy assistant attorney general. Catching them at dinner in the nearby town of Rushville, Nebraska, he arranged for a meeting without delay to finalize the agreement.

The leaders of the American Indian Movement then declared that AIM's job at Wounded Knee was finished and they were through with any further negotiations with the government. They asked their lawyer, Ramon Roubideaux, and CRS's Leo Cardenas to work out the final arrangements for closure.

At 7:00 p.m. that evening, at the junction of Route 18 and Big Foot Trail, Hellstern and Frizzell joined Roubideaux and Cardenas in Roubideaux's station wagon, where the terms of surrender were reviewed and clarified. The final agreement was signed later by Hellstern, Frizzell, and Wayne Colburn for the government and eleven of the elders for the Indians.

On the morning of May 8, seventy-one days after the takeover, the marshals and FBI removed all roadblocks. The Indians in Wounded Knee turned over their weapons to the CRS men, who then drove the occupants, a carload at a time, to a U.S. marshals' checkpoint for processing, in the presence of lawyers representing the Indians. Those with charges against them were sent to Rapid City for the agreed-upon speedy bond hearing. None of AIM's principal leaders were present in Wounded Knee for the surrender. Most of the weapons had also been evacuated cross-country in advance.

On May 17, Brad Patterson, adviser to the president on Indian affairs, led a White House delegation to a meeting on the reservation at the home of Frank Fool's Crow. Following the discussion, he promised to return in two weeks with a response. When the response did come, it was in the form of a letter from Leonard Garment saying that "the days of treaty mak-

21. *New York Times,* May 7, 1973.

ing with American Indians ended in 1871, and that only Congress can re-
scind or change in any way statutes enacted since 1871."[22]

As leaders of the takeover at Wounded Knee, Dennis Banks and Russell Means were tried on a variety of felony counts. After an eight-month
trial in the U.S. District Court in St. Paul, all charges were dismissed by
the judge on the grounds of misconduct on the part of the FBI and the
federal prosecutors. More than one hundred and fifty other participants
at Wounded Knee were brought to trial in several federal courts. In most
cases charges were dismissed. The few cases that went to trial resulted
in acquittals. Later, Leonard Crow Dog and Carter Camp, as leaders at
Wounded Knee, were convicted of being responsible for interfering with
the postal inspectors who had entered the hamlet to investigate charges
of destruction of post office boxes.[23]

The Texas Gulf Coast Shrimping Wars

The abundant shrimp in the Gulf of Mexico had been a source of livelihood for generations of Texans whose boats plied the waters adjacent to
the Gulf Coast towns where they lived. Ten thousand miles away, generations of Vietnamese residing in the Mekong Delta had made their living
in the same way. America's post–Vietnam War program that relocated
Vietnamese refugees to American communities where they might thrive
included the Texas Gulf Coast. This seemingly logical decision had explosive consequences that posed a new challenge for CRS.

The relocation program started in 1975. By 1976 ten thousand Vietnamese had been resettled in Texas, where their sponsoring agencies believed the familiar climate and opportunities in the fishing industry would
help them to make a new start. The numbers grew as the "boat people"
who fled Vietnam in later years were brought to America, and as many
of those who had been transplanted in other parts of the country sought
to reunite with family members in Texas.

Church groups, principally the U.S. Catholic Conference, and other relocation agencies introduced the first of the Vietnamese families to the
area. They were greeted with reserved civility by their neighbors, who sup-
plied them with their old boats—available for sale, although some were of
doubtful economic viability. But trouble arose as soon as it was noted

22. Lazarus, *Black Hills, White Justice,* 310.
23. Means and Wolf, *Where White Men Fear to Tread,* 331, 336.

that the Vietnamese did not fish in the American way, and they were making money with those old boats.

The life of commercial shrimpers in the Gulf of Mexico was growing more difficult even before the arrival of competition from the Vietnamese. The shrimp crop had been diminishing for twenty-five years. In the over-fished waters, it now required two hours to fill a net that could have been filled in only a half hour ten years earlier. Heavy rains in the Houston area for the previous two years further had reduced the yield in the Galveston Bay region.

The additional harvest that the newcomers brought to the market sometimes depressed the price to a point that on some days the Americans felt that it didn't pay to fish. But for the Vietnamese there was never a time when it didn't pay to fish. The Texas fishermen were offended by the fact that their profit margin was eclipsed by that of the newcomers. They bitterly attributed the discrepancy to the simplicity of the Vietnamese lifestyle. Many families lived together in tight quarters, dining on the part of their catch that Americans threw away as "trash" fish. By scrimping and by buying whatever they could for cash instead of credit, the Vietnamese paid off their boats in record time. They drew on their extended families to finance newer boats.

Some Americans admitted publicly that they did not want to work as hard as the competition. The Vietnamese boats left their moorings at 3:00 a.m. in order to be in the most fertile waters at the legal starting time, a half-hour before sunup. Efrain Martinez, who covered all of South Texas for CRS from a one-man office in Houston, noted a scene that typified the problem. Surveying a fishing pier around noon, Martinez saw an American boat come in to unload its cargo. Its skipper had lunch and then proceeded to sort and clean his catch. Then a Vietnamese boat arrived and immediately unloaded, into the arms of the fisherman's waiting family, baskets of shrimp, already cleaned and sorted by size so as to yield the highest price. The Vietnamese boat immediately set out to sea in order to get in one more run before the legal fishing time ended a half-hour after sunset.[24]

Hardest of all for the Americans to take was the Vietnamese violation of the rules of the road—the matrix of law, regulation, and informal custom that helped to preserve the supply and that patterned conduct so as to respect the rights of all. A basic custom was that a boat that found a fruitful fishing spot had exclusive trawling rights within the immediate area. The Vietnamese custom was just the opposite, encouraging the shar-

24. Martinez interview.

ing of good spots. American shouts and hand signals to wave off the intruders were responded to by smiles and signals of language difficulty. The Vietnamese were also accused of other violations ranging from exceeding legal time limits, to using boats with more than the legal five-ton cargo capacity.

Frustration within the white community, fueled by nativist agitation, lit a slow fuse that hit the powder in the summer of 1979 in Seadrift, Texas, a fishing village near Corpus Christi. An American fisherman was killed in a fight with two Vietnamese brothers. In instant retribution, two Vietnamese boats and one home were firebombed. White extremist groups threatened to drive the immigrants out of town.

Martinez responded to the Seadrift situation without delay. His first priority was to mobilize resources for opening up communications channels. This meant drawing into a concerted effort all groups concerned about the problem, including church and other private assistance agencies; local law enforcement; the Texas Department of Wildlife and Fisheries and the U.S. Coast Guard, which administered federal and state laws and regulations governing fishing; the Governor's Task Force on the Resettlement of Indochinese Refugees; as well as the fishermen of both groups.

The fishermen, particularly the whites, recoiled from Martinez's proposal for the formation of a joint fishermen's committee. He wore down their resistance by persistently pressing them to define their self-interest and then realistically addressing the options by which that self-interest might be served. He finally prevailed with the whites by saying, in some anger, "Look, you didn't bring them here. Neither did I. But they're here. And nothing either of us says or does is going to make them go away. So why don't we try to get them to understand why they've got to give up the Vietnamese rules of the road, and play instead by American rules."[25]

Eventually, he did bring together the Seadrift Fisherman's Committee, which lasted for several years as an arena for airing complaints and resolving some of them.

A local task force of interested support groups also came into being. Eventually a comprehensive program took shape. It included the Seadrift Community Council, which was composed of six Americans and four Vietnamese. The task force's main purpose was to serve as a grievance committee and to promote understanding and cooperation among all residents of Seadrift.

Town meetings were held, where community anger could be vented and where authorities would provide answers to the many legitimate questions,

25. Ibid.

as well as refute the misinformation that was circulating about the town.
The U.S. Coast Guard and the state fisheries department were encouraged
to publish translations of fishing laws and regulations and to offer special
classes in Vietnamese. Improved English instruction was initiated in the
schools, and special language classes were started for Vietnamese adults.
Illustrated brochures in English and Vietnamese were published to acquaint the new residents with American customs.[26]

The Seadrift outbreak alerted the entire Texas coast to potential dan-
gers in other communities, and Martinez worked with the most vulnerable jurisdictions to develop contingency plans and to adapt the Seadrift
approach for anticipating and responding to the many interracial tensions that were to plague the Gulf Coast for years to come.

Vietnamese in the small fishing port of Palacios were the next to come
under fire. Klan demonstrations and physical intimidation caused the
refugees to invite the help of the Southern Poverty Law Center, which
was able to get an injunction against harassment by the Klan.

Tensions rose as the refugee population continued to increase, reaching thirty thousand in the Houston area by the end of 1981. Even though
some of the Vietnamese, tired of the stress and danger, said they would
give up shrimping if they could get a good price for their boats and decent jobs elsewhere, the Vietnamese began to make further inroads into
the fishing economy, buying up retail fish stores. It was believed that they
would next move into the wholesale shrimp business. White fishermen,
facing a declining lifestyle, were beginning to withdraw from the fray.

The situation became so threatening that in 1981 the governor was
asked to assign national guard troops to control interracial violence. The
most dangerous arena was Galveston Bay, fifty miles south of Houston.
That vast arm of the Gulf of Mexico had long been a site of prolific shrimp
beds. One-third of the three-hundred-boat fishing fleet in the bay was
Vietnamese.

At a Ku Klux Klan parade in February a mock Vietnamese boat labeled
"Viet Cong" had been burned in effigy. Shortly thereafter, two boats were
burned at their docks in Seadrift, where the 1979 trouble had taken place.
That was followed by three burnings and some false alarms in the Galveston Bay area.

In the twin fishing villages of Seabrook and Kemah, where as many as
forty-two Vietnamese boats tied up at a single mooring area in Kemah
known as "Hanoi Harbor," Martinez worked unsuccessfully for months to
create a joint committee of American and Vietnamese fishermen. The

26. CRS Annual Report, 1980, 14.

most influential person in the local white fishermen's association was the Grand Dragon of the Knights of the White Camellia. He had predicted that if the Vietnamese were not driven out they would one day control the whole industry. The leader of the Vietnamese community was "Colonel" Nam Van Nguyen, his title reflecting his former status in the Vietnamese army. Neither leader had any interest in meeting with the other. Martinez finally decided to try to exploit the considerable machismo of both leaders. He proposed an off-the-record one-on-one meeting, while subtly planting the notion that each man doubted the other had the courage to go head-to-head. The meeting finally took place. When the two leaders discovered that they could work with each other to advance their respective interests, the biracial Seabrook/Kemah Fishermen's Coalition came into being.

Other moves were also afoot to relieve the tension. The state legislature considered a bill to declare a two-year moratorium on the issuance of new commercial fishing licenses. Agencies in the Galveston Bay area set up a school for fish processing occupations to equip fishermen and their families with new skills.

The opening of the shrimping season on May 15 was greatly feared for its potential for violence. Three hundred shrimp boats, one hundred of them owned by Vietnamese, dropped their nets in Galveston Bay under the watchful eye of local, state, and federal law enforcement agencies. There were no untoward occurrences that day. Bad weather for the next few days kept all the boats in their harbors. The rest of the season proceeded without further major outbreaks of violence.

After that, the level of discord in the shrimping industry diminished year by year as the prediction of the Grand Dragon that the Vietnamese would one day dominate the business gradually came to fruition.

Ten

Minorities and the Media

The Conversion of the Image Builders

Before mid-twentieth-century actions by the courts and Congress to uproot the barriers to racial justice, white Americans saw their country as if on a split screen. Large, sharp, and bright was the mainstream portrayal of how white people lived. On a small, grainy segment of the screen, of which the viewer was only vaguely aware, was the depiction of racial minorities. Shown mostly as menials, they appeared less educated, less skilled, less well-spoken, more violent—clearly inferior. This image was reinforced by the media—the broadcasting, film making, news gathering, and publishing industries that influenced people's vision of what America was and, by inference, how it was supposed to be.

The persistence of this image made it easier for some Americans to fight to keep things the way they were. For other Americans, it made it harder to accept the rightness and inevitability of the changes toward side-by-side equality that the law now required. CRS's mandate to promote change without turmoil caused it to focus special attention on ways of working with the media toward that end.

In the early 1960s, radio and television were practically lily-white, and print media were strictly Jim Crow. Discrimination in the image-building business not only perpetuated invidious racial stereotypes, it also barred minorities from employment and ownership opportunities within a major industry. Since the distorted image of blacks and the absence of blacks as journalists helped to reinforce each other, the vision among America's image makers was limited to what could be seen through white eyes.

In its earliest strategic planning CRS recognized that for Americans to understand and accept racial equality, changes within the communications industry were important. Within its first year, CRS initiated a program to encourage early efforts—then barely perceptible within the publishing and broadcasting world—to improve the depth and quality of reporting about minority cultures and to employ minorities as news gatherers and presenters.

CRS began to stake out the ground for a program addressed to the media in 1965. Director LeRoy Collins, as immediate past president of the National Association of Broadcasters, had an insider's credibility with the communications industry. His deputy director, Calvin Kytle (who was to succeed him briefly in the role of acting director), was a journalist and publicist of long standing. Using the platforms offered them by the national associations of media executives, they stimulated the dialogue, then just beginning within the industry, to define the opportunities as well as the obligations of the media, to help America survive the critical period of civil rights transition through which it was passing.

To the media moguls with whom they met, Collins and Kytle held up a mirror to an industry that still perceived only dimly its great opportunity to serve the nation during one of the most critical crises of the century. The more thoughtful in their audience undoubtedly heard, behind their diplomatic language, a bill of particulars that challenged the good newsman to do better.

The nation's leading opinion molders were asked to consider how their failure to depict the Negro people as normal human beings reinforced the myth of white superiority, and how the persistence of that myth made peaceful acceptance of new legal standards more difficult.

To the American Society of Newspaper Editors, Collins attributed the level of racial violence of the previous decade to the reluctance of American leaders, including the media, to support compliance with the Supreme Court's 1954 decision on school desegregation: "This condition encouraged the 'rough element' to get rougher in defiance, the devious to resort to ingenious legal maneuvering, opportunists to ride into power on the hot winds of political demagoguery. . . . Thus little or no national effort was made to lead the American people to understand why racial discrimination is unjust and unconstitutional."[1]

Speaking to the editors and publishers of United Press International, Kytle drew attention to the need to report racial news with the same skill and intensity they addressed to other critical issues. He illustrated their failure by pointing to specific departures from good journalism. He cited the practice by many papers of routinely placing civil rights news on the

1. Collins, text of remarks before American Society of Newspaper Editors, Washington, D.C., April 15, 1965.

same page as the daily crime roundup; stories about civil rights demonstrations that might report "a list of grievances was presented" without bothering to tell what the specific grievances were; failures to seek out good background stories by independently investigating the validity of alleged grievances; failures to seek the views of minority leaders that might differ with the quoted views of the establishment; reluctance to give appropriate coverage to militant groups because of their inflammatory style rather than to present the substance of their viewpoint.[2]

The bottom line stressed the obvious but suppressed truth that a newspaper cannot expect good reporting from reporters who don't know their beat. Citing the paucity of minority newsmen, CRS asked the media leaders to consider how newsrooms and editorial desks might be enriched by the new insights and access to new news sources that would result from minority recruitment and training programs.

Even as they pressed these exhortations for change at the national level in order to focus the attention of news executives on the critical issues, the CRS leaders understood that far more would be needed to bring about change. Persistent demand by minorities themselves and minority-media cooperation at the local level would be needed to hasten the process. Here, too, CRS had a catalytic role to play.

To head this effort Collins chose Ben Holman, a black journalist who had already obtained the distinction of being a barrier-breaking "first of his race." He had been the first black reporter on the *Chicago Daily News* in 1952, when there were no more than five or six blacks in mainstream journalism throughout the country. Ten years later he was the first black on-the-air television reporter, with Chicago's CBS affiliate, WBBM-TV. The network later moved him to New York, where he became one of the first blacks to report the news to a national television network audience.[3]

At CRS, Holman's program was almost blown out of the water before it got started. When the initial draft of a concept paper found its way into the hands of some news-hungry journalists, a cry of concern arose about federal agents planning to exercise undue influence over coverage of the news. Charges of a move to subvert the First Amendment brought agitated inquiries from the White House and Capitol Hill. The teapot tempest was soon resolved, but it put the agency on notice that any effort pertaining to how the news industry did its job would require the delicacy of working in a minefield.

2. Kytle, text of remarks before Sixth Annual Conference, United Press International Editors and Publishers, Washington, D.C., October 5, 1965.

3. Ben Holman, interview with the author.

The program that emerged under Holman's leadership, and that endured for many years, ended up as a cooperative effort between media organizations and the minority community, at both the national and the local levels, with CRS being accepted and saluted as the catalyst that brought it into being and nurtured it.

The job was made easier in many communities where the growing tide of civil disorder was engendering friction between police and the press. Anxious and overstressed police departments, concerned about instances of inflammatory reporting, wanted tight control over the news as a means of riot control. The media, citing the people's right to know, wanted full freedom to report when and what they pleased and from where they pleased. CRS offered to help them work out their differences. In city after city, during periods of calm, CRS initiated media-police conferences to develop mutually agreed upon guidelines for the reporting of racial conflict. A third point of view that CRS insisted be present at these talks was that of the minority community. The meetings did more than work out problems between the police and the news organizations. One byproduct was a recognition of the usefulness of these new federal peacemakers. Another was the development of ongoing relationships between minority leaders and the media. These contacts facilitated the convening of many of the formal media-minority conferences that were to follow.

Holman put together a staff of journalists, including Charles Cogen, Willis Selden, and Lawrence Still, who canvassed the nation identifying news organizations and media executives who had already taken the lead in introducing civil rights awareness into their operations. CRS then sought to reinforce networking among these pioneers and to showcase their efforts throughout the industry.

While the landscape that CRS sought to cultivate was almost bare, it was not a total wasteland. Some news organizations had already made initial ventures, as evidenced by Holman's own experience. Willis Selden, who succeeded Holman in running the CRS media program, has noted other early beginnings.[4] The Associated Press Managing Editors (APME) had a Black News Committee, which, in 1970, published a booklet entitled *Help Wanted: More Black Newsmen*. It listed seventeen special programs and twenty scholarship programs for minority students interested in a career in journalism. The American Newspaper Guild, in 1962, had adopted a nondiscrimination clause in its constitution and directed its locals to seek nondiscrimination clauses in collective bargaining agree-

4. Selden, "Employment and Retention of Black Journalists by Michigan Daily Newspapers." Many of the elements of the CRS media program are chronicled in this thesis.

ments. The Newspaper Fund, a foundation supported by Dow Jones and Company, owner of the *Wall Street Journal* and other publications, in 1968 started programs to train minority high school students for careers in journalism. There were other tentative efforts, but the output was microscopic.

To get its own program off the ground, CRS generated minority-media conferences in a score of cities. These brought broadcasting and publishing executives together with minority and civil rights leaders to focus on two problems: how to bring about fuller and fairer reporting of minority life, and how to achieve more employment opportunities for minorities in the news business.

The way it worked out was typical of how CRS, serving as a catalyst, helped to generate a process of change that would otherwise have taken years longer. While minorities were bitterly resentful of their abuse and neglect by the news media, they accepted it as a given, like so much else of ghetto life. The energy latent in their resentment had nowhere to go until CRS brought it together with a change-making mixture of other elements. These included: a handful of pacesetting captains of the media industry, knowledge of arcane laws and regulations that could provide leverage toward change, expert consultants eager to enlist in a good cause, and a problem-solving process in which the demanders of change could make their case before those capable of making change.

Having been sensitized to journalists' skittishness about the intrusion of the federal government into their business, CRS was careful to confine its role to that of a catalyst and technical resource. Primary sponsorship of local and national conferences came from media and community institutions. A typical scenario called for CRS conciliators on the local scene to excite interest among media leaders and in the minority community. Then, CRS's media experts would make their experience available to the local planning committee. The sponsors of the first national conference, held in New York in October 1967, included the Columbia University Graduate School of Journalism, the American Jewish Committee, and the American Civil Liberties Union. Attendees, in addition to civil rights and community relations organizations, included executives from the major networks and public television, the two major national news services, New York and Washington, D.C., newspapers, some of the mass-circulation magazines, as well as black and Hispanic publications.

While originally focused on the relationships of blacks and the media, these seminars were later enlarged to embrace Hispanic and other minority groups. By 1970 at least twenty-one such events had been conducted in cities across the country. The goal of the local meeting was to create a follow-up program aimed at improved minority employment and improved reporting on minority communities.

A prototype of the CRS-initiated meetings, but organized independently, had taken place in June 1966 in Boston, where basketball great Bill Russell and other Negro leaders initiated a series of discussions with some Boston media executives.[5] These meetings ultimately led to the formation in 1968 of the Boston Media-Community Committee. A history of the committee written in August 1968, as recounted by Selden, noted that media executives reported the following progress in minority hiring: "Channel 4 now has 15 black people (10 in full time, five temporary) as opposed to four in 1967. Channel 5 employs three blacks. Channel 7 has ten full-time, one coming next week, and two summer trainees. . . . Radio reported that eight stations now have 21 black employees compared to a total of five a year ago. . . . The press reported that there are now 110 black employees on four papers, working as columnists, reporters, typesetters, photographers, artists, copy editors and trainees."[6]

Russ Raycroft, a former broadcast executive who worked with the Boston committee, was subsequently used by CRS as a consultant for follow-up programs in other cities. None of these committees, however, lasted as long as the Boston committee, which was still in existence in 1980.[7]

The first meeting of the media with a local Hispanic community took place in San Antonio in 1969, following organizational efforts by CRS's first two Mexican American conciliators, Conzalo Cano and Gilbert Pompa. Subsequent meetings in other cities led a group of Hispanic leaders and journalists to organize a permanent national organization to work for better media coverage of Hispanic life, as well as for recruitment and training of Hispanics for employment in the media. The leader of the effort was Ruben Salazar, an award-winning journalist with the *Los Angeles Times*. With the help of CRS, the group was brought together in June 1970 with the National Urban Coalition's Communications Task Force, a group of the nation's top media leaders. Twenty Hispanics met with a like number of people who were giants in the American communications industry. Some of them, like Katherine Graham of the *Washington Post* and William Randolph Hearst Jr. of Hearst Publications, owned chains of broadcasting outlets as well as major print media.

A direct outgrowth of the meeting was the formation of the National Hispanic Media Council, with Ruben Salazar as its chairman. The president

5. Ibid., 13.
6. History of the Boston Media-Community Committee, June, 1966–October, 1968, cited in ibid.
7. Ibid.

of McGraw-Hill Publications offered to provide office space for a head-quarters, and financial contributions came from Hearst and other sources.[8]

Two months later, Ruben Salazar, while covering a Chicano demonstration against the Vietnam war, was killed by a tear gas shell fired by a Los Angeles deputy sheriff. Bereft of its leader, the National Chicano Media Council continued to function for more than a year, but its achievement failed to match the high hopes that attended its founding.

CRS's media program took on an additional focus in June 1970 when, at the Denver Hispanic-media conference, a speaker awakened the minority community to the availability of a potent tool: the ability of community groups to challenge the license renewals of radio and television stations. Two of the criteria for license renewal, established by the Federal Communications Commission, were hidden weapons, just waiting to be seized: a broadcaster seeking license renewal could be called upon to demonstrate a record of fairness in news presentation and a record of community service. Knowledge of these rarely used provisions, when made available to minority groups of growing political sophistication, was to provide strong leverage for negotiation and change.

An outgrowth of the 1970 Denver conference was the formation of the Colorado Committee on Mass Media and the Spanish Surnamed. Denver-based CRS conciliator Manuel Salinas, with the help of Bill Selden, introduced the committee to the Citizens Communication Center in Washington, D.C., a community advocate in matters of license renewal. Two years later the Colorado Committee was ready to initiate challenges to the license renewals of the four major television stations in Denver. In the negotiations that resulted, the media made commitments to hire Hispanics, and each station engaged a Hispanic coordinator to work with a Hispanic advisory committee.[9] Similar negotiations were conducted by black organizations.

An agreement with more widespread impact, also assisted by the Citizens Communication Center, was negotiated by a group of Hispanic and black organizations with McGraw-Hill, which was moving to buy five television stations from Time-Life. The upshot of the challenge was an arrangement under which McGraw-Hill agreed to increase minority employment and to work with national and local minority advisory committees on employment and programming.[10] Specific provisions of the May 1972 agree-

8. Author unknown, paper on "Hispanics and the Media," copy in author's collection, cites audio tapes by Nick Reyes.

9. Salinas interview.

10. Francisco J. Lewels Jr., *The Uses of the Media by the Chicano Movement* (New York: Praeger Publishers, 1974). As cited in Selden, "Employment and Retention."

ment provided minority employment goals for each station, including the number of blacks and Hispanics in front of and behind the camera. Provisions about programming specified the number of documentaries to be made each year on aspects of minority life and culture, as well as the number of public affairs programs advocating controversial viewpoints on minority issues. In the early seventies other civil rights and religious groups became active, challenging license renewals before the FCC. Within a few years this movement had opened the doors for minority ownership of broadcast stations.

CRS also teamed up with various professional associations to encourage minority employment and training programs. A notable collaboration was in support of a major effort headed by Ossie Davis Jr. within the National Academy of Television Arts and Sciences.

The CRS media program suffered a sudden demise with the termination of the agency's preventive work by the Nixon administration in 1973. Although the media staff was dismantled, experienced staff members continued to be supportive as appropriate opportunities arose. By the end of the seventies, small but measurable changes were being reported within the communications industry. A 1978 survey found that among professional journalists working on daily newspapers, 4 percent were not white. An article in the *Columbia Journalism Review* by Nick Kotz noted that while "Jim Crow is gone, and the number of lily-white newspapers is declining, . . . there has been progress in integrating the newspaper business. But it has been halting, uneven, and far too modest to celebrate . . . two-thirds of the country's 1,762 dailies still have not hired a single minority news professional."[11]

There was still a long way to go, and progress had been slow, but CRS workers such as Ben Holman and Bill Selden, who had sought to build momentum for change, hoped that their efforts had helped to jump-start such movement as had occurred.

11. Kotz, "The Minority Struggle for a Place in the Newsroom," cited in ibid.

Eleven

The Quest for Value

This book was written to tell two previously untold stories. The first is that of the handful of Community Relations Service specialists who, day after day and year after year, were charged with witnessing the details of the civil rights conflict and working for solutions. The second story, woven between the lines, depicts the life of a federal agency whose anonymity prevented the American people from being informed about the work it did and how it did it.

This final chapter will look into some of the nooks and crannies of that federal agency and consider some of the human factors that animated the organization. It attempts a composite personality sketch of the agency and discusses some of the influences that shaped its culture.

The data, drawn from a wide range of CRS activities and concerns, cluster into three themes: (1) The institutional culture of CRS and its effect on agency performance. (2) Costs and benefits of the much vilified federal bureaucracy (as well as the CRS bureaucracy) and the administrative systems that make possible, provide daily nurture to, and magnify the effectiveness of the front-line service programs. (3) The legacy of CRS in resolving racial conflict and advancing the art of community conflict resolution.

These themes are interlaced, often drawing substantiation from the same data. For example, the casework described illustrates how the freedom and trust needed by field representatives to be effective was buttressed by reporting requirements and accountability standards that pushed them to more thoughtfully and rigorously pursue their work. Similarly, without the requirements of performance and outcome measurements, and the documentation of case impact, the long-range achievements of CRS as an agent for change could not be made apparent. So, too, the chapter will note the contribution of rank-and-file staff members to the development of programs of lasting value, as well as the contributions of conciliators and mediators who pioneered techniques that expanded the repertoire of the conflict resolution profession.

Development of the Agency Culture

One of the elements composing the CRS ethos was the fact that many of its personnel harbored a penchant for social justice and social action. Sometime in the late sixties, when Martin Luther King Jr. and Andrew Young were discussing plans for the Poor People's Campaign with Roger Wilkins, Young said to Wilkins, "We regard your agency as the extension of the civil rights movement into the federal government." Recalling that conversation twenty years later, Wilkins said, "And that's what I tried to make it. That surely is how I viewed myself. I viewed us as a voice, inside the government, for the powerless. In the cities around the country, I viewed us as providers of technical assistance and legitimation for groups of powerless people . . . and people who were seeking to represent and to expand the interests of the powerless."[1]

While the impact of Wilkins's drive and focus on the program of the agency lessened with his departure, and as needs changed and as CRS capabilities grew, full recognition of the minority stakeholder as a major partner in the conflict resolution process and of the need for negotiation to take place on a level playing field remained as basic tenets of CRS operations.

A number of staff members, including leaders of the agency, had worked for civil rights organizations before joining CRS, or had been volunteer advocates of minority-centered issues. Among them was Director Gil Pompa. Before entering federal service, he had been a city prosecutor in San Antonio, Texas, and president of the board of the Edgewood Independent School District, one of the poorest in the state. The district was plaintiff in a lawsuit he helped to initiate that ultimately resulted in a State Supreme Court decision equalizing state funding of school districts. Others served voluntary civil rights organizations during their CRS service. Associate Director Roscoe Nix, as president of the NAACP branch in Montgomery County, Maryland, for ten years, helped to build it into a major defender of minority rights; Regional Director Ozell Sutton, as president of Alpha Phi

1. Wilkins interview.

Alpha, the largest national Negro fraternity, presided over the development of a major program in support of improved education and leadership development for black youth; Regional Director Leo Cardenas was a national vice president of the League of United Latin American Citizens (LULAC).

In the early years, some CRS workers were troubled by what they saw as an ethical dilemma. In a conflict between civil rights advocates, who demanded change, and those who resisted change, how could you be a neutral mediator if, deep down, you believed in racial justice?

In time they recognized that this was not a valid dilemma. Both parties expected CRS to be an advocate for compliance with the law. Neutrality had nothing to do with the mediator's feelings about civil rights; it had only to do with the peacemaker's objectivity, honesty, and fairness in guiding the process so that both parties in a conflict would be able to negotiate the best deal they could consistent with the law. Those CRS staff members who longed to be agents of change had to get their satisfaction from knowing that almost all settlements represented movement away from the status quo and toward a situation of greater equality.

As a CRS conciliator on a field assignment, you were on your own in a troubled and bitter world. You could call on your training, a manual full of operational guidelines, the availability of technical support, and a phone line to regional headquarters. But, essentially, you acted on your own initiative, largely dependent on your own resources. It took more than professional skill to carry the load. It took a sturdy ego to venture daily into troubled communities, often as an outsider, to help the conflicting forces calm their raging waters and to work out a resolution for deeply rooted problems.

But the outcome was not always one for the trophy room. The CRS field practitioners knew very well that the resolution of community problems is complex, often involving the interplay of scores of factors: history; public attitudes and opinions; politics; community rivalries; as well as institutional and personal agendas. The task of helping to restore even short-range harmony requires the give-and-take of scores of players. While clear-cut instances of decisive improvement attributable primarily to CRS came often enough to reward the agency's labors, other cases could lead one to wonder: "How much of a difference did we really make?"

Wallace Warfield, an up-through-the-ranks veteran mediator who served as acting director of CRS during the latter part of the Reagan administration, would refer to some conciliation cases as requiring the mediator to "run alongside the case." By that he meant that CRS might participate in a case for weeks or months without finding the opportunity to make a distinctive contribution—until the magic moment when the conciliator's long-cultivated contacts, special skills, and careful trust building enabled him or her to become the critical agent for working out a solution. But sometimes a case might run its full course without that magic moment ever coming.

Two questions were always on the mind of CRS's leaders and employees in the field: Did our intervention do any good? How do we know? Over time a variety of approaches would be used to find the answers.

The concern of CRS staff members that their work "make a difference" was also reflected in the informal culture of the conciliators who continually stretched the operational guidelines when they thought it would help them to do a better job. To supplement the flow of technical assistance and training from headquarters, individual conciliators developed their own direct peer networking. Through this one-on-one give-and-take among fellow professionals across regional lines, they sought and offered solutions for thorny problems by informally sharing methods and contacts. This back-channel network also helped to cement fraternal bonds and maintain a high esprit de corps.

The small size of the agency permitted wide participation in its leadership. The ten regional directors routinely served on or chaired committees and task forces dealing with the most critical problems. Journeyman field representatives also were called upon for input. Regional directors, on many occasions, operating via their own back channels, initiated proposals that became important agency policies or programs.

Like most national organizations with local operations, CRS had to deal with the dynamic tension between the need of headquarters to provide oversight and the insistence of regional offices on maintaining the freedom to manage their own operations.

Field-workers often felt overburdened by what they saw as Washington's incessant demand for information. They believed that headquarters just didn't appreciate the pressures on an overworked staff operating in an atmosphere of continuing crisis, where solving the problem was more important than taking time out to write about it. Moreover, conflict resolution was so complex, and community situations so unique, that the conciliator had to ply his craft with unfettered flexibility. Headquarters, in turn, tried to point out that the very flexibility the conciliator enjoyed was a grant in trust to make good and proper use of the influence that flowed from Washington. Such trust could not be possible without a reliable accountability system involving disciplined operational controls and reporting systems. Differences were reconciled, in part, by including members of the field staff in the design and updating of operational policies and guidelines.

In the mideighties, Director Gilbert Pompa set the performance bar even higher, introducing a quality assurance program to systematize the inquiry into the question of "did we really make a difference," as well as to test the reliability of case reporting. A peer-review process was initiated in which teams of mediators and conciliators were sent into the field to review a sampling of cases closed the previous year. Evaluation interviews were conducted with participants on both sides of the conflict as well as with qualified observers. A critical question when evaluating closed cases was, "Without CRS intervention, how would the outcome have been any different?"

The quality-assurance program succeeded in validating, through the eyes of people in the community, the extent of CRS's contribution to the solution of the conflict. It also certified the reliability of the case reporting system. While the idea of built-in case evaluation generated a measure of anxiety among members of the field staff, the knowledge that their own colleagues were doing the review of their casework provided reassurance as to the fairness of the process. There were other benefits. Some of the mediators found that in evaluating the work of others they acquired insights useful in improving their own case practice; some of the case reviews revealed findings that could be factored into ongoing staff development.

Running the Budget Gauntlet

Even before the agency was out of swaddling clothes, Johnson's own Bureau of the Budget as well as congressional watchdogs of the public treasury were demanding a show of evidence as to the need for the existence of CRS as well as the necessity for every dollar of requested program growth. For a while—during the directorships of LeRoy Collins and Roger Wilkins—anecdotal evidence presented with common sense—and a good deal of charm—was able to carry the day. Moreover, the case was made that the most significant accomplishments of CRS were imponderables. Roger Wilkins wrote, "While we can count the number of communities to which assistance has been given, it is impossible to measure the extent to which antagonisms, conflict and violence were restrained or the degree to which repair of the social fabric and the pace of social change were quickened by our efforts."[2]

The going got heavier after that, with an increasing demand for proof and quantification of achievement. Among the challenges: How to measure

2. CRS Annual Report, 1965, vi.

the success of a case whose outcome was a nonhappening—a confrontation that didn't escalate to a major disorder? How to claim credit as the catalyst of a multicausal event involving a variety of players?

The CRS staff felt that the agency's worth should have been obvious to any sensible observer, even from anecdotal evidence alone: the potential riots that never happened; the civil disturbances that ended days earlier than they might have; the school systems that desegregated without turmoil; the battles for racial equity and justice that were won just a little bit faster and sometimes a little more convincingly than might have happened otherwise; the return of fractured communities to stability a month, or a year, or several years sooner than might have occurred without CRS intervention. In addition, an untold number of communities gained something of lasting value by learning early on, thanks to CRS, to listen and negotiate across racial lines and thus to resolve many problems through their own resources.

But the system didn't work that way. At the annual running of the gauntlet by which agencies proved their worth to administration and congressional budget analysts, and ultimately to congressional appropriations and authorization subcommittees, more rigid measures of proof were often demanded.[3] Gradually, seat-of-the-pants program direction gave way to management via goals and objectives. Those staff members who in their hearts thought the worth of the agency should be measured solely by its "obvious" contributions to keeping the peace learned to talk the talk of the bean counters. It wasn't easy, but CRS ultimately learned how to count what had seemed to be uncountable and how to do program planning for activities that often were rendered on an ad hoc basis in response to emergencies.

Sometimes the answers were found by developing proxy measures of performance—like "objectives achieved." To a congressman's question as to how the agency judges if its case intervention did any good, a CRS director could reply with precise information such as: "We know that in 93 percent of the 243 cases involving police use of excessive force, one or more of our objectives was achieved." That kind of answer was usually enough. But when a skeptical legislator would follow up with, "What is an objective and how do you know when it has been achieved," the director was ready with a description of case process. He could explain that no case could be opened without the regional director's personal approval of the conciliator's assessment; that every assessment included the conciliator's

3. U.S. Department of Justice, Community Relations Service, "Operational Planning System Handbook," 1979.

"verifiable" objectives for resolving the conflict; and that no case was closed without a review of the "outcome" of each objective. Examples of such objectives might include: "to get the parties to the bargaining table"; "to gain a signed, written agreement"; "to bring about a study of the student discipline code and its implementation"; "to negotiate the creation of a minority advisory committee to the police chief"; "adoption of police guidelines for the use of firearms." In learning to satisfy the outside demand for tangible evidence of performance, the agency's advocates for social justice found tools to satisfy their own need for assurance that their work was furthering the cause.

Despite its microscopic budget (which never, even in its most expansive days, reached the $10 million level), the CRS program was often stunted by funding reductions, and at times threatened with extinction. CRS administrators who struggled to keep the agency adequately funded believed that budget analysts in the administrative division of the Justice Department, and in the White House Office of Management and Budget (OMB),[4] thought they won their stripes by recommending budget reductions. These technicians had few opportunities to shine when dealing with the costly programs favored by the department or the administration, or by powerful committee chairs in Congress. It was the runts at the feeding trough, small agencies like CRS that lacked powerful sponsors, that were the easy marks on which a junior analyst might build his reputation.

The ultimate fate of the CRS budget depended on two subcommittees of the House of Representatives that decided each year whether to approve the level of funds requested by the administration. Consistent support came from the Judiciary Committee's Subcommittee on Civil and Constitutional Rights, which had oversight authority over the agency's programs. In its annual reauthorization hearings, members of the committee expressed familiarity and concern with the problems CRS addressed. They often challenged the agency to make even greater efforts and asked how they might be of help. The CRS budget team attributed this support to the pro–civil rights bias of many subcommittee members, which made them comfortable in accepting the worth of CRS achievements at face value. Particularly helpful were those congressmen whose hands-on involvement with civil rights issues in their own district had given them an insider's view of CRS services in times of crisis. Subcommittee Chairman Don Edwards, who presided for many years, and Congressman John Conyers, for example, would often raise questions about CRS's performance in San Jose, California, and Detroit, Michigan.

---

4. OMB was the successor agency to the Bureau of the Budget.

The defenders of the budget had a harder row to hoe in making their case before the Appropriations Committee's Subcommittee on the Departments of State, Commerce, and Justice and the Judiciary. This group, whose members had to examine the budgets of three large departments and more, tended to take a more dispassionate and more challenging view of the needs of CRS, whose operations laid claim to but a smidgen of the budget of just one of the three departments. CRS knew that the appropriations people had the final word on funding but always hoped that a good word from the reauthorization group would help in the formulation of the bottom line.

The agency became something of a political football during the budgeting process, when Democrats on the House Judiciary Committee would praise CRS to the heavens in such a manner as to embarrass a Republican administration for the inadequacies of all its other civil rights programs. At such times the CRS director, in testifying before the committee, would have to become an artful dodger to avoid being cast in the role of a critic of the department and of the president, whose budget he was there to defend. He would pass the ball, when possible, to an administrative official of the Justice Department for the more intricate phases of the repartee. All the players were familiar with the game, in which the congressmen would relent before going too far, since the last thing they wanted to do was to compromise CRS's relations with the department.

The lack of a constituency to lobby for an ample appropriation did not help the CRS budget process. The national civil rights organizations, which would appear to be a natural constituency, focused mostly on the need to defend and expand civil rights. They had little appreciation for the role that conflict resolution played in the cementing of hard-won gains all over the country. The CRS tendency toward self-effacement, resulting from the behind-the-scenes character of its casework, undoubtedly contributed to this low level of regard by those we had looked upon as friends.

During the critical battle for survival in the late seventies, CRS organized a last-ditch effort to stay alive. Key staff members asked civil rights organizations for their help. Regional Director Bob Lamb and I called upon Clarence Mitchell, the lobbyist for the NAACP whose leadership in the fight for civil rights legislation had won him the title "the 101st senator." We were greeted with the challenging remark, "Where have you guys been in the last fifteen years? We wrote you into the law, and then you vanished." After acknowledging the criticism of CRS's low profile, we presented him with a study, especially researched for the occasion, documenting 151 instances, in the previous eighteen months alone, in which CRS had been called on by local NAACP branches around the country to help resolve community civil rights conflicts.[5] Mitchell had no idea of the service CRS was rendering to local branches of his own organization.

Over the years, CRS became reasonably adept at explaining its work, although sometimes it would take more than paper and ink. On one early occasion CRS persuaded an OMB budget analyst to spend a weekend with a conciliator working a case in Baltimore. Afterward the analyst said, with some vehemence, "Now I understand what you were trying to get across in your budget. I kept looking for your 'product.' But it's not just any one thing. It's the process itself that's the product—that draws the parties into a collaborative effort."

CRS learned early on that, in times of budget trouble, the best ally to have in your corner was the attorney general. With the attorney general's support, the full weight of the Department of Justice technicians and lobbyists would push the CRS case among the department's top budgetary priorities. Sometimes even that might not be enough. On several occasions, the agency was saved only by the attorney general's personal intervention at the White House and readiness to take the matter all the way to the president if necessary. During the Carter administration, when OMB came up with a two-year strategy to terminate CRS, Attorney General Griffin Bell personally had to go head-to-head with the budget agency's director to effect a compromise that assured the CRS's continued viability.[6] A few years later, when President Reagan's OMB slated CRS for elimination, it took the intervention of Attorney General Edwin Meese, who threatened to personally take the matter to the president, to assure the agency's continued operation.

Winning the Confidence of the Attorney General

The confidence of the attorney general had to be won anew with each new incumbent. Only a few of the incoming attorneys general were familiar with CRS or had encountered anything quite like it. CRS didn't investigate, litigate, or incarcerate, so what was it doing in the Department of Justice? The very concept of community conflict resolution as an ongoing function of the federal government seemed strange.

Two attorneys general did have personal familiarity with CRS before becoming its boss. Ramsey Clark had worked well with Roger Wilkins in the aftermath of the Watts riot and understood the agency's role at the

5. Gilbert G. Pompa to Benjamin L. Hooks, December 7, 1978.
6. *Washington Star,* December 5, 1978.

operational level. In later years, Janet Reno had worked with CRS on a variety of cases as the state prosecutor in Dade County, Florida. She had personally witnessed the performance of a succession of conciliators, including Fred Crawford, Bob Schroeder, and Tom Battles, at troubled street corners and rancorous conference tables across Dade County.

Attorney General John Mitchell thought it made sense to have a federal agency working to reduce the pressure of racial stress in local communities before they exploded. Ben Holman also felt that Mitchell valued CRS's social analysis of what was happening in the nation's ghettos, as a counterweight to the unevaluated raw data from informants that the FBI often used to depict a threatening and conspiratorial profile of various inner-city problems.[7]

Attorney General Griffin Bell especially valued CRS's ability to use mediation to keep conflict off the streets and out of the courts. Bell, as a federal judge, had been an influential intellectual force seeking to advance the use of alternative dispute resolution techniques to relieve the burden on America's overworked court system. As attorney general, he put the weight of the Justice Department behind that movement. Gil Pompa noted that Bell often teased him about the number of federal judges who wrote to the attorney general commending the work of a CRS mediator to whom he had referred a case that had stubbornly resisted a litigated solution. Pompa felt that while he and the attorney general both suspected that some of the letters may have been solicited, there was no mistaking the judges' enthusiasm for this new and unexpected resource.

William French Smith, early in the Reagan administration, had apparently been impressed with a briefing from Gil Pompa on the work of the agency. Pompa had mentioned, in passing, that each year CRS conducted a review of tension levels in the most troubled cities. At an informal press conference at Union Station, one morning, Smith had been asked whether he anticipated a long hot summer of racial violence. He replied that he wasn't worried because he had an advance warning system. Asked what that warning system was, he replied, "The Community Relations Service."

No one was more shocked than Gil Pompa to read in the *Washington Post* the next day that he had an early warning system. But the announcement did impel the agency to convert its highly informal, highly subjective system of tension-level assessments into a data-based, quasi-scientific process. While the agency was convinced that specific riots were unpredictable, it did believe it was possible to identify cities vulnerable to outbreaks of racial violence and to distinguish cities at high risk from those

7. Holman interview.

facing lower levels of risk. In subsequent years such risk estimates—always treated in the highest confidence—were used to help CRS sharpen the focus of its preventive programming.

Legacy—What Legacy?

None of the congressmen who voted the Community Relations Service into existence—and nobody who worked for it in the years that followed—expected anything more of it than that it would do its job in moderating the turmoil resulting from resistance to the changes brought on by the civil rights laws. The agency was to be a problem solver, helping others to relate more peacefully as they worked out the social changes by which America would make the transition to a more equal society. No one expected the peacemakers to be change makers—to leave any footprints of their own in the sands of time.

Yet the federal troubleshooters, the hand-holders, the community problem solvers could not have done their job for more than a quarter century without having some impact on history. A review of the record finds presumptive evidence that had there not been a CRS, many changes that took place would have occurred more slowly, many would have been worked out less well, and some might never have occurred.

We have seen how CRS, in responding over a score of years to thousands of community conflicts involving police use of deadly force, became a catalyst for improved police practice in hundreds of cities. The resulting national change in standards has undoubtedly helped to bring about a qualitative change in how police relate to minorities. We have also seen that, without CRS assistance to thousands of school districts, the process of school desegregation would have been a far more violent chapter in American history than it has, in fact, turned out to be. In addition, CRS helped to sound the reveille that awakened the broadcast and print media to the need for opening economic opportunities to minorities and for a fuller and fairer portrayal of minorities in American life.

One of the rewards of being a CRS field representative was the latitude within the standard operating procedures to cultivate your own special talents and interests as problem solving tools. Some of these methods became enduring techniques for conflict resolution. Joe Rodriguez, a Central Region conciliator, worked in Missouri, Iowa, Nebraska, and Kansas. During the period of rampant racial violence in the public schools, he was called on to help resolve a bitter and stubborn situation in a large technical high school in Kansas City, Missouri. Over time he was able to organize a program (subsequently to be known nationwide as "peer mediation") in which students themselves, including some who had been leading antagonists, were trained to be conflict resolvers. Within two years the climate of bitterness was gone. The school system then called upon Rodriguez to help introduce peer mediation in all its technical high schools. He used the approach in other high schools in the four-state region and was called upon to consult in other school districts around the country. Peer mediation eventually became a popular program in many American school districts.

Another approach that worked well in some violent schools was used by Arthur Peltz, a former media expert, who worked as a CRS conciliator in California, Arizona, and Nevada. Peltz taught students in racially troubled schools how to write, direct, act in, and produce videos in order to present their grievances with the school and with their fellow students. Rival groups were then helped to respond with videos of their own. The care and thoughtfulness required to state their own position and to understand the position of the other side in order to make an effective response sometimes revealed an identity of views and permitted the face-to-face discussions that followed to get off to a productive start. Peltz enlisted the local TV stations for facilities, equipment, and technical assistance. While the program was effective in reducing interracial friction, as well as enlarging the career interests of the students, CRS found it too time-consuming for widespread use.

Regional Director Julian Klugman encouraged the other troubleshooters of his Western Region to utilize the same principle of sharing grievances and responses between disputing groups in other violence-ridden school settings. CRS would meet separately with antagonistic groups of students, as well as with parent groups and faculty, to help them exchange grievances and responses. The process was successful in creating a less rancorous atmosphere, before opening direct problem-solving sessions. Called the SPIR program (Student Problem Identification and Resolution), it provided a formula for approaching racial disputes in many schools for many years.[8]

The technique of sharing grievances had been adapted by CRS from a program the National Labor Relations Board used in certain industrial situations to forestall labor disputes they might otherwise have had to mediate. Months in advance of contract renewal negotiations, mediators would meet separately with each group to identify grievances and study the other side's response. Later, workers and supervisors would meet to work out solutions.

8. Jonathan Chace, CRS's associate director, noted that the conciliators of the Western Region were still making good use of the SPIR technique in school cases in 2002.

Conciliator John Mathis, who had helped to resolve some thorny racial clashes in state prisons in Oregon, worked with the state corrections authorities to adapt the program as a preventive measure in troubled penal institutions. CRS would meet separately with prisoners and corrections officers to define problems and review the opposing side's perceptions. Then small groups consisting of both guards and prisoners would meet, with the help of a CRS mediator, to work together to define problems and find solutions they could jointly recommend to prison management.

The Art and Science of Community Conflict Resolution

The healing art of community conflict resolution has come a long way since its inception in the midtwentieth century when a few pioneering practitioners arose to meet the need in multicultural urban areas. Since then, the primary development has been in two isolated environments: the Community Relations Service and academia. CRS was enveloped in conflicts that it sought to resolve with intelligence and goodwill. Its methodology grew inductively out of trial and error and developed through usage and pragmatic adaptation into a formal body of practice. The theory and principles of community conflict resolution, on the other hand, were developed in university programs, where they derived from the world of diplomacy and commercial and labor mediation. A handful of private practitioners also made notable contributions to the development of standards and techniques. University-based clinical institutes that taught dispute resolution had only limited opportunities, compared to CRS, to test and develop the skills they taught in actual multiparty conflicts out in the community. CRS, on the other hand, started out with more cases than it could handle but very little theoretical background.

In an early effort to bring the budding profession of community racial conflict resolution, as practiced by CRS, closer to the broader world of conflict resolution, CRS's director in the early seventies, Ben Holman, led a group of CRS staff to the annual conference of SPIDR, the Society of Professionals in Dispute Resolution, an association made up largely of labor and business mediators. At a workshop on the resolution of community disputes, conducted by CRS mediator Ed Howden, only a handful of non-CRS mediators were interested enough to attend. Holman later made a second attempt to bring about a blending of the two communities by developing a proposal for CRS to develop its own academy for the teaching of dispute resolution, but he was unable to win budgetary approval for it.

It was only in later years that community disputes became a major focus of SPIDR meetings.

In the meantime, some blending did occur as men and women with formal dispute resolution training joined the CRS ranks and as some mediators trained via the CRS experience gravitated into private practice or university settings. A number of CRS veterans have moved to leadership roles in the Association for Conflict Resolution (ACR), the successor organization to SPIDR. James Laue was among the first to straddle both worlds. Following his experience at CRS, he founded and directed a clinical institute for the study and practice of community dispute resolution at the University of Missouri–St. Louis. He later helped to organize the Institute for Conflict Analysis and Resolution (ICAR) at George Mason University, where, as Lynch professor of conflict resolution, he established the first doctoral program in conflict resolution in the United States in 1987. Wallace Warfield brought his twenty years of CRS experience to the George Mason faculty and ICAR in 1990.

A significant move to help make the CRS experience available to others via the Internet occurred in 2001. CRS retiree Richard Salem, in cooperation with Heidi and Guy Burgess of the Conflict Research Consortium of the University of Colorado, developed an oral history project to interview retired CRS veterans about techniques they employed in actual community conflict situations.[9] Questions focused on technical problems of interest to others in the profession. Problem areas explored included such matters as goal setting, trust building, identifying underlying issues, dealing with intractable demands, use of the caucus, balancing equity against the need for settlement, dealing with personal attacks, strategies for impasse resolution, maintaining neutrality, dealing with cultural and racial factors, use of outside resources, use of fact finding, handling power differentials between the parties, and so forth.

The interviews reveal the differences in individual style and emphasis that CRS practitioners brought to their casework. The interviewers went to great lengths to explore the situational context of the conflicts that drew forth specific techniques. One such interview is with Nancy Ferrell, one of the conciliators who represented CRS in the states of Texas, Oklahoma, New Mexico, and Arkansas.[10]

In opening a case, Ferrell would first look for case objectives that would involve lasting systemic change, as opposed to objectives designed primar-

9. See http://www.colorado.edu/conflict/civil_rights.
10. See http://www.colorado.edu/conflict/civil_rights/interviews/Nancy_Ferrell.html.

ily to resolve the immediate conflict. Among CRS's case selection criteria, problems involving violence or the threat of violence were accorded first priority. After that, high value was placed on case objectives that held out the hope for influencing long-lasting change. However, such objectives were time-consuming, and successful outcomes were by no means assured. They were a luxury CRS often could not afford. Ferrell was fortunate to have as a regional director John Perez, whose own zest for systemic change enabled him, on occasion, to give her latitude to take on such high-risk, high-potential cases.

Ferrell developed such a case at a large university, where the initial conflict was only the tip of an iceberg. She was drawn to it by a newspaper article describing the high jinks of a traditional fraternity/sorority caper— Plantation Day. Members of one fraternity, in blackface and each with a noose around his neck, placed themselves for a day at the beck and call of the sorority sisters, presumably to the great amusement of all. The newspaper indicated that black students had protested and demanded that the fraternity be banned from the university. The Ku Klux Klan distributed flyers attacking the blacks.

The initial response among some on campus was that the incident was overblown. After all, Plantation Day was a tradition dating back many years, and no one had protested before. There was no deliberate meanness to it. The attempt of the Klan to exploit the situation was meaningless since it was not a part of the university community. The head of the fraternity couldn't understand why anybody would be offended by a bit of innocent fun.

In interviewing faculty members, administrators, and white students, Ferrell perceived an undefined uneasiness about race beneath a surface of goodwill, but no one seemed to know what to do about it. From black and Hispanic students she got a different view. Practices of racial subordination were built into the system. Minorities were virtually excluded from all activities; there was no safe mechanism through which to present grievances and seek remedies. As a result, contrary to the university's intent, the percentage of blacks attending the school was decreasing; and the authorities seemed clueless.

Ferrell concluded that the fraternity incident was just a symptom, and resolution of that problem alone would have little impact on the pervasive institutional racism. Her first objective, therefore, would be to help the university recognize its own problems. If that could be done, work on solutions was likely to follow.

She found a nucleus of support within the administration and faculty. The problem was to get the go-ahead from a resistant university presi-

dent. Ferrell, who tends to be analytic in her approach, sees her methodology as a dance with the client. You can't dance with someone if you're
at one end of the floor and he's at the other. It's hard to dance if he thinks
you're insensitive to his self-interest. For a time you follow his lead, until, in
time, he's comfortable enough to follow yours. It's a matter of timing and
trust building. In meeting with the university president, Ferrell was guided
by two axioms of human behavior she brought to all her cases: (1) no one
can be expected to negotiate to the detriment of self-interest; and (2) all
other things being equal, a person would rather think of himself as wanting to do good than as wanting to do bad.

Thus, she had to find a way to let each side understand that she would
remain sensitive to its needs and that she appreciated any willingness to
make an honest effort to work toward a solution. This belief enabled her
to take other people at their word. Others, in turn, would be reluctant to
break the bond of trust that she offered.

Ferrell said to the president, "I'm here to see if there's any way you
think the Community Relations Service might be able to help." With an
eye on the board of regents, to whom he was accountable, the president
indicated that he didn't want to be seen as "making a federal case of it"
by involving the Justice Department. Ferrell responded that she understood how he felt, but then asked what would happen if there were another racial incident, and it was learned that a CRS offer of assistance
had been rejected because the university thought it didn't need any help.
Then, she tactfully provided him with two thoughts he could offer any detractors. The first was to point out that CRS was a confidential problem-
solving arm of the Justice Department that had been created for the very
purpose of lessening the need for the department to call on its investiga-
tive and prosecuting agencies. Her second thought was: "If you think
there's room for improvement, we're here to help."

Before leaving she asked if he'd like her to stop back after completing her
assessment, in case he would find in it any suggestions for improvement.
He acknowledged, "Well, of course there's always room for improvement."
That became her mantra for continuing her work. The president had set
the tune to which they could dance.

Eventually, the president authorized one of the university vice presidents to work with Ferrell on the formation of a task force to look into
the problem. Ferrell then found herself dancing with many at first reluctant parties. Black students balked at the inclusion in the task force of the
offending fraternity, until convinced that was the only way to get at the
root of the problem. Faculty were fearful of giving more power to students.
Minorities did not trust the student government, from which they felt

excluded. Student organizations did not trust the administration. Some groups thought others might be troublemakers and should be excluded. Many individuals feared facing unfair accusations and angry confrontations. Ferrell made it clear to all groups that she would guarantee a safe environment for all to speak freely and expected in return that all would be heard in good faith.

It took three months of work before Ferrell felt that a representative task force was ready to come together. She then assisted the group for more than a year as it worked through its differences and developed into a cohesive entity that was united in its purpose. A major breakthrough came when the president of the fraternity announced to the group that he finally understood the enormity of Plantation Day, and he was ashamed that he had failed to see how hurtful and demeaning an event it had been.

By the time Ferrell closed the case, the task force had presented a set of recommendations for encouraging and safeguarding the participation of minorities in all aspects of university life. It had enlarged its scope to cover a wide range of relevant problems, such as availability of housing and access for the disabled. It became a mechanism for processing minority grievances and monitoring the remedy process. It was converted into a permanent body, reporting directly to the university president.

A Look Ahead

This final chapter is being written in 2004, fifteen years after the period covered by this book. Patterns of racial conflict and the Community Relations Service's response are the same and yet different.

Police-minority friction is still the number-one source of conflict. While the frequency of such incidents appears to have diminished, acts of police abusiveness still have the power to inflame an entire community. Many scenarios are unchanged: a young black man is shot by police who thought they saw a gun; a Hispanic man dies in police custody. To these have been added the practice of racial profiling of minorities by police, which, to many, appears to be an adaptation of the notorious racially biased stop-and-frisk excesses that were condemned by the Kerner Commission more than three decades earlier. In recent years, hate violence cases have been making up an increasing portion of the CRS caseload.

With a current staff of about fifty-four nationwide, CRS responds to unrelenting calls for its services by spreading its forty-some-odd professional conflict-stoppers—including regional directors—very thin. Although the Department of Justice has cautiously trimmed the size of the agency's budget, it has hedged its gamble, retaining its authority to temporarily enlarge the CRS staff by emergency transfers of funds from other accounts.

This provision was last used in the late 1990s, when outbreaks of hate violence led to the bombing and burning of hundreds of black churches throughout the South. CRS reprised its role of earlier decades in helping to reconcile fractured communities and facilitating access to resources for repair and rebuilding. CRS also provided community liaison for the federal task force appointed by the president to coordinate investigation and prosecution of the crimes. By helping whites to find ways to share in the condemnation of the outrages and participate in the repair process, CRS developed a reconciliation role that will serve the country well to counter outbreaks of hate violence.

These same skills were put to use in June 1998 in Jasper, Texas, when Negro James Byrd was murdered by three white men who dragged him for miles behind a pickup truck. CRS provided an almost continuous presence for two months to help the traumatized rural area deal with its grief and shock as a unified community and to help black and white citizens alike to acknowledge a companionate grief and a shared condemnation of the outrage. CRS also taught local and state officials techniques for managing protest demonstrations staged by outside groups such as the Ku Klux Klan and the New Black Panthers, whose efforts were likely to stir antagonism and violence.[11] The image presented in the national media of blacks and whites in Jasper being joined in their outrage and grief, and the swift justice that followed the crime, helped to neutralize whatever polarizing effect the crime itself may have had.

The impact of America's changing population has triggered a rising number of hate crimes and provides a foretaste of future stress as the nation adjusts to the transition from being predominantly white to being a country in which Caucasians will be in the minority.[12] Demographic changes involve not only immigrants from Asia, Eastern Europe, Mexico, and other Latin American countries. The problem is compounded by a major population shift within the country as "new Americans" follow jobs and relatives to areas of new settlement. Many of these formerly "untouched" communities are in outlying suburbs and in small cities outside metropolitan areas. These population movements have generated a variety of clashes between newcomers and other ethnic groups, and between the newcomers and the Immigration and Naturalization Service. Anxiety

11. Ephraim Martinez, telephone interview with the author.
12. Minorities already outnumber whites in many urban school systems and in a number of cities. The shift is projected to occur for the nation as a whole by the middle of the twenty-first century.

about newcomers, particularly when it comes amid growing economic uncertainty, has reawakened nativist fears. Preventing and responding to hate crimes have become major CRS priorities.[13]

In order to leverage its limited resources, CRS has turned increasingly to programs for building the conflict management capabilities of state and local agencies. CRS trains local police forces and human relations commissions on how to prevent and respond to hate crimes, on dealing with problems of racial profiling, and on how to assess and monitor racial tension. As part of the Justice Department's Task Force on Hate Crime, CRS trained more than three hundred state-certified police trainers. A course on responding to hate crimes is being integrated into police training throughout the country.

Worth Their Weight

U.S. District Court Judge W. Arthur Garrity Jr. had a special relationship with the Community Relations Service. They worked together for more than six years on one of America's most notorious episodes involving violent resistance to civil rights changes required by the Constitution. The school desegregation case in Boston drew the attention of the entire world, and the struggle over its resolution was helpful to many other cities in forestalling violent resistance to their own school desegregation.

In 1975 Judge Garrity endorsed the nomination of CRS mediator Silke Hansen for a Federal Woman's Award. His letter bore eyewitness testimony to some of the detail of CRS case activity:

> One of the principal stabilizing forces in the city during the present school year has been a network of racial-ethnic councils of parents and students at racially troubled schools. I sought and benefitted from Miss Hansen's advice in establishing these councils. . . . she, more than anyone else, was responsible for the functioning and progress of these councils. Her perseverance in initiating and promoting meetings of black and white parents after repeated rejections has been remarkable. . . . By way of illustration, there has been almost fanatical resistance to desegregation in South Boston, which has been a scene of violence and ugly confrontations. White parents and students at the high school there refused to participate in the formation of a biracial council for many reasons. . . . Only Miss Hansen remained undiscouraged. By patience and the force of her forthright personality and skill and judgement . . . she succeeded in organizing a biracial group there which has kept open lines of communication between hostile factions. . . . A city-

13. Community Relations Service, U.S. Department of Justice, Bulletin, "Hate Crime: The Violence of Intolerance," 1998.

wide parents' advisory group has been elected to assist local groups. . . . I attended and addressed one of its meetings. . . . It was readily observable that she enjoyed the confidence and trust of all fourteen members of the city-wide group. They obviously valued her suggestions and comments. Some of the members were at swords' points on various substantive questions, but they seemed disposed to discover peaceful resolutions under her influence.[14]

Three years later, Judge Garrity again evoked the CRS's role in the Boston school case, this time in a letter to President Jimmy Carter, in response to press reports that the administration was weighing the termination of CRS. The judge said: "At the outset of school desegregation here, and on several occasions thereafter, local officials simply didn't know which way to turn. CRS was able to . . . provide counsel and leadership not only to school officials but to the police and other municipal departments as well, and to avoid widespread violence." Calling the contemplated move penny wise but pound foolish, the judge went on: "According to the newspapers the annual budget of CRS is under $6,000,000. Why, the cost of police overtime at a single city high school during the first two years was over $10,000,000."[15]

On January 20, 1959, Lyndon B. Johnson, then majority leader of the Senate, introduced a bill to create a community relations service. The proposal was not acted upon, but its provisions ultimately became law as Title Ten of the Civil Rights Act of 1964. In his speech presenting the 1959 bill, Johnson said: "In any protracted controversy there is the stage of stalemate, a stalemate so bad that people cannot talk to each other. At this point . . . a conciliator would be worth his weight in gold. A man who could be trusted and who could come into the community and go back and forth between the leaders could break the log jam in communications. . . . And the people themselves would settle the controversy."[16]

Many objective observers reading that quote might salute Johnson's prescience—with due allowance, perhaps, for a bit of overstatement with regard to the weight-in-gold business. Judge Garrity, however, quite likely would have endorsed Johnson's valuation without qualification.

14. Judge W. Arthur Garrity Jr. to Community Relations Service, March 31, 1975, copy in author's collection.

15. Judge W. Arthur Garrity Jr. to President Jimmy Carter, December 6, 1978, copy in author's collection.

16. S. 499, 86th Cong., 1st sess., 1959, *Congressional Record* 105, pt. 1:876.

Selected Bibliography

Adams, John P. *At the Heart of the Whirlwind.* New York: Harper and Row, 1976.

Branch, Taylor. *Parting the Waters: America in the King Years, 1954–63.* New York: Simon and Schuster, 1988.

Burns, James MacGregor, ed. *To Heal and to Build: The Programs of President Lyndon B. Johnson.* New York: McGraw-Hill, 1968.

Chestnut, J. L., Jr., and Julia Cass. *Black in Selma: The Uncommon Life of J. L. Chestnut, Jr.* New York: Farrar, Straus and Giroux, 1990.

Clark, Ramsey. *Crime in America: Observations on Its Nature, Causes, Prevention, and Control.* New York: Simon and Schuster, 1970.

Davidowicz, Lucy S. "Civil Rights and Intergroup Tensions." In *The American Jewish Yearbook, 1965.* New York: American Jewish Committee and Jewish Publication Society of America, 1965.

Deloria, Vine. *Behind the Trail of Broken Treaties: An Indian Declaration of Independence.* New York: Dell, 1974.

Dibrell, George. "Mediation in Civil Rights Issues: The Port Arthur Experience." *Police Chief Magazine,* November 1976.

Edwards, George. *The Police on the Urban Frontier: A Guide to Community Understanding.* New York: American Jewish Committee, 1968.

Finney, Graham S. "Desegregating the Schools in Dayton." In *Round Table Justice: Case Studies in Conflict Resolution,* Reports to the Ford Foundation, ed. Robert B. Goldmann. Westview Special Studies in Peace, Conflict and Conflict Resolution, 1980.

Good, Paul. "A White Look at Black Power." *Nation,* August 8, 1966, 112–17.

Evans, Rowland, and Robert Novak. *Lyndon B. Johnson: The Exercise of Power.* New York: New American Library, 1966.

Fleming, Harold C., with Virginia Fleming. *The Potomac Chronicle: Public Policy and Civil Rights from Kennedy to Reagan.* Athens: University of Georgia Press, 1996.

Greenwald, Robert F. "CRS: Dispute Resolution through Mediation." *Journal of the American Bar Association,* August 1978, pp. 1250–54.

Halberstam, David. *The Children.* New York: Random House, 1998.

Hampton, Henry, and Steve Fayer. *Voices of Freedom: An Oral History of the Civil Rights Movement from the 1950s through the 1980s.* New York: Bantam Books, 1990.

King, Martin Luther, Jr. *Where Do We Go from Here: Chaos or Community.* New York: Harper and Row, 1967.

Kotz, Nick. "The Minority Struggle for a Place in the Newsroom." *Columbia Journalism Review* 17, no. 6 (March/April 1979): 23–31.

Lazarus, Edward. *Black Hills, White Justice: The Sioux Nation versus the United States, 1975 to the Present.* New York: HarperCollins, 1991.

Lewis, John. *Walking with the Wind: A Memoir of the Movement.* New York: Simon and Schuster, 1998.

Means, Russell, and Marvin J. Wolf. *Where White Men Fear to Tread: The Autobiography of Russell Means.* New York: St. Martins Press, 1995.

National Advisory Commission on Civil Disorders (Kerner Commission). *Report of the National Advisory Commission on Civil Disorders.* Washington, D.C.: U.S. Government Printing Office, 1968.

National Citizens Committee for Community Relations, Community Relations Service, U.S. Department of Justice. *Putting the Hard-core Unemployed into Jobs.* Washington, D.C.: U.S. Government Printing Office. 1968.

President's Commission on Law Enforcement and Administration of Justice. *Commission Report: The Challenge of Crime in a Free Society.* Washington, D.C.: U.S. Government Printing Office, 1967.

——. *Task Force Report: The Police.* Washington, D.C.: U.S. Government Printing Office, 1967.

Raines, Howell. *My Soul Is Rested: Movement Days in the Deep South Remembered.* New York: G. P. Putnam's Sons, 1977.

Rustin, Bayard. "Black Power and Coalition Politics." *Commentary,* September 1966.

Selden, Willis A. "Employment and Retention of Black Journalists by Michigan Daily Newspapers." Master's thesis, Michigan State University School of Journalism, 1980.

Sorensen, Theodore C. *Kennedy.* New York: Harper and Row, 1965.

U.S. Department of Justice, Community Relations Service. *Police Use of Deadly Force: A Conciliation Handbook for Citizens and Police.* Washington, D.C.: U.S. Government Printing Office, 1982.

——. Annual Reports for Fiscal Years 1965 to 1989.

Whalen, Charles, and Barbara Whalen. *The Longest Debate: A Legislative History of the 1964 Civil Rights Act.* Washington, D.C.: Seven Locks Press, 1985.

Williams, Juan. *Eyes on the Prize: America's Civil Rights Years, 1954–1965.* New York: Viking, 1987.

Wofford, Harris. *Of Kennedys and Kings: Making Sense of the Sixties.* New York: Farrar, Straus and Giroux, 1980.

Woodhead, Henry. "Red-neck at the Bridge." *Atlanta Journal and Constitution Magazine,* May 12, 1974.

Young, Andrew. *An Easy Burden: The Civil Rights Movement and the Transformation of America.* New York: HarperCollins, 1996.

Index

Abernathy, Ralph, 91, 94
Abram, Morris B., 17
Adams, Hank, 200
Adams, John P., 210
Adams County, Miss., 37–38
AFL-CIO, 176, 178
Agencies, city, 164, 171
Ahern, James, 115
Akron, Ohio, 143
Alabama, 5, 34, 44; voting discrimination in, 52, 60. *See also* Selma
Alcatraz: Sioux takeover of, 198
Alinsky, Saul, 81
American Civil Liberties Union (ACLU), 114
American Dilemma, An (Myrdal with Rose), 102
American Indian Movement (AIM), 199–213
American Jewish Committee, 178
American Nazi Party, 53
American Newspaper Guild, 221
American Society of Newspaper Editors, 219
Andreotti, Dante, 130–31
Anti-Defamation League, of B'nai B'rith, 180
Antipoverty programs, federal, 76; laws for, 102–3; in Rochester, 79, 82; from Vice President's Summer Task Force, 78–79
Aronson, Arnold, 8–9, 13
Ashcroft, John, 179

Ashford, Laplois (Lakey), 82
Ashmore, Robert T., 13
Assessment and fact-finding, in CRS methods, 25, 27, 43, 49, 231–32
Associated Press Managing Editors (APME), 221
Association for Conflict Resolution (ACR), 239
Association for the Preservation of the White Race, 37
Atlanta, Ga., 186–88
Atlantic City, N.J., 131
Attorneys general, 83, 234–36. *See also* Justice, Department of

Bad Heart Bull, Wesley, 201
Baker, J. Wilson, 50, 58; and demonstrations, 52, 55–57, 68–70; negotiations by, 59, 61; relations with other police, 59–63, 72; trying to avoid confrontations, 53–54, 68–69
Banks, Dennis, 202–3, 211, 213
Barnett, Ross, 60
Barry, Marion, 135
Barton, Robert, 139
Bell, Griffin, 234–35
Berioz, Hector, 206
Bevel, James, 55–56
Birmingham, Ala., 5, 10–11, 22
Black Panthers, 114–16
Black power movement, 116–22
Blough, Roger, 17
Blount, Winton, 34, 71–72

Boggs, Hale, 30–31
Bonilla, Reuben, Jr., 141–42
Boston, Mass., 223; racism in, 179–80; school desegregation in, 155–56, 160–70, 179, 244–45
Boston Committee, 180
Boycotts: of Coors, 188, 190; and counterboycotts, 40; to demand civil rights, 38, 40, 47, 56–57, 60; by students, 47, 56, 165, 172
Boynton, Amelia, 48, 50, 54, 73
Boynton, Sam, 47, 48
Broomfield, Tyree, 176
Brotherhood of Sleeping Car Porters, 118–19
Brown, H. Rap, 117, 120–22
Brown, Lee, 131, 134n11, 145
Brown Berets, 140
Buffalo, N.Y., 106–7
BUILD (in Buffalo), 106
Bureau of Indian Affairs (BIA), 198–99, 201–2, 204
Burger, Warren, 159
Burgess, Heidi and Guy, 239
Business leaders, 14, 49, 52; and boycotts, 38, 40; on effects of racial tensions, 27, 50–51, 187; of media, 33, 219–20, 222–24; in National Citizens Committee for Community Relations, 17, 33; in negotiations with minority communities, 10–11, 190–91; and school desegregation, 159, 170, 174, 178; support for civil rights among, 15–17, 33–34; using civic responsibility of, 27–28. See also National Citizens Committee for Community Relations
Business Press Advisory Council, 33–34
Byrd, James, 243

Cabell, Ed, 171
Cahners, Norman, 33–34
Cairo, Ill., 185–86
Califano, Joe, 83, 94
Callon, Ben, 39
Cambridge, Md., 120–22
Camp, Carter, 213
Cano, Conzalo, 223
Cardenas, Leo, 189, 212, 228
Carmichael, Stokely, 116–18
Carter, Jimmy, 234, 245
Carter, Lisle, 86
Celler, Emanuel, 12–14

Chace, Jonathan, 208, 237n8
Chambers of commerce, 16–17, 40, 72–73
Chaney, James E., 37
Chestnut, J. L., Jr., 48n4
Chicago, Ill., 78, 104, 106n7
Child Development Group of Mississippi (CDGM), 42–43
Christopher, Warren, 109
Churches, 47; attacks on, 4, 37, 243
Cincinnati, Ohio, 93
Citizens Communication Center, 224
Citizens Council, 45, 60
Civic leaders, 53, 56, 132; and black grievances, 41, 88; CRS working with, 27–28, 41; negotiations by, 27–28, 49, 61, 115; and school desegregation, 159, 170, 174, 177
Civil Rights Act of 1957, 6, 9
Civil Rights Act of 1960, 52–53
Civil Rights Act of 1964, 90; CRS in, 2, 13–15, 95–96, 245; compliance with, 17, 54; content of, 4, 39, 158; fears about, 3, 5; fears of noncompliance with, 11–12, 15–17, 23; hotlines for complaints about, 23; Johnson's involvement in, 7, 9–10, 17; passage of, 3, 5; on public accommodations, 21–22, 54; struggle preceding, 3, 12–15; support for, 12, 15–17, 102
Civil Rights Commission, U.S., 6–7, 9, 38
Civil Rights Division, of Justice Department, 23, 48, 84; and criminal justice system, 135, 184; enforcing school desegregation, 156–58
Civil rights movement, 31, 83, 130; and Civil Rights Act, 13, 16; on distributive justice, 89, 95; effects of, 104, 123; feelings about Johnson, 8–10; focus of, 5–6, 13, 46–47, 74–75, 89; goals of, vs. CRS goals, 54–55; media coverage of, 10, 48, 54, 72, 88, 219–20; splits within, 43, 75, 102; tactics of, 4–5; white support for, 75, 101–2
Civil rights organizations: and CRS, 222–23, 233–34; on integration vs. black power, 118–19; and media, 222–23, 225; and school desegregation, 87, 168; welcome for whites in, 117, 119–20
Clark, James, 45, 47–48, 54n10, 57, 72; arrests by, 54, 56; as embarrassment to civic leaders, 51, 55–56; and law-

and-order issue in demonstrations, 50, 52; and march from Selma to Montgomery, 62–63, 65–66, 69–70

Clark, Ramsey, 134; on CRS, 84, 97; and march to Montgomery, 71–72; and murder of King, 91–92; and Poor Peoples Campaign, 93–94; and riot in Detroit, 108–10; Wilkins's friendship with, 85–86, 234

Cloud, John, 62, 66

Cogen, Charles, 221

Colburn, Wayne, 204, 212

Collins, LeRoy, 76, 230; and CRS in Selma, 61, 64–69, 71–72, 84; on CRS's role, 32–33, 79, 83–84, 95, 219; as first CRS director, 17–20, 24; and Johnson, 64–72; and school desegregation, 28–31

Colorado Committee on Mass Media and the Spanish Surnamed, 224

Commerce, Department of, 23; CRS transferred from, 35n17, 84; CRS under, 4, 12, 24, 83

Community conflict prevention: CRS programs for, 96–100, 225

Community conflict resolution, 194; conciliators' methods in, 25–27, 236–42; CRS focus on, 96–97, 234; CRS expertise in, 43, 244; university programs for, 238–39

Community Relations Service (CRS): appreciation for, 43, 234–36, 244–45; backgrounds of staff, 227–28, 239; budgets of, 43, 99–100, 192, 230–34, 242–43, 245; cases of, 1–2, 44, 104, 146, 157; civil rights movement's lack of attention to, 5–6, 13; conciliation vs. mediation by, 136, 181–83; conferences sponsored by, 134–35, 147–48, 222–23; as coordinator of executive programs, 76, 83; creation of, 2, 9, 12–15, 245; credibility of, 30–31, 82, 85–86, 131–32, 161, 189; crisis response vs. long-term conciliation by, 67, 240; crisis response vs. preventative work, 155–57, 168, 170; culture of, 227–30; directors of, 17–20, 84–86, 126n2, 146, 184, 230; effectiveness of, 40–41, 52n8, 67, 104, 159–60, 191–92, 228–34; expansion of, 95, 97, 159; expectations for, 236; focus of, 35, 76–78, 84–85, 95–96, 146–47, 227; Johnson's focus on, 4–7, 9–10,

17, 24; under Justice Department, 35n17, 83–84, 234–36; limitations of, 35, 43, 104; mandate of, 14, 193, 196; methods of, 43–44, 97–98, 222, 238–42; networking by, 32–35, 134, 221–23, 229; number of cases handled by, 21, 183; objectives for cases of, 54, 75, 157–60, 168, 231–32, 239–40; organization of, 35, 79, 81–82, 229; preventative programs of, 32–35, 97–100, 159–60, 179, 225; quick start-up of, 23–24; recruitment of staff for, 24, 84–85, 126n2; reports by, 43, 151n35, 226, 229–30; risk analysis by, 23–24, 104n5; roles of, 71n71, 75–76, 90, 177–78, 243–44; rumor control by, 115n17, 121; selection criteria for cases of, 30–31, 86–87, 192, 240; source of cases of, 132, 242; staff of, 79n5, 236–37, 242; support for creation of, 10, 12; training by, 151–52, 244; use of technical specialists by, 115, 130–31. See also specific locales and issues

Conciliation, 83; civil rights vs., 28–29; requests for, 21, 23; vs. mediation, 136, 181–83

Conciliators, CRS, 29n11; attributes of, 21, 24–25, 228; backgrounds of, 106, 182, 227–28; methods of, 21, 25–27, 39–40, 49, 80, 217, 236–37; oral history of, 239–42; recruitment of, 24, 78–79; reporting requirements for, 226, 229–30; training for, 79n5, 228. See also Community Relations Service; specific locales and issues

Conference on Desegregation without Turmoil, 177–78

Congress of Racial Equality (CORE), 22, 26, 46n2, 86–87, 117, 119

Connor, Bull, 10

Convissor, Sam, 81–82

Conyers, John, 232

Cook County Jail, 184–85

Coors, Peter, 190

Coors Company, 188–91

Crow Dog, Leonard, 209, 213

Culberson, George, 96

Cummings, Milton, 34

Dade County, Fla., 235

Daley, Richard, 78, 87–89

Dallas, Tex., 177

Dallas County, Ala., 46, 52–53, 55–57.
  See also Selma
Dallas County Voters League (DVL), 46,
  50, 52
Davis, Ossie, Jr., 225
Dayton, Ohio, 173–77
Dean, Arthur, 18
Dean, John, 114
Deloria, Vine, Jr., 198
Delta Ministry, of the National Council
  of Churches, 42–43
DeMascio, Robert E., 170, 172
Dennis, Sam, 88
Denver, Colo., 224
Desegregation: as focus of civil rights
  movement, 13; of hotels, 22–23, 27;
  of public accommodations, 21–22, 26,
  48, 53–54; resistance to, 4, 10–11;
  tactics for, in North, 88–89. *See also*
  School desegregation
Detroit, Mich., 93; police practices in,
  110–11, 133, 150; riots in, 107–11,
  113; school desegregation in, 170–73,
  177; in Vice President's Summer Task
  Force, 78–79
Development programs, 42–43, 97–100
Dibrell, George, 136, 140
Dirksen, William McKinley, 14
Distributive justice, 74–75, 89, 94–95.
  See also Poor Peoples Campaign
Dixmoor, Ill., 104
Doar, John, 48–49, 71–72, 83–84
Draper, Jim, 28–29, 38–40, 42
Dyson, Frank, 142

Edelman, Marian Wright, 86
Edwards, Don, 232
Edwards, George, 125
Eisenhower, Dwight, 122
Elizabeth, N.J., 104
Ellington, Buford, 17
Elliott, Osborn, 123–24
Employment, 112; affirmative action
  plans for, 40, 50–51, 73, 190–91; lack
  of, for youth, 106–7; of minorities in
  law enforcement, 129, 137–40, 143–
  45, 159; of minorities in media, 220–
  25; and minority empowerment, 97–
  98; NCC programs for, 33–35
Employment discrimination, 51, 75, 104;
  and Coors, 188, 190–91; ending, 4,
  40; in law enforcement, 127–28, 147;
  in media, 218–20

Equal Employment Opportunities
  Commission, 4, 10
Erickson, Ralph, 204–5
Evans, Rowland, 6
Evers, Charles, 38–41
Evers, Medgar, 38

Faith, Michael, 167, 169
Farmworkers, 71n71, 99
Fayette, Miss., 41
Federal courts, 114, 183–84, 235;
  enforcing school desegregation, 156,
  160–69, 174–75; on march from
  Selma to Montgomery, 64, 66–67,
  69; Native Americans in, 197, 213;
  use of CRS mediation by, 191–92
Federal troops, 5; protecting civil rights
  activists, 71, 117n18; use in urban
  riots, 107–10, 113–16
Ferrell, Nancy, 239–42
FIGHT (Freedom, Integration, God,
  Honor, Today), 80
Finney, Graham, 175–76
Fleming, Harold, 16, 20, 24, 29–31,
  33, 83
Florence, Franklin, 79–81
Flynn, Ray, 180
Fool's Crow, Frank, 211–12
Foreman, James, 185
Fort Laramie treaty of 1868, 199
Frazier, Charles, 28
Freedom houses, 29n10, 37–38
Freedom rides, 4
Freedom Summer, 5, 37
Frizzell, Kent, 210–11

Garment, Leonard, 201, 211–13
Garrity, W. Arthur, 155, 179–80; and
  school desegregation, 160–69; sup-
  port for CRS, 244–45
Gary, Ind., 78
Gaynett, Gustavo, 126, 136, 171
Gibson, John, 120–21
Glatt, Charles, 174–75
Goldberg, Arthur, 6
Good, Paul, 118
Goodman, Andrew, 37
Gordon, Jack M., 184
Graham, Katherine, 223
Greater Boston Civil Rights Coalition, 180
Greenberg, Jack, 18–19
Greenspan, Burt, 206
Greenwald, Robert, 136–41, 182–84

Gregory, Dick, 27
Gregory, Hayden, 161
Griffin, John, 25, 96

Hansen, Silke, 167, 189, 244–45
Hardy, Willie, 135
Hare, James, 48, 51
Health, Education, and Welfare,
    Department of (HEW), 158–60
Hearst, Randolph, Jr., 223–24
Heilbron, Jerome (Jerry), 23–25
Heinz, John, 48
Hellstern, Richard R., 212
Help Wanted: More Black Newsmen (As-
    sociated Press Managing Editors), 221
Hicks, Louise Day, 162, 165
Hilton, Conrad, 17–18
Hilton Head, S.C., 28
Hispanic Association on Corporate
    Responsibility, 191
Hispanics: on CRS staff, 84–85, 126n2;
    and media, 223–24; and police, 140–
    43, 146; vs. Coors, 188–91
Hodges, Luther, 17, 24, 83
Holman, Ben, 126n2, 235, 238–39; and
    media, 220–21, 225; on mediation vs.
    conciliation, 182; and school desegre-
    gation, 161, 171
Holman, Carl, 86
Howard, Ransom, 138
Howden, Ed, 187, 209, 238
Hughes, Robert, 193, 195
Humphrey, Hubert, 14, 76, 83
Hunting and fishing rights: conflicts
    over, 194–96, 213–17

Idaho Fish and Game Commission,
    194–96
Indian Reorganization Act of 1934, 198
Industrial Areas Foundation (IAF), 81
Institute for Conflict Analysis and Reso-
    lution (ICAR), 239
Institute for Indian Law and Jurisdic-
    tion, 196
International Association of Chiefs of
    Police (IACP), 129, 134–35, 137
International Association of City
    Managers, 178
Irvin, Sam, 14–15

Jackson, Andrew, 197
Jackson, Jimmie Lee, 57, 60
Jackson, Sullivan, 64, 67

Janis, Jay, 23–25, 28
Jasper, Tex., 243
Jefferson County, Miss., 41
Jefferson Parish, La., 184
Jersey City, N.J., 104
Johnson, Frank, 64–65, 70
Johnson, Lyndon B., 71; and Civil Rights
    Act, 3, 14, 17; civil rights activists'
    feelings about, 8–10; civil rights goals
    of, 2, 4, 74–75, 122; and compliance
    with Civil Rights Act, 5, 17; and
    creation of CRS, 6–7, 245; and CRS,
    32, 84, 230; focus on CRS, 4–6, 9–10,
    17, 20; and National Advisory Com-
    mission on Civil Disorders, 111–12;
    and NCC, 17–18, 32, 35; and poverty,
    75, 94; and struggle in Selma, 64–65,
    67–68, 71; and urban riots, 108–9,
    113; and voting rights legislation, 56,
    70; and War on Poverty, 76, 101; and
    Wilkins as CRS director, 84, 86
Johnson, Paul B., Jr., 38–40
Joint Center for Political Studies
    (JCPS), 145
Jones, Tommie, 175–76
Jonesboro, La., 28–29
Justice, Department of, 5, 22; and Civil
    Disturbance Task Force, 113–16; and
    Civil Rights Act, 7–8, 11–12, 15; and
    CRS budget, 233–34, 242–43; CRS
    under, 35n17, 83–84, 95, 241; and
    police-community relations, 134, 148;
    and school desegregation, 159, 177;
    Task Force on Hate Crime, 244; and
    urban riots, 109, 113; on voting rights,
    46–47, 186. See also Attorneys
    general; Civil Rights Division, of
    Justice Department

Katzenbach, Nicholas D., 22–23, 83–
    84, 132
Keller, Charles, 17
Kennedy, Edward, 163
Kennedy, John F., 7–10, 15–16
Kennedy, Robert, 31
Kerner, Otto, 97, 111
Kerner Commission. See National Advi-
    sory Commission on Civil Disorders
Kerrigan, John J., 162, 168
King, Martin Luther, Jr., 10, 90; at-
    tacks on and threats to, 52, 60, 72;
    on black power, 119–20; vs. Daley, in
    Chicago, 87–89; and Johnson, 56, 70;

and march from Selma to Montgomery, 64–66; murder of, 91–93,
122; and SCLC influence, 87–89, 93;
in Selma, 49, 52–53, 54n10, 55–57,
60; and voting rights, 49, 53, 55–57
King, Matthew, 211
Kleindienst, Richard, 97
Klugman, Julian, 237
Kotz, Nick, 225
Ku Klux Klan (KKK), 37, 41, 45, 216,
240; CRS and, 42, 243; and power
elite, 39–40; and school desegregation, 155–56
Kunstler, William, 120
Kytle, Calvin, 57, 83, 219–20

Labor movement, 176, 178, 188, 237
Lafayette, Bernard, 46–47
Lamb, Robert, Jr., 130–31, 145, 147,
196, 210, 233
Laue, James, 40, 44, 91, 239; in
Chicago, 88–89; in Selma, 59, 61;
and tension around H. Rap Brown's
arrests, 120–21
Law Enforcement Assistance Adminis-
tration (LEAA), 134–35, 139, 152
Le Maistre, George, 34
Leadership Conference on Civil Rights,
8–9
League of United Latin American
Citizens (LULAC), 141, 148, 189
League of Women Voters, 177
Lee, James, 135
"Letter from a Selma Jail" (King), 55
Lewis, John, 62–63
Lewis, Milton, 104–5
Liburd, Joshua, 115
Lindsay, John, 112
Lingo, Al, 48, 61–63, 65–67
Little Rock, Ark., 4–5
Los Angeles, Calif., 78, 85, 110
Louisiana, 152, 181, 183–84
Louisville, Ky., 188

Macy, John, 24
Magnuson, Warren, 20
Manger, Julius, 18, 26–27, 33
Mansfield, Mike, 14
March on Washington (1963), 5
Marcus, Stanley, 34–35
Marks, Miss., 92
Marquez, Pasqual, 206

Marshall, Burke, 8, 49, 71; on CRS's
role, 83–84; effectiveness of media-
tion by, 10–11; and fears of non-
compliance with Civil Rights Act,
11, 16, 23
Marshall, John, 197
Marshall, Thurgood, 18–19
Martinez, Efrain, 202; on Texas shrimp-
ing conflict, 214–17; at Wounded
Knee, 203, 207–8
Mason, Phil, 88
Mathis, John, 238
McClure, Ed, 161
McCormick, John, 12–13
McCulloch, William, 12–14
McGraw-Hill, 224–25
Means, Russell, 199–203, 211, 213
Meany, George, 17, 178
Media, 55; CRS working with, 132,
218–25, 236; minority employment in,
220–25; and minority empowerment,
97–98; and police, 221; and minority
communities, 221–22, 224–25; and
school desegregation, 156, 159, 171,
174, 177–78; and white perceptions
of minorities, 218–19
Media coverage: of black power move-
ment, 114, 118; of civil disorders,
106, 221; of civil rights activities, 10,
48, 54, 72, 88, 219–20; of H. Rap
Brown's arrests, 120–21; of minority
communities, 33, 222–25; in Selma,
45, 48, 51, 53–54, 54n10; of standoff
at Wounded Knee, 205, 207, 209
Meese, Edwin, 234
Memphis, Tenn., 91–92
Meredith, James, 117
Metcalfe, George, 38
Metropolitan Churches United, 174, 176
Mexican American Legal Defense and
Education Fund (MALDEF), 141
Miami, Fla., 78
Michigan, 144. See also Detroit
Middleton, Jack, 115
Migrant workers, 71n71, 99
Miller, Fred, 60, 63, 67, 69
Mills, Wilbur, 94
Minority organizations, 132, 170; and
media reform, 222–25
Mississippi, 5, 36–43, 44, 117
Mississippi Freedom Democratic Party
(MFDP), 36

Mitchell, Clarence, 233–34
Mitchell, John, 35, 97, 235
*Monell v. Department of Social
  Services,* 149–51
Montgomery, Ala., 4; march from Selma
  to, 60–72
Morgan, Carl, 61
Mould, Christopher, 104
Mount Rushmore, 199
Moye, Charles A., 187
Murphy, Patrick V., 129, 152
Myrdal, Gunnar, 102

Natchez, Miss., 37–41
National Advisory Commission on Civil
  Disorders (Kerner Commission), 96–
  97, 104, 107; mission of, 111–12;
  report by, 112–13, 122–23
National Association for the Advance-
  ment of Colored People (NAACP),
  18–19, 40–41, 46n2, 77; and CRS,
  86, 233–34; emphasis on integration,
  118–19; and school desegregation, 38,
  155, 162, 174
National Association of Police Community Relations Officers (NAPCRO), 139
National Association of School Superintendents, 178
National Association of Secondary
  School Principals, 178
National Center for Quality Integrated
  Education, 178
National Chicano Media Council, 224
National Citizens Committee for Community Relations (NCC), 17; committees of, 33, 34–35; continued involvement of, 26–28; CRS networking
  with, 32–35; demise of, 35; employment programs of, 33–35
National Consultation on Safety and
  Force, 148
National Council of Churches, 48, 205,
  209–10
National Council of La Raza, 190
National Guard: abuse of minority
  residents by, 110–11; in Alabama,
  71; at Black Panthers trial, 114, 116;
  federalized, 71, 109; sent to keep
  order, 38, 216; and urban riots, 104,
  107–10, 120
National Hispanic Media Council,
  223–24

National Institute on Police and
  Community Relations, 129
National Labor Relations Board, 237
National Minority Advisory Council on
  Criminal Justice, 152
National Organization of Black Law
  Enforcement Executives (NOBLE),
  145, 147–48
National Rifle Association (NRA), 122
National States Rights Party, 52–53
National Urban League, 86–87, 118–19,
  148, 180
Native Americans: CRS work with,
  71n71, 193–96; grievances of, 196–98,
  210–11; rivalries among, 202–3, 212;
  support for AIM at Wounded Knee,
  207, 209; vs. federal government,
  198–213
New Black Panthers, 243
New Detroit coalition, 170
New Haven, Conn., 114–16
New Jersey, 104
New Mexico, 34
New York City, N.Y., 75, 78, 103, 146
Newark, N.J., 78, 107
Newspaper Fund, 222
Newsweek, 123–24
Nez Percé, 193, 194–96
Nix, Roscoe, 227
Nixon, Richard, 113–14; and CRS, 97,
  225; and Native American treaty
  rights, 200–201; and school
  desegregation, 158–59
Nosser, John, 37–38
Novak, Robert, 6

Oakland, Calif., 78
Oberdorfer, Louis, 16
Oglala Sioux Civil Rights Organization
  (OSCRO), 202–3
Ollie's Barbeque, 22
Omaha, Neb., 104–5
Orange, James, 69
Oregon, 238
Ortiz, Maurillo (Moe), 141
Our Common Heritage (OCH), 176

Padgett, Gail, 151–52
Paterson, N.J., 104
Patterson, Brad, 212
Peer mediation, 237
Peltz, Arthur, 237

Pennsylvania, 152
People and Responsible Organization for
    Detroit (PRO Detroit), 170, 172
Perez, John, 151–52, 240
Perry, John, 68–69, 110
Philadelphia, Pa., 78, 104, 146
Phillips, Cabell, 12
Pine Ridge reservation, 201–2
Police, 221; conferences for, 147–48,
    196; CRS credibility with, 131–32;
    CRS mediating between minority
    communities and, 106–7, 136–40;
    CRS technical specialists on, 115,
    130–31; CRS working with, 26, 127,
    236; divisiveness among, 59–61, 72,
    207–9; effects of bad community
    relations on work of, 128, 132–33;
    and H. Rap Brown, 120–22; improved
    practices of, 61, 236; and march from
    Selma to Montgomery, 62–63, 65–66;
    and minority empowerment, 97–99;
    minority officers in, 143–45, 153, 159,
    186–87; and Native Americans, 193–
    96, 199, 201–4, 207–9; and Poor
    Peoples Campaign, 92–94; racial
    tension within departments, 127–28,
    186–88; response to demonstrations,
    5, 10, 47–50; in school desegregation,
    164–66, 168–69, 172–73, 176; in
    Selma, 49–51, 53–54, 58–61, 72; in
    Texas shrimping conflict, 215, 217;
    training for, 151–52, 244; and urban
    riots, 103, 107–8, 111–13, 122, 127–
    28; use of deadly force by, 147–48,
    152–53; use of force by, 137, 139–40,
    148–52; and voter registration, 55–57
Police Foundation, 145, 148, 152
Police-community relations: effects of
    bad, 128, 132–33; police resistance
    to change in, 129, 131; efforts to im-
    prove, 134–35, 147–48; report on,
    132–33; and use of deadly force, 147
Police-community relations programs:
    creation of, 129, 159; CRS negotiation
    of, 137, 139; recommendations for,
    106, 128, 143
Police-minority relations, 125; abuse in,
    110–11, 128, 133; CRS work in, 120–
    21, 136, 236, 242; efforts to improve,
    128–29, 134, 143; grievances in, 51,
    125–26, 130, 132, 136; with Hispanics,
    140–43; improvements in, 152–54; and
    use of deadly force, 145–48, 152–53

Politics, 233; blacks' power in, 36, 41,
    47, 117–18, 185–86; conciliators' sepa-
    ration from, 29–31; effects of threat
    of violence on, 116; over Civil Rights
    Act, 12–15; over school desegrega-
    tion, 155, 162–63, 165, 174; over use
    of federal troops, 113; poor people's
    lack of power in, 93, 129–30; power
    of business leaders in, 49; race in, 36,
    180; split between moderate and
    extremist whites in, 49–50
Pollard, William, 178
Pompa, Gilbert, 126n2, 152, 223, 227,
    235; as CRS director, 146, 184, 230
Poor Peoples Campaign, 71n71, 89–90,
    92–95
Port Arthur, Tex., 125–26, 136–40
Potomac Institute, 16, 20
Pouissant, Alvin, 127
Pratt, John H., 160
President's Commission on Law Enforce-
    ment and Administration of Justice,
    132–33
President's Council on Equal Opportu-
    nity, 76, 78, 83
Prince George's County, Md., 177
Prisons: civil rights in, 181, 183–85;
    mediation in, 238
Project Compliance, 16, 20, 22–23
Public accommodations, desegregation
    of: challenges to law, 21–22; in Civil
    Rights Act, 10–11, 13; compliance
    with, 22–23, 40, 51; demonstrations
    for, 48, 53–54; fears of resistance to,
    16–18; injunctive relief for, 14;
    resistance to, 10–11

Racial Imbalance Act (1965), 162
Rackley, Alex, 114
Randolph, A. Philip, 118–19
Rauh, Joseph, 9–10
Raycroft, Russ, 223
Reagan, Ronald, 122, 234
Reeb, James, 67–68, 70
Reese, Frederick Douglas, 50, 61
Reno, Janet, 235
Resor, Stanley, 108
Resurrection City (Poor Peoples encamp-
    ment in Washington), 93–94
ROAR (Restore Our Alienated Rights),
    162
Rochester, N.Y., 78, 82; riots in, 75, 79,
    81, 104

Rockwell, George Lincoln, 53
Rodriguez, Joe, 236–37
Romney, George, 108–9, 113
Rose, Arnold M., 102
Roubideaux, Ramon, 212
Rubin, Carl B., 174–75
Ruckelshaus, William, 114
Russell, Bill, 223
Russell, Richard, 15
Rustin, Bayard, 119–20

Salazar, Ruben, 223–24
Salem, Richard: oral history of concilia-
    tors by, 239–42; and school desegre-
    gation, 171, 175; at Wounded Knee,
    206, 210
Salinas, Manuel, 224
Samet, Seymour, 25–26
San Diego, Calif., 133
San Francisco, Calif., 78, 130–31, 150
Sargent, Francis, 162, 167
School desegregation, 13, 51, 82; in
    Boston, 155–56, 160–70; civic volun-
    teers in, 173–74, 176–78; CRS goals
    in, 157–60, 168; CRS in, 28, 168, 179,
    236, 244–45; in Dayton, 173–76; in
    Detroit, 170–73; effects of violence in,
    30–31; efforts to foster acceptance of,
    6–7, 171–72, 177–78; federal govern-
    ment enforcing, 4–5, 117n18, 156–58;
    pace of increased, 158–60; planning
    for, 158, 170–75; resistance to, 4,
    8n7, 15, 45, 156, 158–60, 162–69,
    173–74, 176, 219; in St. Helena
    Parish, 29–31; white response to
    demand for, 38
Schwerner, Michael H., 37
Scott, Rita, 171
Seale, Bobby, 114–16
Seadrift, Tex., 214–16
Seattle, Wash., 93
Secrest, Andrew MacDowd (Mac), 26;
    personality of, 24, 52n8; in Rochester,
    79; and second march from Selma to
    Montgomery, 65–67; in Selma, 27, 49,
    51–52, 54, 57–58, 61, 69–70, 73
Selden, Armistead I., 13
Selden, Willis, 221, 223–25
Selma, Ala., 27; black grievances in,
    51–52; conciliation efforts in, 54, 72,
    84; cooling-off period in, 61–62;
    demonstrations in, 47–48, 56–57;
    law enforcement factions in, 59–61;

march to Montgomery from, 60–63,
    70–72; mass meetings in, 47–48, 53,
    57, 60; media covering racial violence
    in, 45, 51; racial disparity in, 46, 51,
    59; racial factions in, 49–51; racial
    tension increasing in, 53–54, 68–69;
    second march to Montgomery from,
    63–67; violence in, 45, 51, 67–68;
    voter registration in, 46–47, 57–58;
    voting rights in, 48–49, 52, 54–57, 70
Selma Ministerial Association, 49–50
Shores, Arthur, 34
Shrimping: Texas conflict over, 213–17
Shriver, Sergeant, 93–94
Siegal, Gerald, 6
Sikes, Melvyn, 129
Sioux, 198–99
Smith, William French, 235
Smitherman, Joe, 49, 69, 73
Society of Professionals in Dispute Reso-
    lution (SPIDR), 238–39
Sorenson, Theodore C., 7
Southern Christian Leadership
    Conference (SCLC), 4, 50;
    demonstrations by, 56, 69, 117; goals
    of, 52, 55, 61, 89; influence of, 87–91;
    marches from Selma to Montgomery
    by, 61–64; and Poor Peoples Cam-
    paign, 89–90, 92–95; tactics of, 51,
    58–59; working for voting rights,
    46n2, 49, 52–53, 55
Southern Governors Association, 17, 19
Southern Manifesto, 8n7
Southern Poverty Law Center, 216
Southern Regional Council, 20
St. Augustine, Fla., 5
St. Helena Parish, La., 29–31
St. Louis, Mo., 129
St. Petersburg, Fla., 146–47
Steering Committee on Texas Law
    Enforcement and Community Rela-
    tions, 142–43
Stewart, John, 15
Still, Lawrence, 221
Student Nonviolent Coordinating
    Committee (SNCC), 4; and black
    power movement, 117, 121; and CRS's
    choice of venues, 86–87; marches by,
    62, 117; relations with other organiza-
    tions, 50, 119; voting rights work by,
    46, 49, 52, 53
Supreme Court, U.S.: on excessive
    police force, 149; on Native American

treaty rights, 194, 197; on public accommodations laws, 22; resistance to school desegregation orders of, 8n7, 45, 219; school desegregation orders of, 4, 156, 158–60
Sutton, Ozell, 147, 187, 227–28
Swift, Leroy, 139
Sylvester, Ed, 86

Task Force on Hate Crime, of Justice Department, 244
Taylor, Jesse, 182, 184
Technical specialists, CRS use of, 130–31
Terronez, John, 201, 203–4
Texas: conflict over shrimping in, 213–17; police practices in, 137, 140–43, 151–52
Thomas, Daniel H., 55, 61, 69–70
Thurmond, Strom, 15, 19–20
Till, Emmett, 4
Trail of Broken Treaties, 200–201
Treaty rights, Native American, 196–98, 200, 202
Trimbach, Joseph, 204
Turner, James, 114

United Press International, 219–20

Vance, Cyrus, 109
Venable, Abraham, 25
Vice President's Summer Task Force on Urban Problems, 76, 78–79
Vietnamese refugees: in Texas, 213–17
Vivian, C. T., 57
Voter Education Project (VEP), 46
Voter registration, 60; attempts to speed up, 57–58, 61; discrimination in, 46, 48, 52–53, 55

Wallace, George, 5, 61; ban on night marches, 59–60; and marches from Selma to Montgomery, 62, 64, 66, 71; popularity of, 72, 102
Walsh, Martin, 160–61, 179–80, 204–6
Warfield, Wallace, 228–29, 239
War on Poverty, 76, 101–3, 202
Washington, D.C., 122, 150, 201; Poor Peoples Campaign in, 89–90, 92–94
Washington, Willie, 37–38
Webster, William, 147–48
West, E. Gordon, 181, 183
Whalen, Charles and Barbara, 13–14
Wheeler, John, 18, 28
White, Kevin, 163–64, 167, 179–80
White, Lee, 7, 17
White Citizens Council, 4, 156
Wilkins, Roger, 57, 134; background of, 76–77; on focus of CRS, 83, 95–96, 227; friendship with Ramsey Clark, 85–86, 234; and King, 90–92; police abuse of, 110–11; and Poor Peoples Campaign, 93–94; reputation of, 85–86; role in CRS, 77–78, 84–86, 230; and urban riots, 104, 109
Wilkins, Roy, 86, 112, 118–19
Will, Hubert L., 184
Williams, Hosea, 59, 62–63, 70
Wilson, Dick, 201–2, 206–7
Wilson, Kemmons, 17–18, 27
Wofford, Harris, 6–7
Wood, Harlington, 209–10
Worcester v. Georgia, 197–98
Wounded Knee, S.D.: standoff at, 203–13

Yarborough, Ralph, 20
Yellow Thunder, Raymond, 200
Yorty, Samuel, 78
Young, Andrew, 227; and King, 72, 91; and march from Selma to Montgomery, 63, 65; in Selma, 59–62
Young, Whitney, 118–19
Yzaguirre, Raul, 190

Permissions